THE INFINITE THOUGHT
PROJECTIONS OF JESUS

Books by Alton E. Carpenter

The Infinite Thought Projections of Jesus
Twenty-three Keys to Inner Peace

The Infinite Thought Projections of Jesus

Alton E. Carpenter,

B.A., Th.B, Th.M., Th.D.
President, Scottsdale Memorial Hospital
Scottsdale, Arizona

EXPOSITION PRESS   HICKSVILLE, N.Y.

To my wife, Cecil Alice

First Edition

© 1975 by Alton E. Carpenter

ISBN 0-682-48356-7

Printed in the United States of America

Contents

Preface

The parables of Jesus have always held a fascination for this writer. At times, when he was a boy, as he sat in Sunday school listening to a poorly prepared teacher, the Bible seemed uninteresting; but when the lesson had to do with a parable—well, even a poorly prepared teacher could not lessen its appeal to his boyish mind. Here was something that a boy could get his teeth into!

The word "parable" meant nothing to that boy, but the stories of the New Testament did! Years later, as a student of theology in the seminary, after an exposure to the field of science, which left an unerasable imprint and a thirst for answers of certainty for the unanswerable questions of life, that boy, now a man, met a professor of Greek who further stimulated his curiosity concerning the parables of Jesus. In the study of the New Testament in the original Greek language, this professor made each parable a jewel that sparkled with the richness of the mind of Christ. This professor had the knack of sending his students out of the seminary searching for the hidden diamonds of Christ to be found in the New Testament. This search had led to the writing of this book.

Undergraduate and graduate work in the fields of psychology and sociology became fertile soil in which the parabolic seeds could germinate and bring forth more profitable spiritual dividends as the writer continued his study in psychological principles being employed by Jesus, the Master Psychologist, as He made theological application in these parables to the needs He saw in the lives of the people with whom He came into daily contact.

A by-product of this study was the discovery of the thought projection method Jesus was using. This method opened a completely new field in thought procedure study. It was to this writer in his study of theology what Albert Einstein's theory of relativity was to the field of science. It gave a new dimension to theology—a new key to unlock the mind of God as Jesus revealed God's mind to us. It also removed the "narrative" fence from around the parables built by theologians through the ages. To many scholars of the Bible, a parable was only a story, a narrative told by Jesus. If it were not in the form of a story it was not considered a parable. I believe the *thought projection method*, which we shall use in this book, will remove this narrative fence from around all the parables. When this is done, new and unlimited theological horizons are opened to the student of the Bible as he searches the mind of Christ for the great truths of God.

In the Gospel of Matthew there are only twenty-one *narrative* thought projections (parables), but there are one hundred and thirty *pure* thought projections! Each of these pure thought projections of Jesus is a spiritual diamond of great value and should demand of the reader the same attention he gives to the other twenty-one parables found in Matthew's Gospel. Many of these have been neglected and undeveloped because the Bible student has been searching only for the obvious—the "story-form" parables. The narrative-type parables make up only a fraction of the great spiritual wealth stored by Jesus in His thought projections. This spiritual pool has yet to be tapped and put on the theological markets of the world to meet the demands and needs of a spiritually hungry world. This is the basic reason for writing this book.

Besides these one hundred and fifty-one thought projections in Matthew, there are more than two hundred thought projections in the other Gospels. These will be presented in a second volume on the thought projections of Jesus as found in Mark, Luke, and John.

It is impossible to give credit to all to whom it is due or to the many who have made some contribution toward this book. Thirty years of study and research have gone into this volume and thirty years can be a very effective "eraser" regarding the original sources of thoughts and facts gathered and placed within the covers of this book.

I shall always be grateful and greatly indebted to Dr. Elmer Haight, my brilliant and unassuming professor of Greek under whom I studied in the seminary, for placing the feet of this writer on the parable road which has led me into the "Thought Projection Reservation of Theology."

I have reduced all footnotes to a very minimum, believing that footnotes add nothing to the understanding of the subject matter under consideration, but do detract from and interrupt thought flow in reading. This author reacts to them as a surgeon would in the operating room if the attending nurse, handing him an instrument would at the same time give him the name of the maker and distributor of each instrument. All sources used will be found in the bibliography at the end of the book.

I am grateful for the many patient students who have passed through my course, Re-402, over the years at Arizona State University. Their eager minds challenged me to provide the spiritual and intellectual stimulus that they needed to motivate greater "in-depth" study of the matchless teachings of the Master.

Without the patient understanding and encouragement of my wife, Cecil Alice, this volume would have never become a reality. It is dedicated to her for the glory it might bring the Master whom we both love and serve.

Paradise Valley, Arizona

Introduction

The name of this book, *The Infinite Thought Projections of Jesus*, should be clarified and justified. This is done in a later chapter of the book. I am deliberate in avoiding calling it "The Parables of Jesus," for I believe theologians have limited and restricted the word "parable" by applying it to only the narratives spoken by Jesus. The Hebrew and Greek words for "parable" do not have this restriction. For this reason I have disassociated the word from its historically restricted application and have used the broader term, "thought projections of Jesus." When this term is used, I am referring to either one of the two general forms of thought projections: the narrative thought projection (parables), or the pure thought projection non-narrative form.

The material in this book has been divided into two parts. Part I deals with the background materials needed by the average reader in order for him to receive the most profit from his study or from the reading of this book. Part II locates, explains, identifies the figure of speech used; classifies and offers applications for the one hundred and fifty-one thought projections recorded in the Gospel of Matthew.

In chapter 1 of Part I, I take a look at the reader and his Bible. How should one approach the New Testament, the book of Matthew? Can it be used in the same way as a textbook in another subject? What about the many disturbing questions being raised today about the Bible? What should be our attitude? In this chapter I attempt to set forth some guidelines to help the reader or the student face up to these and other questions regarding the Bible. This chapter should help us to avoid reading into the Bible something it does not say, or reading out the things it is saying to us. We must let the Bible speak for itself. It is most difficult to read and interpret the Bible without the use of our "theological background glasses." These must come off if the Bible is to speak to us clearly.

In chapter 2 I consider the questions: "Whence cometh our

Bible?" "What is revelation, inspiration, and interpretation?" An analysis is made of these questions and an attempt to reduce them down to a theological level that can be understood by the average layman.

In chapter 3 a brief survey is made of church history. The infant Christian movement is traced from its beginning to our present age. What we know today as Christianity is not only the product of its founder, Jesus Christ, but is also a by-product of the environment in which it has lived through its two thousand years of growth. When the Christian movement left the hills and valleys of its founder, the Galilean, it moved into the cities of the Roman and Greek world, attracting and absorbing people from many cultures and religions. It was, in turn, conditioned in its theology by these new forces. This change was felt in its theology and the application of this theology. Certain changes in theological direction are quite obvious to any reader of church history; and in our brief trip through church history we take notice of these changes and try to understand the reasons for them. I believe that we can better appreciate what is happening today in the field of theology after this brief survey of the history of the Christian movement.

Chapter 4 is given over to a review of the historical interpretations of the thought projections (parables) of Jesus. I have divided history into six periods for this study. I believe that each period is characterized theologically by the interpretations made of the parables of Jesus. I indicate these characteristics and the men who exercised great influence upon their period of history. I believe that the thought projections of Jesus (parables) have had more influence upon schools of theology through the ages than any one factor in the New Testament. This is the burden of this chapter.

In chapter 5 I make a study of a thought projection. I attempt to justify my usage of this term in place of the word "parable." We take a look at the root meaning of the Hebrew and Greek words for "parable." It is pointed out in this chapter what a parable is not and what it is; the figures of speech making up all thought projections are discussed. This prepares us for our search of the Gospels for the many thought projections used by Jesus to reveal to man the hidden things of God.

In chapter 6 the question is raised, "Why did Jesus use thought projections (parables)?" In answering this question several psychological reasons are suggested because of the many sound and modern psychological principles behind the use of this technique. In using the thought projection method, Jesus was far ahead of His time in conveying new ideas to man. We could use His method today with great profit in preaching and teaching.

Chapter 7 has to do with the same question asked in chapter 6, "Why did Jesus use thought projections (parables)?" Several theological reasons are given in answering this question. When asked by His disciples why He used the parabolic method of teaching, Jesus replied, "To reveal to you the mysteries of the kingdom hidden since the foundations of the world were laid" (Matt. 13:35). A study of these thought projections of Jesus will alert us to new truths concerning God and His relationship to man. We will discover many new characteristics of God in such a study. A study of these thought projections of Jesus, as found in the four Gospels, will enhance our knowledge of God, and will help remove God from the theological shadows men have placed around Him in trying to protect His holiness and deity. They become the spotlights on the theological stage of the ages to direct our attention upon HIM.

In chapter 8 I examine some of the psychological procedures underlying the thought projection method of interpretation. A brief study is made of motivations, stimuli, instincts, conditioned reflexes, and emotions as these things relate themselves to the spiritual decisions we must make in life. I suggest certain rules to follow in the study of the thought projections of Jesus. This chapter should be helpful to preacher, teacher, public speaker, and soul winner. The use of some of these suggested ideas will help us avoid many errors in trying to get another person to respond to what we are trying to sell to or share with him.

In chapter 9 I have classified all the thought projections we have uncovered in the Gospel of Matthew. These are classified by subject, what is being illustrated by Jesus, the figure of speech employed by Jesus to form His thought projection, and the final classification of each thought projection. This should be helpful to anyone seeking a certain subject or an illustration for a subject under study that needs more light upon it.

The second division, or Part II is given over to a study of all the thought projections found in the Gospel of Matthew. I give a brief summary of the six chapters (1, 2, 3, 14, 27, and 28) which contain no thought projections. This is done to give continuity to the study of the book of Matthew. Each chapter contains all the

thought projections in a specific chapter of Matthew. This procedure
is used again to avoid breaking the continuity of the Gospel story
as told by Matthew. No attempt is made to fully develop each
thought projection for the reader. I have left this challenge to the
student, the Bible scholar, or the preacher. I address my effort in this
book to the "mining operation"—the locating and bringing to the
surface these thoughts of Jesus. All twenty-one narrative thought
projections (parables) are familar to most readers of the Bible, but
the other one hundred and thirty pure thought projections are perhaps not so familiar, at least under this classification.

Twenty-two chapters in the Gospel of Matthew contain two or
more thought projections each, and six chapters have no thought
projections in them. These are chapters 1, 2, 3, 14, 27, and 28.
Chapters 1, 2, and 3 deal with John the forerunner, with the birth
of Jesus, and with Jesus' baptism. He did no teaching until after
His baptism. Chapter 14 deals with the feeding of the five thousand,
the storm at sea, and Jesus walking on the water. Jesus does no
teaching in this chapter. Chapters 27 and 28 tell of the trial, death,
and the resurrection of Jesus. Jesus had finished His instructions,
both to His disciples and to the world, before His death. He had
little to add after His resurrection.

PART I:

Background Material

1

The Reader and His Bible

The Bible is many things to many people. To some it is a book to lend religious dignity to the home and is to be found in a prominent place in the living room to impress all who might enter. It may or may not be opened, the latter being the general rule. It is there not to be read, but to impress. It is a showpiece, a symbol of a religious culture maintained in that home. It is there for effect—window dressing for the public, but nothing more.

The Bible for some people is nothing more than a recorder for the family history. In it you will find the name and date of each child born, the dates of weddings of members of the family, and the dates of their deaths. It is not a maker of history for that family—only a recorder of it. It exercises no influence nor works any miracle of change in the lives of the people it should be serving. Its message of hope is never learned nor its precepts for a better and fuller life ever discovered. Its value to its owner can be measured only in the amount of space it contains to record the history of that family. It is not a living book for them—only a blank one on the living room table.

The Bible is many things to many people. To some it is an instrument used to extend their egos. It is a book which they memorize so that it might be used by them in debate. It is quoted to support their pet theological positions. This approach is not limited to persons wanting to be known as "debaters," for even some so-called theologians use the Bible merely to gain a victory over other theologians or a congregation. The points argued, or even proved, lose their value to such persons when victory is gained. They do not attempt to apply such truths to their own lives. They want to be known as "masters" of the Bible, but they never let the message of the Bible master them.

The Bible can become nothing more than a textbook to a student in college or seminary, lessons to be learned and examinations to be passed, the source for a devotional message, or the text for a sermon on Sunday. It is a springboard to be used to justify every whim or fancy of our day.

To millions of people, the Bible is a book of devotional food to which they turn daily for spiritual strength. It is their meat and drink, their light in darkness. It is the stairway into the mind of God, a mirror of their own limitations, and a reminder of their dependence upon the grace of God. It is a living book, a book of inspiration, and it is loved not for its name, but for its message. It is the first book in their lives and the last. They will live by it and die by it. It is the living Word of God for them. It gives them their standard of morals, the inspiration to live up to these morals, and the direction for their lives.

It is all these things to such people, but it is even more. It is their link with the eternal God and His contact with them. It is their link with eternity and their bridge across the chasm of death. It is their daily hope which gives real meaning to life itself—not only to life, but even to death. If the Bible were removed from their lives, they would find no real values left in life to make life worth the struggle and sacrifice to continue.

What should be the attitude of a reader of the Bible, or a student of the Bible? How should we approach our study of the Bible, God's Holy Word? We are living in the age of science, and many questions about the Bible are being thrust into our lives from every side. Many questions are being asked about the Bible today that distress the honest and sincere Bible student. Because of these things, we would like to suggest several things that should be kept in mind when one approaches the Bible, either as a book of devotion or a text book for study.

We should always remember that there are many different fields of science and study. All fields of knowledge do not use the same criteria to measure and test the truth they are seeking to discover. Each will use the method common to and accepted by its particular field. The engineer will use mathematics to prove the accuracy of his study, and he will always find a slide rule and pencil within reach of his hands; whereas, the chemist will use test tubes and formulas to test the accuracy of his experiment. He is not concerned with inches and feet, as is the engineer, but he is more interested in what happens in the test tube, and he will use the results of such tests for his future formulas.

The same principles apply to the field of humanity studies. The sociologist uses neither criterion in his work, nor does the psychologist. The student of electronics will not use the same measuring devices in his work as the theologian will use in his. Not any one of the fields of science is less so because it does not use the particular instrument to prove its validity that all others use. Such a demand would make the men in that field the laughing stock of all other fields.

There is one thing that all fields of science have in common—must have in common—to be scientifically correct in their procedures. Each and all must always be consistent in their results. Two parts hydrogen and one part oxygen must always make water when these two elements are brought together in that ratio under the same conditions anywhere in the world. The Bible has nothing to fear from the field of science or from the application of this principle to itself. One basic error made by those who declare that the Bible is not a reliable guide for life, or is "out of date," is to be found in this area. They are attempting to measure the truth of the Bible by a slide rule, a test tube, or the principal measuring device common to some particular field.

We believe that each field in the many areas of knowledge which we have at our command should be left to speak for itself and in its own terminology. We should not attempt to force rules of our discipline upon another. We do not demand that authorities in the field of geology speak for the men who are masters in the field of psychology—nor even to speak for the men in the field of botany, as closely related as these two areas of knowledge might seem to be. And yet, it is not uncommon to hear professors in some particular field in a university trying to make theology and theologians conform to their own thought patterns, but these same professors never attempt to discredit the subject matter taught by fellow professors in other fields unrelated to their own. If such conformity were practiced in our universities today, there would be little learning or teaching done in them—the students would leave each classroom in a state of confusion and frustration.

Each field of science and each field in the humanity area has its own textbooks and teaches its subject from these. If the Bible had undergone as much change as textbooks in other fields of science have undergone during the past twenty years, it would have destroyed itself. If the Bible had as many of its truths, which had been taught as truths, proven to be untruths, and had as many changes made in its "theories" as every field of science has had during the last ten years, the Bible would have been destroyed as a book of divine truth. No one would believe in it—nor should he.

As you read the Bible, hold in suspension that which you cannot or do not understand. Few people would have finished any course they started in college if they were required to understand the entire book the first day they opened it. Many students do not understand much of their textbook after they have spent a year in the course under the lecturing of a master teacher in that particular subject! Many do not learn enough to even pass the course successfully!

Your ability to understand God's Word will increase with study. You will have to attend many classes and go often into God's laboratory of life to put to the test many of the things you discover about God and about yourself. The Bible and God can stand any test you may make concerning God's divine truths. We are told by God through His Holy Word to "try me, test me, and prove me" (Malachi 3:10).

We should also remember that in every field of knowledge, certain basic facts must be accepted on faith. As cold and precise as mathematics is, faith must be exercised by the mathematician before he can start to use this tool: 2 and 2 equals 4; 1 and 1 equals 2. We cannot prove this, nor can he. We just accept this on faith and take off from there. Believing this makes possible miracles in this field—reject this first step, and your career in this field of science ends there. No man has ever seen an atom. But the Greeks 600 to 300 years before Christ, without any of our modern electronic devices, not only discovered the atom by pure reason, but predicted that some day man would learn how to split one. It took Einstein's theory, in our generation, to prove them right—2000 years after an unseen thing called an "atom" was discovered by pure reasoning of the human mind!

Faith in the Bible as the Word of God should be considered not a weakness but an area of strength. It is the starting point for the Christian. A person is not being "peculiar" by exercising faith in the Word of God. He, like the men of science, is using faith as his starting point in his search for the truths of God. He will have this faith justified if he will use it and put it to the test in the laboratory of God, living it day by day.

Man must have some source of authority for everything he does. If man rejects the Bible as his guide and authority in morals and in religion, he will find another. This might be the philosophy of some persons or persons. It can be a combination of many ideas from many sources, or it can be that he has set himself up as his own authority. To reject the Bible as his authority is merely to substitute it for another. To reject God is to place someone human above God or to place one's own mind above that of God. It is to declare oneself superior to the divine mind of God.

Since this book has to do with a study of the thought projections of Jesus located in the Gospel of Matthew, the reader should not let the question raised about the Old Testament disturb him. Genesis has been a book under fire from both theologians and men from the fields of science for many generations, and the Bible has been ably defended by men from each and both of these schools of thought. Like an old and experienced, but bloody, warrior, the Bible seems to outlive all those who attack it, and the casualty of this fight is always the attacker and not the attacked. When the final chapter of this battle is written, the world will not be surprised to see that nothing will happen to change such results.

The Bible has never claimed for itself the title of "A Book of Science"; nor has it ever attempted to explain the "hows" of God's creation of this world. It concerns itself only with the fact that God was behind the creation of the world. The Bible says that God was the creator, and the Bible is quite willing to listen to the explanation of the scientists as to how this was done. There is no conflict with the true scientist and the honest theologian over what the Bible teaches about creation.

We ought to approach the Bible with open minds as we do any other subject under study. We should allow the Bible to speak for itself on all subjects and should not permit men, ancient or modern, to speak for the Bible. It is quite capable of revealing its own mind without interpretations from man as to what it is saying.

We need to remove our "theological eye glasses" when we approach the Bible to study or to read as a devotional book. The most dangerous enemy the Bible has is not from the world of science, but from its own theologians and from its own defenders. It is most distressing to hear someone trying to explain to another what you really meant when that is not what you meant at all! This is the

position in which the Bible is placed by many of its friends—its defenders. Let us try to be silent when we study our Bibles and listen
to the voice of the Bible as it speaks to us of its author—God.

Since so much has been said in recent years regarding the Bible
and science, listen to the voice of one of our greatest living scientists
as he speaks to us through an article appearing in the *Arizona Re-
public,* Phoenix, Arizona, July 18, 1965. Wernher Von Braun is
talking about science and God. His subject for this article is faith.

Science and faith are the two dominant forces in this century. We
must try to understand their nature if we are to comprehend some of the
most serious problems of the era in which we live.

The mainspring of science is curiosity. Since time immemorial, there
have always been men and women who felt a burning desire to know
what was under the rock, beyond the hills, across the oceans. This restless breed now want to know what makes an atom work, through what
process life reproduces itself, or what is on the far side of the moon.

But also, there would not be a single great accomplishment in the
history of mankind without faith. Any man who strives to accomplish
something needs a degree of faith in himself. And whenever he takes on
a challenge that requires more moral strength than he can muster with
his own limited mental and spiritual resources, he needs faith in God.

One of the most crucial issues of our time lies in the fact that modern
science, along with miracle drugs and communications satellites, has also
produced nuclear bombs. It cannot be denied that science has failed to
provide a practical answer on how to cope with them. As a result, science
and scientists have often been blamed for the desperate dilemma in
which mankind finds itself today.

Science, by itself, has no moral dimension. The drug which cures
when taken in small doses may kill when taken in excess. The nuclear
energies that produce cheap electrical power when harnessed in a reactor
may kill when abruptly released in a bomb. Thus it does not make sense
to ask a scientist whether his poison or his nuclear energy is 'good' or
'bad' for mankind.

And so, the realization that science is unable to control the possible
abuse of the forces it has made available has led hundreds of millions in
the world to a new interest in religion. This religious revival shows that
there is a widespread realization that in the nuclear age man has a desperate need for stronger ethical control of the immeasurable physical
forces he has unleashed.

But many people find the churches, those old ramparts of faith, badly
battered by the onslaught of three hundred years of scientific skepticism.
This has led many to believe that science and religion are not compatible,
that 'knowing' and 'believing' cannot live side by side.

Nothing could be further from the truth. Science and religion are
not antagonists. On the contrary, they are sisters. While science tries to
learn more about the creation, religion tries to better understand the
Creator. While, through science, man tries to harness the forces of na-

ture around him, through religion he tries to harness the forces of nature within him.

Science may not have a moral dimension. But I am certain that science, in its search for new insights into the nature of the creation, has produced new ethical values of its own. Most certainly science has fostered veracity and humility. Again, it is a mark of all true science that its findings are valid and objective for all times and all peoples; that these findings demand unconditional acceptance and that once proved correct, they are universally embraced. If man has ever come close to finding an answer to Pontius Pilate's question, 'What is truth?' science has shown the way. Personally, I believe in the ultimate victory of truth. I am confident that to the extent that we shall learn more about nature, we shall not only arrive at universally accepted scientific findings, but also at a set of universally accepted rules and standards of human behavior.

The materialists of the nineteenth century and their Marxist heirs of the twentieth, tried to tell us that, as science gives us more knowledge about the creation, we could live without faith in a Creator. Yet so far, with every new answer, we have discovered new questions. *The better we understand the intricacies of the atomic structure, the nature of life, or the master plan of the galaxies, the more reason we have found to marvel at the wonder of God's creation.*

But our need for God is not based on awe alone. Man needs faith just as he needs food, water or air.

With all the science in the world, we need faith in God, whenever faith in ourselves has reached its limit.

The question is often asked, "How can we be sure that the Bible we now have is the pure text of the original manuscripts?" This is a valid question and should be answered.

Jesus spoke in Aramaic, a modified form of Hebrew spoken in the first century by the Jews. Most of the original manuscripts were written in the Greek language. Previous to 330 B.C., the Greek language was confined to the small country of Greece; many dialects were spoken, but these were generally merged into one common Greek language (Koine). After the conquests of Alexander the Great spread the Greek language around the known world, it became the language of commerce and the "second" language of people in other lands.

The New Testament was copied by hand, and passed on to the next generation for fifteen hundred years, until the invention of the printing press. During this long period of hand copying, mistakes crept into these manuscripts. Through the labor of textual critics through the years, these mistakes have been eliminated. Biblical scholars tell us that in the best texts of the Greek New Testament today, 999 words out of 1000 are the same as those in the original manuscripts, the thousandth word which might be in question is of minor value and would have no historical effect on fact or doctrine.

These textual critics had more than 14,000 ancient manuscripts with which to work. Four thousand of these were Greek manuscripts that go back to the third century in an unbroken succession. Eight thousand of these manuscripts were copies of the Latin Vulgate, and 2000 others were copies of the New Testament in other languages. Tertullian tells us that original manuscripts were in existence in A.D. 200. Chester Beatty recently discovered manuscripts dating back to between A.D. 200-300.

"No other book in all history has been criticized, studied, attacked by friend and foe, or subjected to as many tests to prove its validity. What we have in our possession is a book which has been refined by every critical test known to man. The dross, gathered by the passing of time, has been separated from our New Testament, and the writers of the first century would find little that differs from what they laboriously inscribed on paper scrolls with a stylus."[1]

---

[1]Kenneth Wuest, *Wuest's Word Studies* (Grand Rapids, Michigan: Wm. B. Eerdmans Publishing Co., 1953) pp. 20-21.

2

Whence Cometh Our Bible?

Whence cometh our Bible? Before we can begin an intellectual search for the answer to this question, we must face two other questions. When we find the answers to these two, we have the answer to our first question, "Whence cometh our Bible?" The two questions are: "Why does man need the Bible?" and "What motivations within man cause him to search for moral and spiritual standards not found within himself?" In other words, what has created man's need for the Bible?

Why does man need the Bible? If man evolved from a lower form of animal life through the processes of evolution, the same physical process that supplied all his physical needs ought to have supplied all his moral and spiritual needs, too. He, like other animals, should have been supplied from within himself with all the tools needed to satisfy all his basic needs. The fish of the sea were supplied with organisms with which to meet the basic needs of their environment. Nature gave to the fish, not legs with which to walk, but fins so it could swim. Birds of the air were given wings that make it possible for them to navigate the heavens. Man was given a sex drive, and God furnished man with the means of satisfying this drive.

The dog has been a domesticated animal for thousands of years. He has been associated with the inherited basic needs nature gave him—food, shelter, reproduction (it is doubtful if the dog knows the results of his sex act), and attention from his master. As far as it can be determined, dogs have no outside ambitions to become "better dogs," "rulers of men," and so on. In other words, a dog merely wants to be a dog. Not so with man, he is never satisfied with the status quo. He is always reaching out for something better and higher not found within himself. Whence cometh this ambition, this drive, and this feeling of disappointment with a static life?

In all cultures, there are found methods used by members of that culture to give expression to some form of worship. This is

25

found in the most primitive culture yet discovered. Man is constantly reaching out toward some power, being, or god he believes exists outside of his own cultural pattern. His hands might be extended as hands of a beggar, as hands of a grateful receiver of some favor he thinks his god has bestowed upon him, or it might be hands extended in simple worship—an act of fellowship and communication.

There is another question which is closely akin to our second. Where did man get this spiritual and moral motivation, drive, or desire? We should expand this question to include a supporting question. Who or what implanted it within his nature? What causes him to attempt to improve his own moral and spiritual concepts, and what motivates him with the desire to share these with others within his own cultural pattern? These cannot come from man's basic physical nature, for man is basically selfish. A female dog may fight other animals to save her pups, but later this same mother may fight and kill that pup when it is grown. It soon becomes just another dog against whom she must defend herself.

I believe that this drive that motivates man to reach out from himself and from outside of his social pattern was implanted in man by God. I believe that the answer is to be found in the words of the Bible . . . "Let us make man in our image, after our likeness, and let him have dominion over the fish of the sea . . ." (Gen. 1:26). "So God created man in his own image, in the image of God he created him; male and female He created them" (Gen. 1:27). I believe that the answer to the three questions raised are to be found in these two verses of scripture.

When the Bible speaks of God making man in God's own image, I do not believe that the Bible is proclaiming the physical processes God used to make man, nor do I believe that the Bible is giving us a description of the finished physical product of this creation. Neither do I believe that man began as a single cell, emerging by stages of evolution from the dust of the earth, and that after a long period of time, man emerged as a human being to become an "anthropos"— a creature who walks with his face upward toward God. We cannot accept the theory of evolution, for this theory raises more questions than it can answer. To accept the theory that God made the first man and provided natural laws to continue this life-producing process, I believe, does no violence either to the Holy Bible or to science.

I believe this "image of God" does not refer to man's physical likeness to God, for the Bible teaches that God is a Spirit and is not to be limited to a physical form possessed by man. The physical form of man is only the early house for the spirit of man. God needs no such house. The implanted image of God in man is the implantation in man of the divine. By this act of God, man received a spiritual-responding nature possessed by no other created thing on earth. This spiritual-responding nature possessed by man can never be satisfied until it is liberated to respond to spiritual impulses emanating from God's nature. When man's spiritual nature is synchronized with the spirit of God, when spiritual communication and spiritual fellowship is established between an individual and God, man realizes the spiritual peace for which he is seeking. Sin breaks man's communication with God and God's communication with man. Sin ruins the spiritual-responding nature of man. Christ's mission on earth was to restore this relationship. We will not attempt to give a theological explanation of the atonement here. This is given in many of the thought projections found in the four Gospels, and will be dealt with in our study of these thought projections later in this book.

Whence cometh the Bible and why does man need the Bible? The Bible is the compass that guides man in his search for the moral and spiritual needs he finds within himself, but for which he has no answer within himself, nor within the range of his experience in life. The Bible is to man what nature is to the creatures of this world. Nature provokes a need, and nature supplies an answer to that need. Within the Bible is to be found the answer to the spiritual needs of man. God planted in man a spiritual need for fellowship with himself. Man knows not what lies behind this spiritual desire. The Bible is God's gift to man so that man might know how to have this spiritual need satisfied.

The Bible is a historical recording of God's attempt to satisfy all of man's spiritual and moral needs. It is a record of God's many attempts to break through to man to deliver the spiritual equipment man requires to be victorious in life. The Bible is not a book of history nor of science. It is a library containing sixty-six books. It is a book with one author—God. It is a book that took 1500 years to write and compile, and although a book with one author, God, it was recorded by many men. It is a book with one continuous theme —the love of God. God is pictured throughout its pages as a loving father seeking to find and reclaim his lost sons (Luke 15:11-32).

We are now ready to face the most important question of any we have asked. Is the Bible the Word of God? This question raises a legion of questions. How can we be sure that the Bible is the Word of God and not the wishful thinking of man through the ages? Is the Bible the child of man's own rationalization for something he wanted—life extended beyond this earthly life? Is the Bible the Word of God or of man? This is the question that must be resolved before the Bible can become of value to man. Three words hold the key to the truth we are seeking to unlock this door of the mind, and it is essential that we understand their meaning and application to the Bible. They are *revelation, inspiration,* and *interpretation* (sometimes called "illumination").

If the Bible is the Word of God, how did God reveal Himself and His Word to man? The word "revelation" opens this window for us. When man received a revelation from God, what safeguarded the accuracy of his recording of this revelation? The word "inspiration" as it is applied to our Bible must be understood and accepted by a Bible student before the Bible becomes the Word of God to him. The third word needed to complete our spiritual triangle is the word "interpretation." God has spoken to men of other ages. These men have recorded in the language of their day these revelations from God. How is man to interpret the Scriptures today? Who is to interpret for us the words of the Bible? It is the purpose of the author to clarify these questions of theology in this chapter.

Revelation has to do with the process of causing another to see something unknown to him. Man can know nothing about God unless God chooses to reveal Himself to man. The Bible says, "The heavens declare the glory of God . . ." (Psa. 19:1). The heavens can declare the glory of God, but they cannot nor do they reveal God Himself as God. Jesus said, "If you have seen me you have seen the Father" (John 14:9). God has revealed Himself to man through the voice of prophecy and the prophets. Prophets were charged by God to reveal God's concepts, desires, and behavior patterns for man. The prophets were more concerned in calling God's people back to God— those who had forsaken the laws of God—than they were in predicting future events, for the former was the basic desire of God. They did both upon certain occasions. God identified Himself with His message to His prophets and others by performing miracles for them or through them. Jesus used the same technique to establish before men His own relationship with God the Father.

Jesus was the supreme and last revelation of God Himself to man. Henceforth, knowledge of God must come from the study of God's Word. The Word of God, the Holy Bible, becomes the source of our knowledge of God. Jesus proved his relationship to God by His miracles and by the prophecies He made of certain events that were to come. History has validated His claims to be the "one sent from God." The New Testament is the official recording of this historical visit of Christ to earth and the interpretation of it. We repeat, the Bible is not a book of general history nor a book of science, but a book of God's divine revelation of Himself to man. The New Testament was closed and all writings excluded from it upon the death of the last of the disciples of Christ. The New Testament is a "verified" book by eye witnesses. The word "Canon" (kavwv) means a "measuring reed"; hence, a rule or a standard. It is a book, if believed and lived, that will measure our lives to the standards of God. It says to us, "This is the life that pleases God." If man is to know how to live to please God, the Bible is his rule of measurement. If man would realize the highest form of living, the Bible gives him the patterns to follow. Revelation is God's method of revealing Himself to man. Revelation is God breaking through the barrier of divine silence to speak to man—the creature He created and with whom He could share Himself and have communion with through all the ages to come.

The word *inspiration* has to do with the mechanics employed by God to properly have His revelation recorded for the human race. It deals with the problem of "selecting" and "retaining" and "recording" the right material God is revealing to man. It is in this area that many theologians differ. It is easy to confuse the meaning of the words *revelation, inspiration,* and *interpretation.* Man must be inspired by the Holy Spirit to receive the revelations of God, and it must also be the responsibility of the Holy Spirit to see that God's revelation is properly recorded by man. The Holy Spirit is also responsible for the selection of the material recorded. We have an excellent example of this in the experience of Peter when he responded to the question asked by Jesus, "Whom do men say that I am?" (Matt. 16:16). Peter replied, "Thou art the Christ, the Son of the Living God." Peter gave Jesus the answer He wanted to hear—it was the right answer.

Jesus lays down a spiritual principle regarding inspiration in verse seventeen of the sixteenth chapter of Matthew when He said,

"Blessed are you, Simon Barjona! For flesh and blood has not revealed this to you, but my Father in heaven." Peter had received
the divine revelation in respect to the person of Jesus, and the Holy
Spirit had confirmed this revelation. It was not a revelation by, or of,
men—no, not even a group of men. Peter had not figured all this
out by human logic. He had not gone to the Jewish historical computer of Israel and after feeding into this computer all the data he
had learned from history plus all the experiences he had with Jesus
up to this moment, he did not press a button and learn the answer
regarding the person of Christ. The Holy Spirit was God's computer
for him.

Dr. Strong defines inspiration of the Scriptures as "that special
divine influence upon the minds of the Scripture writers in virtue of
which their production, apart from error of transcription, and when
rightly interpreted, together constitute an infallible and sufficient rule
of faith and practice.[1]

God speaks to man (revelation) and man records the truth of the
message God is conveying to man under the guiding influence of
the Holy Spirit (inspiration). The writers of the New Testament
had been promised the coming of the Holy Spirit and that the Holy
Spirit would *reveal, teach,* and *direct* their lives (John 15:26, 27;
John 20:21, 22; Matt. 10:19, 20, and Gal. 1:12). Paul sums up
his own concept of inspiration as it is related to revelation in Gal.
1:11, 12: "For I would have you know, brethren, that the gospel
which was preached by me is not man's gospel. For I did not receive
it from man, nor was I taught it, but it came through a revelation
of Jesus Christ."

There has been much speculation concerning the doctrine of the
divine inspiration of the Scriptures. These theories rise and fall like
the tides of the sea. They reappear in some new form in each new
generation, but their substance is always the same. It shall be our
purpose to group each theory in respect to its substance, not by its
style or form. Our modern age had added nothing new to the theological stream in this area except to cast a new cloak over some old
dead bodies. However, we believe that this method will be more
knowledgeable to our modern reader. I recognize it is impossible

---

[1]Augustus Hopkins Strong, *Systematic Theology* (New York: Armstrong and Son,
1889), p. 95.

to keep these theories from overlapping or "spilling over" from one classification to another.

We shall group the several theories of *inspiration* under four subjects and give to each a classification. These classifications are: (1) THE INTELLECTUAL AND EMOTIONAL INSPIRA- TION THEORY (this includes the old "intuition" theory and the "general inspiration" theory); (2) THE GENERAL SPIRITUAL INSPIRATION THEORY (this includes the "illumination" and "mechanical" theories); (3) THE ROBOT THEORY (this in- cludes the "verbal" and "dictation" theories); and (4) THE SPIRITUAL COOPERATIONAL THEORY (under this classifi- cation are the "plenary" and "dynamical" theories). We believe that all other theories would fall into one of these four categories.

1. THE INTELLECTUAL AND EMOTIONAL INSPI- RATION THEORY. The general inspiration and intuition theories both suggest much of the same ideas regarding inspiration, namely, it is merely a higher development of the natural insight into truth which all men possess to some degree. It is this kind of inspiration that produces our artists, men of science, writers, etc. This suggests that inspiration is but a higher development of man's natural in- tellectual ability to filter out and discover truths beyond the normal range of the mind. All men possess this potential to a degree. This theory suggests that the writers of our Bible were such men. This theory relates itself to the Pelagian and the rationalistic view of man's independence of God. Man replaces God's revelation with man's own intellectual and emotional inspiration—born in the mind of man and brought to the surface by man's emotions.

I reject this theory when it is applied to the Bible, for it is based upon the flow of human emotions which are aroused by physical stimuli. The individual's brain, glands, and emotions are stimulated into a response by physical stimuli found in his immediate environ- ment at the time of the experience. The stimulation could come from the response of the audience he is addressing. It could be a response to the speaker's own voice coming back to him—bouncing back from the faces of those before him—or it could be the result of his own reactions to the physical "props" of the building, the background music, or lighting effects skillfully created to build a "crowd mood." A man might be stimulated to paint, write, or speak, far beyond his known ability, by the beauty of a sunset, the whisper of a soft breeze, or the moonlight seen dancing on the surface of a beautiful lake. His stimulation could be a response to the fragrance of a spring garden. Moments of great joy or great sorrow create inspiration. Men can rise, and have risen, to superhuman heights under such circumstances. Inspiration can come from the hours or days spent with the great minds of the ages (books).

There is nothing wrong with such inspiration—man was made to be able to respond to such stimuli. But the Bible did not come to man that way. It came to man from the mind of God. The heavens and even the lilies declare the glory of God (Matt. 6:22-24). But each is incapable of declaring the nature, beauty, or the personality of God. God's mind cannot be revealed to man by such means (Romans 1:17-25).

This type of inspiration does not assure the accuracy of the thing spoken or written. Many religious poems and religious hymns are things of beauty, and they offer emotional inspiration to people, but many of their truths break down in the light of truth itself. The Bible is not a book of intellectual and emotional inspiration; if it were, it could not have stood the test of the ages. It is not a record of man's response to his physical environment. Man is a prisoner of his physical world, and the inspiration he receives from the stimuli of his physical prison can help lift his vision above the physical norm, but it cannot nor does it qualify his utterances to bear the mark of the divine. The Bible is man's spiritual response to the divine—to a spiritual stimulus outside of himself and his physical world. Man lacks the capacity to reach out to the divine—but the divine can and does reach down to man, and the response to this meeting is divine inspiration. Intellectual and emotional inspiration cause man to reach out from himself to other men. The Bible is not a book that found its origin in the mind of man. It came to man from the mind of God.

2. THE GENERAL SPIRITUAL INSPIRATION THEORY. The "illumination" and "mechanical" theories would feel comfortable under this umbrella. It claims inspiration for all Christians; Christians differ only in degrees of inspiration. This theory dates back to the Arminian view of inspiration. The Christian is said to have been cooperating with God in producing the Scriptures. It is claimed that the Bible is not the word of God, but that it contains the word of God, and that the words of the Bible are not inspired but the writers were inspired.

It says that the spiritual man has the same inspirational potential that man has intellectually. One man (Christian) can lift himself up to a higher inspirational level than other men. The way he responds to the Holy Spirit's leadership determines the degree of his inspiration. It teaches that the preacher of any age is just as inspired as Paul was when he wrote the Book of Romans. To believe this is to add confusion to eternal truth.

I cannot accept this theory, for I believe that the Holy Spirit reveals no new truths today from God that are not already recorded in the Scriptures. The Holy Spirit reveals only to modern man revelations of God already contained in the Scriptures, and modern man cannot add to these revelations by his own spiritual inspirations.

3. THE ROBOT THEORY. We would have to include the Dictation Theory and the Verbal Theory of inspiration under this classification. Man is merely a machine recording the words of God. Man is not aware of what he is writing, nor does he have any control of the words or phrases he uses. He is a human secretary for God. He holds the pen but God guides his hand as he writes. Both theories have much to commend them, but both are weakened by the extremes to which they are carried by their advocates. To the casual reader of the Bible—and to many devout Christians—"verbal inspiration" means that every word of the King James translation is divinely selected. This is why I have suggested a fourth classification.

The words of the Bible, with man writing the words, are inspired. God does the selection of not only the thoughts for the writer, but also the words to record these thoughts. I cannot accept this theory, for it reduces man to a machine without mind or emotions. It does not place God in a very favorable position in His relationship to a spirit-led child that He uses to do his mechanical work of recording. It also charges God with all the errors of spelling, grammar, questionable dates, and changes in theological views expressed. For example, Paul wrote concerning the early expectance of the return of Christ, but later he wrote of the delayed return of Christ. Which view was inspired of the Holy Spirit and which view was not?

4. THE SPIRITUAL COOPERATIONAL THEORY. The "plenary" and the "dynamical" theories make up this theory. The word "plenary" means "complete" or "entire," and "dynamical" has to do with the supernatural work of God in revealing to spiritually sensitive men the message He wanted them to record about Himself. It told that inspiration is not a natural but a supernatural fact of a

Holy God working in the life of spiritual man to produce the Bible. It is man cooperating with God on the highest level to produce a spiritual masterpiece unmatched in all history—the Holy Bible.

We believe that this is in keeping with the words of Peter: "No prophecy ever came except as the Holy men spake from God, being moved by the Holy Spirit" (2 Peter 1:21). God spoke to certain men concerning His Holy Truths, and these men recorded them, but did so only within the command they had of their own language and in the light of their knowledge of the scientific truths of their day. God's power to make his truth known to men is not in ratio to their literary abilities or inabilities. However, man's spiritual and intellectual limitations have placed restrictions on the recording of God's truth. God chose certain men, and these men recorded the messages of God within the framework of their own culture. To properly understand what these spirit-led men recorded, one must also understand their social, political, cultural, and religious backgrounds. The amazing thing about the Bible is that although it was recorded over a span of more than 1500 years in languages of many cultures and was recorded by men of many cultural patterns, its messages come through "clear and plain" and "understandable in every age," and this does not exclude our highly scientific age of today. It had to be of God to do this!

Dr. Augustus Strong sums up this theory by saying, "The Scriptures contain a human as well as a divine element, so that while they constitute a body of infallible truth, this truth is shaped in human molds and adaptable to ordinary human intelligence . . . in short, inspiration is neither natural, partial, nor mechanical, but supernatural, plenary, and dynamical."[2]

Dr. Strong hands down two cardinal principles in respect to inspiration: "Principles: (A) The human mind can be inhabited and energized by God while yet attaining and retaining therein its own highest intelligence and freedom. (B) The Scripture, being the work of one God, as well as of the man in whom God moved and dwelt, constitutes an articulated and organic unity. Question: (A) Is any part of Scripture uninspired? Answer: Every part of Scripture is inspired in its connection and relation with every other part. (B) Are there degrees of inspiration? Answer: There are degrees of value, but not of inspiration. Each part in its connection with the rest is

---

[2]Strong, *Systematic Theology*, pp. 99-100.

made completely true, and completeness has no degree. It has been said, 'The Scriptures are given to teach us, not how the heavens go, but how to go to heaven.' "[3]

Dr. Weatherhead sums it up in another way when he says, "The Biblical historian is not as eager to be accurate as to show God at work in history. The psalmist is not so eager to write good poetry as to proclaim the glory of God."[4]

The third word of our spiritual triangle must not be excluded in our search for the answer to "Whence cometh our Bible?" This is the word "interpretation." Dr. Kenneth Wuest calls it "illumination."[5] If God revealed a message, and this message was recorded by men inspired by the Holy Spirit, who is to interpret what is revealed and recorded? Jesus gives us our clue when he said to His disciples that men of old and men of every age "would have eyes to see, but they could not see; they would have ears to hear, but could not hear" (Matt. 13:17). The Holy Spirit, who has taken up his abode in the life of every Christian, is to act as the teacher. To the Christian, the Bible is not merely another book—no, not even another religious book. It is our only source of knowledge concerning God. We would caution our readers that the Holy Spirit will not open the Scriptures to anyone who is not willing to pay the intellectual price as well as the spiritual price to understand the word of God. The Holy Spirit will not teach you the Greek language of the New Testament; no, He will not even teach you how to read the English Bible! Your understanding of the Bible will be in direct ratio to your willingness to pay the price for your spiritual and intellectual development; neither can be ignored without cost in knowledge of God's word. The parables of Jesus cannot be understood in all their richness, unless something is known about the background of each parable. Each is built upon some known object of that day and each had some special materialistic meaning that Jesus wanted to bring over into the spiritual world to help His listeners understand some spiritual truth. One must know the meaning of the "needle's eye" to understand the full spiritual application Jesus was making in the parable of the camel and the needle's

---

[3]*Ibid.*, p. 104.

[4]Leslie D. Weatherhead, *The Christian Agnostic* (New York: Abingdon Press, 1965), p. 197.

[5]Kenneth Wuest, *Wuest's Word Studies* (Grand Rapids, Michigan: Wm. B. Eerdmans Publishing Co., 1953).

eye. The Holy Spirit can use only the tools available to Him. If a person's mind is sharpened to a keen edge by study, and his spirit is warmly alive in responding to the leadership of the Holy Spirit, much is revealed to him of the great truths to be found in the Bible. If either one of these two is missing in the life of the student, the Bible has little to say to him.

We are told that the Scriptures are to be studied for a spiritual profit. They are trustworthy. If the Bible is not God's word to us, and if it is not to be trusted—what is left for the Christian to follow? There is no other source of divine wisdom to be found: All else is of man himself.

3

The Imprint of
the Changing Ages
upon Christianity

If Peter, James, John, or Paul should return to earth for a short visit, each would be staggered at the changes which have taken place within the framework of the Christian movement. Many things that they would see and hear under the name of "the church" would shock and amaze them. The Christian movement has been a changing organization since Jesus left it in the hands of His early disciples. In some areas of Christianity, the only thing its church has in common with the first-century church is the name "Christ"— and some Christians are not too proud of that. How and why did all this happen? Was this change a part of God's plan? If the change was not of God's choosing, why did He permit it to take place?

Let us face the last question first. When Christ left His movement in the hands of men, He could control its direction only as long as He was able to control those to whom the responsibilities of the church movement were given. Men still possessed their human weaknesses. At times, some of the leaders were not even spirit-born. Men were brought into the church from many kinds of backgrounds and training, and each brought these differences into the church itself. When these things are considered in a study of church history, we shall find the answer to our first question, "Why and how did the Christian movement change from the simple program of preaching the Gospel of the first century (the story of the life, death, and resurrection of Jesus) to what we see in the world today?"

The first few years after the resurrection and ascension of Christ there was no written word; no, not even the New Testament. There was no need for this as there were the eleven Christ-trained disciples who could give their own personal testimonies of what later became the recorded Gospel. They all expected an early return of Christ to earth; why then should they take time out to write about matters known to so many and which were witnessed by persons to whom they were preaching about Christ? To write these things down would be a waste of energy and time.

When the great persecutor of the early Christians, Saul of Tarsus, was converted to Christianity, the Christian movement made its first change. Paul, too, thought that Christ would speedily return. He was a zealous proclaimer of The Christ across Asia Minor and later in Europe. He had one message: *Christ the Messiah, the Saviour, who came and lived among men was nailed to a Roman cross, and in so dying, He became the One who died for all. Through and by His death, man could now have his broken fellowship with God restored by exercising faith in Christ.* Paul came to know this Jesus himself in a personal way on the road to Damascus. He wanted to share the good news with everyone.

Paul believed in the early return of Christ as did all the early Christians. They misunderstood the timetable of Christ, however, and when Christ failed to return, serious questions began to arise in the minds of those early Christians. Paul knew one thing—he had had a personal experience with Christ, and he had seen thousands of other lives changed by contact with Christ. Paul shifted his emphasis from the early return of Christ to the fact that Christ was already living in the lives of all Christians on earth. It was true that He would return some day, He had given His personal promise (John 14:3). But Christians did not have to wait for death or for that day to have Christ with them. They could enjoy daily fellowship with Christ, for He was alive within their lives. "For me to live is for Christ to live . . . He lives in me . . . We are the temples of God . . ." These statements of Paul give us the key to his theology; namely Christ lives within the lives of all His children. This is the spirit, henceforth, of all of Paul's writings.

When the Christian movement moved into the Mediterranean world, it drew into its ranks Syrians, Egyptians, Greeks, Romans, and peoples from many lands. In turn, Christianity adopted many of the previous ideas and practices of these people. The Christian movement appealed to the Greek mind as well as to the Roman mind, and, in turn, the movement was conditioned by the various schools of thought represented by these people.

Dr. Luther Rice, in summing up this period of church history in an article of November 26, 1965, writes,

This was the very message that the sin-sick and weary Roman world needed. Faith in the old gods of mythology had been lost, and the Roman mind and heart were reaching out for some satisfaction, for some answer to the eternal questions which in every age intuitively stir in the human heart. They were ready for some religion that could take the place of the faith that had fallen.

From Egypt and the East had come the most attractive ritualistic religions, whose advocates sought to satisfy these longings with the things which they could give. The Cybele-Attis cult, with its elaborate rites, came from Phrygia. Certain Syrian nature cults came from that land of dreams. The Isis-Seraphis cult came from Egypt; and probably greatest of all, came the cult of Mithra, which reached its greatest influence contemporaneously with the beginnings of Christianity. Plutarch tells us that Pompey found traces of Mithra among the Cilician pirates in the first century B.C., and the armies of Rome came under the influence of the teachings of all these occult faiths, even before their priests and apostles brought them to the Capital City.

Now these religions all emphasized the idea of personal immortality, and because of the natural longings of the human heart for satisfaction to its intuitive faith in another world, the Romans were at first much drawn to these cults. These religions all taught a possible union of men with the life of the gods, through the efficacy and power of certain visible ceremonies and sacraments. And yet, at last, the Roman mind was a practical mind. They demanded reality. Hence they were not satisfied by these things. The cultured Roman was more and more offended by this frenzied worship, as he went more deeply into it. Though he was powerfully impressed by the promises which were made and which corresponded so much to his own intuitive hopes and longings, he nevertheless despised these mutilated, effeminate priests; while over it all was the absence of positive proof for their claims, and the lack of reality, which above everything else the Roman craved.

Just at this time, then, with this vacuum in the intellectual and spiritual life of the Empire needing to be filled by something, and this appetite for reality, and this longing for the assurance of immortality—about which Cicero theorized so beautifully—just at this time, I say, these men who had seen the risen Christ, brought to the attention of the Roman world the beautiful faith, founded upon fact, which He came to bring to our earth, and for which He lived and died and rose again. They did not come with pomp and ceremony. They were not fat, and slick, and well fed. They were not "hale-fellows-well-met" with the leading politicians. They were not given a reception and banquet by the ruling classes. They came not with silken robes and swinging censers, nor with vague promises, founded only upon shadowy hopes. No! They came with the marks of stripes upon their backs, with chains upon their limbs, with the very fervor of God in their hearts, and the ring of reality in their voices, as they said to the Roman world: 'Cast us into prison, if you wish, burn us and crucify us if you will, but we come to tell you the truth. We give you a faith that is not founded upon hearsay or theory. We give you reality. *We have seen the risen Christ*, and for the sake of this testimony, we prove our sincerity by the willingness to lay down our lives!'

"Jews and Christians were both influenced religiously by the religions of conquered and conquering nations, and frequently these religions almost suffocated Judaism and Christianity and led to explosive reactions in both of them."[1]

The Roman Catholic Church still bears the mark of the Roman Empire in its form of control of its members and in its constitution. It was influenced by the mystics of Asia who were attracted to the Christian movement by the mysteries of the Lord's Supper, baptism, and the promises of the Spirit of the Living God within the human frame. They, in turn, brought their own influence to play in molding the early church.

By the twelfth century, the theology of the Roman Church dominated the entire Christian movement. It tolerated no opposition in doctrine nor in its form of organization. William A. Gifford makes this observation of this period of history:

> After four hundred years, when the church seemed to have reached the saturation point, St. Vincent of Lerins thought it time to rule out further novelties, at least in theology. Only that was to be regarded as Catholic was truth which had been believed everywhere, always and by all. This became the Catholic mind. Nevertheless, further adjustments were required to be made. For example, when the writings of Aristotle came back to Europe by way of the Arabs of Spain, a few Catholic scholars saw that they could not be ignored; and within fifty years Albert the Great and Thomas Aquinas succeeded in incorporating Aristotle into the Catholic system.
>
> It was believed that all this vast system, Catholicism, was implicit in certain writings adopted by the church quite early as authoritative, or canonical. Catholicism, it was thought, was simply those Scriptures . . . the Bible made explicit.
>
> Catholicism was, by the twelfth century, a very comprehensive and impressive system; and the Catholic Christians were just the population itself participating in mysteries they did not understand, and submitting to a discipline that made them somewhat better here and much safer hereafter.[2]

This Catholicism remained unchanged, though attempts were made, without success, at three General Church Councils in 1500 to bring about reforms within the church and to turn back to the teachings of the New Testament. It took a German monk named

---

[1]Paul Tillich, *The Future of Religion* (New York: Harper and Row, 1966), p. 84.

[2]Wm. A. Gifford, *The Story of Faith* (New York: The Macmillan Co., 1946), pp. 578-80.

Luther, who, after trying to call the church's attention to abuses within the church, found himself charged by the church as a heretic for this attempt to bring about theological and moral change. In defending himself, Luther arrived at what is known as Protestantism. He rejected useless discussions of the theological schools and actions of church councils, and went back to the Scriptures for his authority. Henceforth, for Luther, Scholasticism and Canon Law were replaced by the Bible.

This created a vigorous and fresh examination of the Bible. It was discovered that the Bible was not A book, but a *library* of books, and that it was not a book of law on morals and religion, but a record of ancient men and their experiences with God and His with them. The New Testament was not church dogma to be followed blindly, but a record of the life, death, and resurrection of Christ as recorded in the four Gospels, and the rest of the New Testament was composed of letters written to churches or individuals (with the exception of the book of Revelation) to help them understand the meaning of what they had in Christ Jesus, what kind of life would honor Christ, and what Christ expected of them.

Preaching had died in the churches around the beginning of the fifth century and had been replaced by rituals to be performed and ceremonies to be conducted. The church spoke on all questions: at first in the area of spiritual matters and morals, but as it grew more powerful, on all matters with divine authority. The church did not speak through preaching, but through utterances of popes and church councils. Now, with the rediscovery of the Bible, preaching again was revived. The preacher had to do more than quote the church for his authority, or even the Bible. He had to justify what he said by a conviction born out of study of the Bible. Again, common men were being preached to after a thousand years of silence. They were hearing again what Paul said "by the foolishness of preaching" men were to be saved. (2 Cor. 11:21)

Three hundred years later there was another movement in the Christian world. Again, it was a backward turning to the Bible. Before they had turned from Canon Law and Scholasticism to the Bible; now they went back to the Bible—behind it—to the historical Christ of the Bible. They wanted to see what Jesus had to say concerning man in his relationship to other men. Men looked at their society and saw child labor, sweatshops, slavery, filth, disease, and moral decay and realized that something was still missing from human society. The social gospel and modern missions came forth as a result of the new emphasis.

Interest in the parables of Jesus and the Sermon on the Mount became the new focal points of study. What was learned from these studies awakened emotions to the plight of men everywhere. Modern missions became a moving force in the world. Cary went to India and Livingstone went to Africa; the lives of these two men became a challenge to the Christian churches of the world. This period became a golden one for all non-Roman Catholic churches. The Protestant churches and the Baptist churches of America became great spiritual forces for the first time in history, and not only in America; for their influence was felt around the world in schools, colleges, hospitals, and in their preaching ministry. Then, the wheels of this movement began to slow down at the end of World War II. Something began to happen, something was lacking in our religious emphasis as we faced two new forces in our world. Too many church theologians and church leaders are still unaware of what is happening to Christianity in our day.

Man for the first time faced the awful fact that he had within his hands—for the first time in all history—the power to destroy the world. Man had learned how to harness and release the awesome power of the atom. This was not disturbing as long as only the United States, a Christian nation, had this secret but when non-Christians, such as the Soviet Union and China, learned our secret, we knew that our world would never be the same.

The second force we face today is our new technology. It has been said that the computer has done more, and will do more, to change civilization than anything in history since the discovery of the wheel. This may or may not be so, but it is at least a symbol of this new scientific age. It is said that today 75 percent of all medicines we take were not known ten years ago, and that within twenty years, 85 percent of the working force of America will be working in jobs that are not now in existence. We have become a mobile people. We buy homes as we buy cars. No longer is homeownership a symbol of stability. A new word, "urbanization," describes our new society. We hide our personalities from the world in great cities.

Textbooks of ten years ago in some fields of science are now worthless. New ones have been written in light of new discoveries to replace those that are not only out of date, but stand in direct contradiction to new facts. This has had its effect on all fields of knowledge. We are on the threshold of new and unlimited knowledge in almost every known field. Have we come to a new threshold of theological knowledge? When we walk into this new room stacked with this new theological knowledge, will we find ourselves embarrassed, as some scientists have been in their particular fields. Will these new discoveries, if they are made, reaffirm our present convictions concerning the Bible, God, and Christ, or will they shatter these beliefs beyond recovery?

These considerations are sending some theologians into nontheological fields to find the answer. To take this direction is the same as if a man of medicine were to feel that to know more about the human body he must study astronomy. Some of these men will never survive the icy caves of their own doubts, for they have turned to the wrong sources of information. Others will return forever dazed by the glare of these nontheological lamps. (The Bible is still the only recorded source of God's approach to man.) All other books record the footprints of God as seen in His creative powers, but you will never find God that way. If these books are accurate and honest, they will help you in your search for the One who made those tracks, but you will have to return to the Book of Books—the Bible —for your final answer.

Jesus was once asked why He used the thought projection method (parables). He said that they would reveal the mysteries of God, mysteries which have been hidden since the day of creation (Matt. 10:1-17, Matt. 13:34-35). We need to return to the Bible, get behind the Bible to the Christ who is the center of it, sit at His feet again and listen to these thought projections, for they will give us the mysteries to match the mysteries being discovered by the men of science. And suppose we find not that which we are seeking? Suppose we draw a spiritual blank? What then? To whom or to what should we turn? Jesus once watched sadly as some of his early "would-be disciples" turned away from Him. They were not willing to pay the cost of following Him. They could not intellectually pay the price He demanded—believe in Him to the point of "eating His body"—sharing His death. Jesus looked at their retreating backs and asked the twelve disciples, "Will you, too, join their ranks?" (John 6:68.) One gave this answer; and it still rings clearly down through the ages and is magnified by all the advancements of science:

"To whom shall we go, to whom can we go? who has the words of life? If you do not have this for us, there is no hope anywhere else— it is you or nothing!" (John 6:68-70)

Those who would throw the New Testament overboard in the stormy sea in which we are living—to what and to whom can they turn? Their own minds? The mind of another mortal man, such as they, or to a group of mortal men? Far better to go overboard with the New Testament and take your chances with it as support than to attempt the stormy seas of life and eternity in your own finite wisdom, or to pit the mind of mortal man against the wisdom of God as revealed in His only earthly recorded revelation—the Bible.

4

Historical Interpretation
of the Thought Projections
# of Jesus and Their
Influence on Molding
the Christian Movement

In another chapter, we presented a brief survey of the growth and development of the Christian movement. A brief glance was taken at some of the external influences that came into the Christian church which helped mold many of the present-day theological views held by many Christians. To even a casual reader of church history it is apparent that the influence of the methods used to interpret Scripture has much to do with what is taught and believed in the church. In this chapter, we will examine the various approaches made in certain periods of church history in interpreting the thought projections of Jesus. There is a relationship to each of these periods with the external forces which came to exert their influence upon the church movement from within and from without the church.

It is now believed that many of the writings of Paul preceded the writing of the four Gospels. The "living historians"—Matthew, Mark, Luke, and John—gave not only personal witness to the life and teachings of Jesus, but also verification to these facts when spoken by other Christian leaders of the first century.

It was not until the conviction had grown into a strong certainty among the early church leaders that Christ might not come back within their own lifetime that the need arose for recording these historical events. In the meantime, Paul had been writing letters to the churches he was instrumental in organizing in Asia and in Europe.

It is often charged by those who would either reject the New Testament as the supreme authority for the doctrines of their church or put the traditions of their church on the same inspirational level with the New Testament that their church preceded the New Testament. They are not in error in thinking this if we think of the New Testament's birthday as the day its written form was completed. They are in great error, however, to assume that the life and teachings of Jesus preceded the formal organization of the church or that what Paul wrote only became truth for the churches of his age after he signed his name to each epistle.

The gospel is the gospel when it was lived and spoken by Jesus. Recording it on paper did not suddenly transform it into becoming THE GOSPEL. The truths enunciated by Paul in his letters to various churches did not suddenly become truths when he inked his name to each epistle.

We have divided the history of interpretation into six periods so that each might be considered in the light of its particular age. The first period is *the age of utterance* (verbal). This covers the life of Christ and up to the death of His disciples. Each thought projection was accepted by the people in the light of the time and place of its utterance. Jesus was asked to explain but a few of these sayings to His own disciples, and we do not have anyone outside of this family circle asking Him for an explanation.

The second period would extend from A.D. 100, the end of the first century, to the end of the fifth century. During this period *the allegorical method* was employed by theologians. This is the method of interpreting what is said by looking for a meaning different from the literal one. The one lost sheep is not a lost sheep at all—it can be a nation, an individual, and so on.

The third period runs from 500 to 1500. All theology during this period was based, not upon what the New Testament said about a subject, but upon what had been interpreted from the Scriptures on this subject by the early church fathers. No new interpretations could be offered contrary to what was taught by these early church fathers. I have called the period the *age of imprisonment of the Scriptures.*

The fourth period of history is from 1500 to 1800. This is the period *of liberation of the Scriptures from their theological prison* into which traditions of the church had cast it.

The fifth period is from 1800 to 1950. This is the period of the beginning of Biblical criticism. Careful comparisons were made of various Scriptures and their original sources, and the Bible had to be its own defense, from within and from without. This can be called the early *modern period.*

We now come to the sixth period, the age of nuclear science or the late *modern period.* It is the age of reaching out into the unknowns of life for answers to questions we have been afraid to ask for fear that the answers might not be of our choosing. They might force us to rewrite our theological concepts, and we were satisfied with the neat way such things had been pigeonholed for us by others from other ages.

Let us examine each of the periods in more detail in respect to what each contributed to the interpretations of thought projections of Jesus. The book is written with the belief that it, too, might make its own contribution to this last period. Could it be called the *thought projection period?*

1. THE AGE OF ORIGINAL UTTERANCES (A.D. 1-100). Jesus spoke His thought projections to many crowds and to His disciples in private. These were repeated by His disciples and others who had heard them. They were recorded by the writers of the four Gospels. Some utterances were duplicated; some were omitted by one, two, or three; and some were given by one writer while unstressed by the others. It seems that these thought projections were presented by these early disciples in somewhat the same manner as Jesus gave them. The hearers were left to draw their own conclusions and make their own applications. They had not yet been colored with "theology." It is reasonable to assume that the people of that century were familiar enough with the background of each of these thought projections to have a reasonable understanding of the thought Jesus had projected. Only when these teachings of Jesus were carried over into a different culture and to people with a different social, political, and cultural background did an interpretation and explanation become necessary.

2. THE ALLEGORICAL METHOD PERIOD (A.D. 100-500). When the church movement pushed out into the Greek world and began to have its ranks swelled by converts from Greek culture, the church soon felt the impact of this culture. The Greeks had been trained to accept their literature as sacred, creating problems for them with the gods of their literature. In the works of Homer, the gods did not always act in their moral conduct as gods should; thus, in order to protect their own spiritual natures, and that of their gods, some explanation had to be made for such "ungodly" conduct.

The allegorical method of interpretation of Homer's works and of all their literature gave them the perfect answer. So we have Zeus becoming the "upper air," Hera becoming the "lower air" and Poseidon becoming "water." This same method of interpretation became the method of the early church fathers in their study of the parabolic teachings of Jesus.

Mystery concepts of religion were brought into the Christian movement by converts from mystics of the Far East. The teachings of Christ regarding His own death and resurrection, the meaning of the Lord's Supper, baptism, and Paul's teaching of the indwelling Christ in the life of every Christian called for an allegorical interpretation of some Scriptures by the early church to justify some of these mystic ideas and doctrines.

Because of the many crosscurrents flowing across the unchanneled baby church, certain un-Biblical doctrines were being practiced. Some of these came from former religious backgrounds with only a thin coat of Christian veneer lightly brushed on, and some justification had to be found in the Scriptures for them. The Greek method of allegory became for the Christian theologians what it had been for the Greek apologists when they were called upon to defend questionable acts of their gods. Whenever a doctrine stood in contradiction with the Bible, the allegorical technique was applied to that Scripture. To read some of the things that were read into the thought projection spoken by Jesus would make a good comedy play if it were not in the field of religion. It was easier to change the meaning of the Scriptures than to change a doctrine!

Some of the outstanding church fathers who used this method were Irenaeus (130-200), Tertullian (160-220), Clement (150-215), Origen (185-254), and Augustine (340-430). An example of how this method was used by Augustine is in the story of the Good Samaritan. The wounded man of this story is a picture of a man who is "half-alive" in his knowledge and understanding of God and "half-dead" to sin. The act of binding up his wounds is seen by Augustine as an act which signifies Christ's restraint of sin. The act of pouring wine and oil into the man's wound is the "comfort coming from good works and an exhortation to spiritual work." The innkeeper is revealed by Augustine's X-ray eyes as the Apostle Paul, and the two pence given to the innkeeper are two commands of love!

Such approaches as these did not go unchallenged, but without success. They were challenged by men like Theodore of Mopsuestia

(350-428), John Chrysostom (347-407), and men from the Antioch School, but they could not stem the tide. Thus the foundation was laid for men to build their theological houses on the Bible without regard to what the Bible really taught or meant. The end justified their theological means. They could eat their theological cake and have it too. They could have their theological beliefs, and still claim the Bible to be their authority.

3. THE AGE OF IMPRISONMENT OF THE SCRIPTURES (500-1500). This period covers the centuries from the Dark Ages to the Renaissance and the Reformation. It was the period of such men as the Venerable Bede of Jarrow (673-735) and Thomas Aquinas (1175-1274). The church would not allow any interpretations of the Scriptures to be made that were not in keeping with those already made by the early church fathers. Theology of the Roman Catholic church became the master of the Holy Bible. The voice of the early church fathers and not the Scriptures, was the only voice to be followed. It was a dark age for the Word of God, for the Word was put to rest for a thousand years, not to be disturbed until the age of Luther. This was the age when it was more popular, and healthier, not to think than to think.

When we review the work of 1000 years on the parables of Jesus, one must say of these theologians what Emperor Galerius said of an archer he saw firing twenty successive arrows at a target and missing with all, "May I congratulate you on your splendid talent of missing."

4. THE PERIOD OF LIBERATION OF THE SCRIPTURES FROM THEIR THEOLOGICAL PRISON (1500-1800). This period extended from the Renaissance and Reformation to the Early Modern period. What produced this transition from the Dark Ages to the Early Modern period were the invention of the printing press (men everywhere now had an opportunity to read, whereas before, reading was limited to a few), the revival of learning, the general revolt against the Roman Catholic church, and the appearance of the Scriptures in the vernacular.

The Scriptures could again speak for themselves. Men discovered that the Bible was not a book, but a library of many books. Men began to compare Scriptures and to examine their findings with relation to discoveries in other fields that had bearing on religion. No longer did men have to stop at the library doors of the early church fathers in their search for spiritual truths. Now they did not even have to stop at their churches, but could push on directly into the Word of God itself. The Bible became their textbook and their authority.

Thought projections were no longer allegories, nor were they to be treated as such. Each could speak for itself. The treatment given to these teachings of Jesus by the early church fathers was no longer acceptable. Fve men stand out in this period; one gave his life. John Huss (1373-1415) was condemned by the Council of Constance and his body burned. His death made it possible later for Luther (1483-1546) to escape the same fate, but it was his work and that of Wycliff (1320?-1384) in England that prepared the soil for the reformation that, under the leadership of Luther, was to sweep Europe. John Calvin (1509-1564) and Juan Maldonado (1533-1583) caught the torch set afire by Wycliff and Huss and fanned by Luther, until this light could be seen by all men for ages to come. The hole these men burned in the theological curtain can never be repaired.

5. THE EARLY MODERN PERIOD (1800-1950). This is the age of modern missions and the rise of the social gospel. Theologians began another critical study of the Bible in an attempt to rediscover Christ's and God's attitude toward man. Man's personal interest in man was the focal point of attention. The Christian Church was awakened to the fact that the Bible taught that men everywhere were lost. This gave birth to the modern mission programs of the Baptist and Protestant groups. Missions became the keynote of the pulpit. Schools, hospitals, and colleges bearing the name of Christ sprang up all over the world.

A second thing came out of this study—a new social gospel. Man-to-man relationship was given a new look through the eyes of the New Testament. This wrought profound changes in the social structure of America. Children were taken out of workshops and put into school, working days were reduced, and working hours began to shrink. Man's value of man began to rise.

And then came World War II and Korea, followed by Vietnam. Former allies became enemies, and enemies became new allies. Nationalism became the focal point of the eyes of the world. Africa rose up in revolt, and new nations were born overnight. This same spirit of revolt spread into the national life and the minority groups within our society. And above the heads of all mankind, hanging by a human hair, is the bomb that can wipe out our entire civilization.

We ask ourselves, "What happened to our spirit of missions and what has happened to the social gospel? Before, we hated as a nation, but now we hate and resist our fellowman as an individual." We now face another age, another different period of history, and we ask ourselves, "Do we have the spiritual tools for it?"

Three men who have been outstanding in their interpretations of thought projections during this period and who have made the most outstanding contributions are Richard Trench, A. B. Bruce, and Adolf Julicher. Many theologians have added their contributions to this period, such as Albert Schweitzer (1875-1965), Walter Rauschen- busch (1861-1918), William Temple (1881-1944), Sören Kierke- gaard (1813-1855), Karl Barth (1886-1968) and Rudolph Bultmann (1884-   ), Emil Bruner (1889-1966), Reinhold Niebuhr (1892- 1971), and Paul Tillich (1886-1965). We do not stand in agreement with all that these men taught and believed, but each is a product of the theological trends of his day. We can summarize this period in regard to the change in thought projection interpretation by saying that it was the accepted opinion of most of the theologians of this period that thought projections were not allegorical in nature, but were similitudes. Each thought projection was looked upon as a figure of speech setting forth a single truth, easily understood by the crowd. Each thought projection had one central theme or point of interest. But who was to determine this one point? Which point was the right point? This was the weakness of this approach. The narrative was still the accepted definition of a parable, but some thought was given to the metaphors as "parable seeds." We have come a long way in understanding the thought projections of Jesus, but we still have one big gulf to cross. This is now being crossed by our sixth period (1950-   ).

6. THE LATE MODERN PERIOD (1950-   ) or the *Thought Projection Period.* It could also be known as the "age of the computer" or the "age of nuclear science."

The narrative fence is removed from the parables of Jesus, and because of the association of the word *parable* with the narrative form of a parable, the words *thought projections of Jesus* are sub- stituted. This term is more in keeping with the Greek word for "parable." By using this method to locate the thought projections of Jesus, we have a tool that for the first time helps us to recognize every one of these golden gems which fell from the lips of Jesus. They can be gathered one by one and studied for the mysteries hidden from the minds of man since the foundations of the world were laid down by God (Matt. 13:34-35). Each of these jewels is found in one of the four figures of speech used by Jesus: the simile, the metaphor, the allegory, or the proverb.

In the Gospel of Matthew there are *twenty-one* narrative parables or thought projections. Thus, if we use the old parable criteria to locate a thought projection, this Gospel would yield only twenty-one jewels from the mind of Christ, but when we use the thought projection method we will find *one hundred and thirty-one* pure thought projections plus the twenty-one thought projections which are narrative parables, for a total of *one hundred and fifty-two* of God's diamonds in the Gospel of Matthew alone! Instead of having twenty-one thought projections to think upon, we have one hundred fifty-two to challenge our minds.

The men who have laid the foundation for this method by their contributions in the field of parables are Dodd C. Campbell Morgan, Jermias, Herbert Lockyer, and others. The thought projection method is this author's contribution born out of thirty years of study of the parables of Jesus.

5

What Is a Thought Projection?

What is a parable? Almost any Sunday school pupil would give you an answer something like this: "A parable is an earthly story with a heavenly meaning." When this definition is placed beside the so-called parables in the New Testament it is quite adequate in its application. But an examination of the word "parable" itself would quickly reveal the limitation of such a definition, for a parable is more than what is suggested by this definition.

What is a parable? It would profit us in our search for a definition to examine what a parable is not. *It is not a fable.* Most dictionaries will define a fable as "a brief story or tale embodying a moral, and introducing persons, animals, or inanimate things as speakers and actors," or "a foolish or improbable story."

Richard C. Trench in his book *Notes on the Parables of Our Lord* makes this comparison between a parable and a fable.

> The parable is constructed to set forth a truth spiritually and heavenly; this, the fable, with all its value, is not. It is essentially of the earth, and never lifts itself above the earth. It never has a higher aim than to inculcate maxims of prudential morality, industry, caution, foresight, and the like; and these will sometimes recommend even at the expense of the higher self-forgetting virtues. The fable just reaches that pitch of morality which the world will understand and approve. But it has no place in the Scriptures and in the nature of things could have none, the purpose of Scriptures excludes it; that purpose being the awakening of man to a consciousness of a divine origin, the education of the reason, and of all which is spiritual in man, and not, except incidentally, the sharpening of the understanding.[1]

Every parable spoken by Jesus came out of an experience common to those to whom He was speaking. A parable is born out of a human experience; it is never a creature of a vivid imagination, and

---

[1]Richard C. Trench, *Notes On the Parables of Our Lord* (Westwood, N.J.: Fleming H. Revell Co.), pp. 3-4.

it is grounded in reality. A fable is a created child of an imaginative mind with no factual foundation, and it is created to give emphasis to some moral value being stressed. It is often an instrument of entertainment. A parable is never used by Jesus for this purpose.

A parable is not a myth (mythus). A myth is a vehicle for truth, but it can be made up of an untruth mixed with the truth. One cannot often distinguish between the two. A parable is a vehicle *only* for a spiritual truth—it is never mixed with an untruth. In the Parable of the Unjust Judge (Luke 18:1-8), God is pictured as the judge. God cannot be "just" and "unjust." This parable is simply illustrating man's part in prayer. The judge adjusted the grievances of the woman against whom he had ruled previously. She did not give up her "pleading" until she had received what she wanted. Prayer was the subject under discussion. Jesus begins this parable with these words, "He spake a parable to them to this end, that they ought always to pray, and not to faint" (Luke 18:1). A parable has to be the truth "all the way." It must portray a truth in the subject selected as the vehicle, and a truth must be in its conclusion or application.

A parable is never a story told to entertain or to amuse. It is not a story told just for the telling. There is a spiritual purpose in every parable Jesus spoke. Each parable came from the mind of Christ to answer a spiritual need He saw in the hearts of those around Him. Jesus was not an actor on a stage to entertain those who came out to hear and see Him. He was not concerned about establishing a reputation as a great public speaker or being a "jolly good fellow." He was a spiritual surgeon using words as His scalpel to remove the sin-tumor from their souls.

It is suggested by many theologians that a parable is not an allegory nor a proverb. I do not share this view because I believe that the word "parable" itself in the original Hebrew (*mashal*) and Greek (*parabole*) languages carries the same idea as the proverb— "be like." Jesus takes ancient proverbs and turns them into New Testament parables. Examples of this are "Physician, heal thyself" (Luke 4:23) and "The things which come out of a man are what defile him" (Matt. 15:11). We contend that these are parables in their basic nature and in the true definition of the words *mashal* and *parabole.* Six such parables are found in Matthew's Gospel.

We see Jesus using an allegory in His construction of the parable known as the Parable of the Sower (Matt. 13:3-9, 19-23). We have twenty-three such parables whose origins begin as allegories. We traced elsewhere in this book the history of the interpretation of parables and how, for many centuries, the allegorical emphasis dominated every interpretation of the utterances of Jesus.

We now come back to the basic question, "What is a parable?" Again we turn to the Hebrew word *mashal* and its Aramaic equivalent, *mathla*. Each is derived from a verb meaning "to be like"—a very broad label that covers several figures of speech. The Greek word *parabole*, para (beside) + *ballo* (throw or cast), suggests the casting down of one thing beside another thing. A familiar comparison is drawn so that the message might be understood. There are four ways used by Jesus in the New Testament to do this: They are the PROVERB plus three figures of speech, SIMILE, METAPHOR, and ALLEGORY. The idea of a "narrative association" has nothing to do with the definition of a parable.

The familiar parables are given in narrative form. Because of the limitation that the narrative idea imposes upon our study of the parables of Jesus, we suggest a different classification for these utterances of Jesus. We suggest the classification THOUGHT PROJECTIONS OF JESUS. Henceforth, we shall use this term in this book as the final classification of all the parables of Jesus, regardless of whether they appear in narrative form or not. We believe it would be correct to classify all parables as THOUGHT PROJECTIONS with a further subclassification of "narrative thought projections" (parables) and "pure thought projections" (nonnarrative form). A thought projection may be "contrastable" or "historical" in nature. There are five historical and one contrastable thought projections found in the Gospel of Matthew (see chapter 9, "Classification of the Thought Projections in Matthew").

Jesus projects thoughts for people to absorb into their own minds, and from this process of assimilation by word-stimulation, the people must determine for themselves the course of action they choose to take. Jesus is saying to them, "Here is the need I see in your life. Take this thought I am casting down beside that need. The answer to your need is to be found within that thought. You draw your own parable and you will find your own answer within that parable." He said to them on one occasion, "Who is the real neighbor? [Parable of the Good Samaritan (Luke 10:30-37)]. You tell me the conclusion you have drawn from the story. What is your answer?"

"I am the bread of life" (John 6:35). Jesus is throwing out a metaphor for them to mull over in their minds. When they find the answer by placing the idea of bread alongside of Christ, they will come up with some startling answers about themselves (their hunger for food) and Christ (He will supply that need). They will discover, too, that bread is of no value to the hungry unless eaten. This is a THOUGHT PROJECTION IN ACTION. This is a parable. Jesus gives them the "ready or instant mix," and they need only to add water (think it through) and out comes a perfect parable.

What is a parable? We must conclude from these studies that a parable is more than a narrative placed alongside a spiritual fact by Jesus so that people might understand that truth and act upon it. It is any thought projected by Jesus into the minds of His hearers that will cause them to place it beside a need in their lives and which stimulates them into forming a conclusion for themselves. Man has to make a decision with every thought projection of Jesus. Each demands an answer from the hearer. Each will be given an answer by the hearer.

These thought projections (parables) of Jesus are developed by Jesus in four ways in the New Testament. Three are figures of speech and the fourth way is through the proverb.* If we go searching only for the narrative parables of Jesus, we will miss most of the thought projections uttered by Him. It would be like hunting for iron ore and passing up diamonds! So we go searching the Gospel, not for narratives, but for the similes, metaphors, allegories, and proverbs, for in each is to be found a precious jewel from the lips of Jesus. The work may be tedious, but it is richly rewarding for the searcher.

What is a proverb (pro—before, verbun—word; thus, "words spoken before"), and how does Jesus use a proverb to project a thought? A proverb is a pithy saying ("a rolling stone gathers no moss," etc.), especially one condensing the wisdom of experience. Jesus takes an ancient proverb and uses it as a parable. He makes a parable out of it by placing it alongside a spiritual unknown to reveal its truth to the hearers. Two examples are: "Physician, heal thyself" (Luke 4:23), or "A prophet is not without honor save in his own country" (Matt. 13:57). When Jesus said, "The well need no physician" (Matt. 9:10-13), he was using a proverb to paint a picture of the self-righteous people who were blind to their own

---

*For the sake of convenience, I am including proverbs with the figures of speech.

need of Him. The healthy people did not seek out a doctor in the days of Christ—only the very sick did this. Find the proverbs used by Jesus and you will find a thought projection or a parable pearl within its structure.

Almost all the narrative-type parables of Jesus were constructed from similes. This is a figure of speech expressing comparison or likeness by the use of such term as *like, as, like as, so,* etc. The thought projection (parable) of the ten virgins is an example. These are easily located because Jesus begins almost all narrative thought projections with *as, like,* and *like unto.* Alertness to these many similes as we read the Gospels will bring its own reward in the discovery of many new and penetrating thoughts from the mind of Christ. There are twenty-eight similes in the Gospel of Matthew.

Jesus used many metaphors to plant His thought projections in the minds of his audiences. Matthew's Gospel abounds in these. There are ninety-three of these in Matthew's Gospel. A metaphor is a figure of speech in which one object is likened to another by speaking of it as if it were the other. It is distinguished from a simile by not employing any word of comparison such as *like, as, like unto,* etc. The word *metaphor* is of Greek origin. The preposition *meta* (over) and the verb *pherein* (to carry) means to carry over one thing into the other. Jesus uses it to transfer the identity of one object to another so the other is understood. "Beware of the leaven of the Pharisees" (Matt. 16:6). The evil influence of the Pharisees is identified with the Pharisee himself. "Ye are the light of the world" (Matt. 5:14). Jesus is using a metaphor to show the disciples the responsibility of their influence. They are compared to light shining in a world of darkness. It will not be denied, and it will be seen by others.

The first parable to which Jesus offered an explanation after a request from His disciples was built upon an allegory (Matt. 13:3-9; 19-23). This is the Parable of the Sower. Later he was asked to explain another parable (Matt. 13:24-30; 36-43), the Parable of the Wheat and the Tares. The Gospel of Matthew contains twenty-three such thought projections (parables) built upon allegories. This figure of speech still gives the student of the New Testament the most trouble; however, this has not been limited to the modern scholar!

"An allegory [*allos* (other) + *agoreoein* (to speak in public assembly-forum)] is the setting forth of a subject or the telling of a

story in figurative or symbolic language requiring interpretation, . . .
a story or narrative, as a fable, in which a moral principle or abstract
truth is presented by means of fictional character, events, etc.," says
a modern dictionary.[2] It means basically to interpret a text in terms
of something else. The Greeks made this approach very popular in
their attempts to interpret the works of Homer. The early church
fathers, in their attempts to justify some of their doctrines, used this
method to get around Scriptures that did not square up to their
doctrines. We still must be on guard so as not to fall into the
same pit as we try to interpret the allegorical thought projections
(parables) of Jesus.

E. W. Bullinger sums up the simile, the metaphor, and the
allegory as they relate themselves to each other, this way: "META-
PHOR is a comparison by REPRESENTATION, COMPARISON
IS SUBSTITUTED; SIMILE is a comparison by RESEMBLANCE,
COMPARISON IS STATED; ALLEGORY is a comparison by
IMPLICATION, COMPARISON IS IMPLIED."[3]

We come back to our original question with which we began
this chapter, "What is a parable?" It is a method used by Jesus to
bring to light a hidden spiritual truth to His hearers which they
seek to answer a personal need in their own lives. This was done by
the use of figures of speech and proverbs that made it possible for
Him to take a familiar circumstance of their daily lives and place it
alongside a hidden spiritual truth so that it could be recognized and
used by them to answer a need in their hearts. This familiar circumstance became identified with the hidden spiritual truth.

The figures of speech employed by Jesus to do this were the
metaphor, simile, allegory, and proverb. Jesus constructed some of
the parables for them and presented them to the people in narrative
form, but in most cases, He gave them the material (thought projections)—the easel and the brush to paint and hang their own
pictures (parables). This parabolic method we call the *thought projection* approach. Each thought projection is a parable in its truest
sense, for it performs the function of the root meaning of the word
"parable."

---

[2]*The Reader's Digest Great Encyclopedic Dictionary* (Pleasantville, N.Y.: The
Reader's Digest Association, 1966), p. 37.

[3]E. W. Bullinger, *Figures of Speech in the Bible*, p. 16, as quoted by Herbert
Lockyer in his *Parables of the Bible* (Grand Rapids, Michigan: Zondervan Publishing
House, n.d.), p. 16.

6

Some Psychological Reasons for the Thought Projection Method

"And He said unto them, unto you it is given to know the mystery of the Kingdom of God: but unto them that are without, all these things are done in parables. That seeing they may see, and not perceive; and hearing they may hear, and not understand: lest at anytime they should be converted, and their sins should be forgiven them" (Mark 4:11-12).

Why did Jesus use thought projections (parables)? Why did he tuck away great truths in obscure similes, metaphors, proverbs, and allegories? Why did not Jesus speak in simple and clear language the truths he wanted the people to hear? Surely, He must have had important reasons for not doing so. I believe Jesus did have good reasons for speaking as He did in thought projections (parables). We shall examine some of these reasons in this chapter.

Two of the reasons are negative in nature. Jesus was deliberate in using thought projections to hide great truths from those who would misuse or abuse them. Such persons would have used what He taught, not only against Him, but later against His followers. He justified this attitude by quoting His reasons from the Old Testament. Jesus was never blind to basic truth, nor was he blind to the hard facts of life: the hardness and unchangeableness of some men to the great things of God. He knew the history of His own people too well to be blinded to these truths. To such men, his thought projections did not make sense. Their true meaning and their truths were lost to them. They could not understand what He was trying to say, nor did they care.

A second negative reason why Jesus spoke in thought projections was that He did not want those who would only hate the truths He was trying to reveal to understand them. They simply lacked the spiritual capacity to appreciate them. His precious eternal truths should not be wasted—would not be wasted on the spiritually blind who wished to remain in that condition. He had nothing to reveal from God the Father to those who had not developed a spiritual sense of value for Godly things.

Jesus used a thought projection to illustrate this fact to His disciples. He warned them not to cast pearls before swine, for swine not only fail to appreciate the value of such pearls and trample them into the mud of their pigpen, but they turn and attempt to kill the giver of pearls in their disappointment. They want "slop," not "pearls." Those hogs had not developed a true sense of value for the finer things of life; nor did they have the capacity to do so, and it would be wasteful to give them pearls. Pearls would be lost and no good would come from this generous act.

Jesus was saying, "People can be like hogs; some do not have, nor care to have, a sense of value for spiritual things." The Gospel message is wasted on people who do not have, nor desire to have, a spiritual concept of fellowship with God. They are quite satisfied to live and die in a spiritual vacuum. These people to whom Jesus spoke had eyes to see and ears to hear the same things that John, Matthew, and Paul heard and saw, but they lacked the spiritual capacity and the moral desire of these men. John and Matthew were in the same crowd as those who rejected Jesus; all heard the same words from the lips of Jesus, but they all did not hear the same thing. They heard the same words, but the words did not hold the same value for each.

There are several positive reasons why Jesus used the thought projection method in His teaching and preaching. These are still valid today and are worthy of consideration.

1. *It is easier to teach an unknown fact by associating it with a known fact* than it is to try to explain the unknown fact by any other method. The root word for parable means "to place something alongside of another thing." Jesus would look at his audience, appraise its general background, and then select the type of thought projection most familiar to the most people. Trying to explain the great mystery of God to men who were either herdsmen or familiar with the relationship of the shepherd to his sheep, Jesus makes a comparison of God to a shepherd, sheep to people. This is the technique of teaching by association. This transference of knowledge from the known object to an unknown object tells much about the unknown.

2. Closely parallel to this reason is another: *It is using a known fact to throw "light" upon a dark unknown.* This acts in the same way a spotlight does when it is thrown on a dark stage. The actor is standing on the stage but can not be seen by the audience, for he is lost in the darkness of the stage. Then a brilliant spotlight reaches out its fingers of light and captures him, and there he is for all to see! "When ye pray," say "our Father . . ." (Matt. 6:9), said Jesus. Here the spotlight is the word "Father", which is thrown on God. Each who heard Jesus speaking had a father of his own. Each knew what this meant: love, protection, understanding, companionship, and so on. They could understand God, if God was like a Father. If Jesus had said that God was, "omnipotent," "omniscient," and "omnipresent," these words would have meant nothing to fishermen and housewives who could not read nor write. Jesus would not have communicated with those He was trying to reach. The modern preacher today could learn from the teaching example of Jesus.

3. *The thought projection method used by Jesus forced His listeners to think for themselves.* The average man does not like to think for himself. Jesus challenged His hearers to arrive at some definite conclusion. This is a learning experience He thrust upon the people. So He tells the story of the traveler who was set upon by thieves, left to die, and bypassed by two religious men; but a religious outcast stopped, gave first aid, then carried him to an inn to recover, paying his bill and offering to return and pay any other cost that might be incurred by the wounded man.

Here we see the Master Teacher at His best. "You asked me a question, Who really is one's neighbor? You heard this story. What did you think of the characters in it? Of the three men in the story who could have given aid to the stricken man, Which of the three was a true neighbor?" His listeners were forced to do their own thinking and to arrive at the answer for themselves. Jesus made them think through for themselves, and His story became the blackboard upon which they could solve their own problem.

4. *The thought projection technique used by Jesus is an excellent method to gain the attention of a crowd.* Just watch the faces in any audience when a speaker starts telling a story, that is, using an illustration to give emphasis to what he is saying. Not only will the children come awake, but also the sleepy adults will sit up and give the speaker their complete and undivided attention. The skilled teacher knows that this attention must be converted very quickly

into interest or its effect is quickly lost. No one can turn away from a good story, and Jesus changed milling street crowds into interested audiences by the use of this technique. It must not be overlooked that Jesus never told a story just to be telling one, but that He always told one to illustrate the needs of the people He saw standing before Him.

5. *An illustration, a story, not only quickly gets attention, but is remembered by an audience long after the people of that audience have forgotten the subject or text of the speech or sermon.* Try reviewing at dinner a sermon the family has just heard at the morning worship service on any given Sunday. Not many will recall the text or the subject; a few will give a general summary of the message; but all will remember the illustrations used by the minister.

6. *The thought projection technique nails down great theological truths with parabolic nails.* If the illustrations are the things remembered longest in a sermon, it follows that the thing being illustrated will also be associated in our minds with the illustration.

7. Jesus used the parabolic method in his teaching and preaching because *It is easier to arouse and excite the emotions of people by words used this way than by any other method.* We hear with our minds, but the seed planted in our minds by way of the spoken word will not bear fruit unless it is watered by our emotions. These emotions—fear, hate, love, etc.—will give motivation to what we hear and see, and the degree of our reaction will be in ratio to the degree they have stirred us emotionally.

A leader of a great religious denomination, addressing the executive board charged with the raising of the budget for that particular year, said: "I wish it were as easy to raise money for the total budget which includes our colleges, mission work, and all our other activities, as it is to raise $200,000 we need to operate our Orphaned Children's Home." What this man of many years of experience in this type of work was saying was that "it is easier to get money for a cause if the emotions of our people are stirred. Who can fail to be stirred when orphaned children are being considered?" Millions of dollars each year are being fleeced from emotionally stirred American citizens.

8. *A good story bears repeating.* Whenever a thought projection was placed before a crowd by Jesus, the subconscious minds of the people in that crowd went on "standby alert" to record for future use the story or illustration used. "Now, I must remember this

story and tell it to my wife or my friends later." Is this not your reaction to an illustration or a good story you hear? Ministers who attend conventions always come back to their churches with many good stories that they use in the next several sermons, and they are well fortified with all the latest jokes. It is amazing how quickly a good story or a good joke spreads across the United States. This was true even before the age of the radio and television.

It is interesting to notice that men in public life who reject the Bible as a way of life will often quote a familiar parable from the Bible to prove a point. The leaders of Russia, of the past and present, have not been exceptions to this.

9. *Thought projections of Jesus force people to think for themselves,* and in so doing they associate themselves with the subject. A thinker becomes "owner" of his conclusions. The average child has to be made to study for himself, and we train the human mind for many years just to make men think. A thought projection or a narrative parable forces the hearer to "think it through" for himself. When you have done this, the thought you get from this learning activity becomes your own personal thought. This is your conclusion, and it becomes your own personal property. We are no longer a bystander, but have become involved. We will defend that which belongs to us.

No one can possess a book by merely buying it with money. You may have ownership of that book, but until you have read it yourself, you do not possess it for yourself. Legal claim to physical possession has little or no true value; if its contents are lost to you, it is not really yours to claim.

10. *Thought projections of Jesus demand a decision from every hearer.* You cannot brush them aside easily. They demand some decision, and Jesus gave each illustration expecting some decision upon the part of the hearer. Jesus never told a story just to entertain people. He saw the need in their lives for something. He placed the answer to that need in parabolic form; he asked them to study it through, and would then ask, "What answer did you find to meet your need"?

11. *Each thought projection Jesus cast before the people not only met a need He saw in their lives, but revealed something about God, the Heavenly Father.* Jesus was not interested in performing psychological tricks for the crowd nor in demonstrating to them the latest in psychiatry. He was not trying to turn man's thought inward or

outward, but upward. He wanted man to realize that God the Father was standing ready to come to the aid of all those who would turn and acknowledge Him in their lives.

12. *A story, an illustration called by any name—thought projection or parable, appeals to all ages and to all types of people.* It is universal in its appeal. Jesus quickly gained the attention of the children, adults, freemen, and slaves; men of the fields, of the shops, and even the teachers of his day by the simple use of parabolic illustrations. It matters not if the figure of speech used was a simile, metaphor, or an allegory, or if a proverb was used, when Jesus turned one of these into a thought projection He had the attention of the crowd, and thus could reveal to them something of the great hidden mysteries of God.

Jesus was falsely accused of many things, but he was never accused of being a dull or boresome preacher or teacher, nor of preaching "over the heads" of his audience.

7

Some Theological
Reasons for the Thought
Projection Method

"All these things spake Jesus unto the multitude in parables; and without a parable spake He not unto them: That it might be fulfilled which was spoken by the prophet, saying, 'I will open my mouth in parables; I will utter things which have been kept secret from the foundation of the world' " (Matt. 13:34-35).

"And to make all men see what is the fellowship of the mystery, which from the beginning of the world hath been hid in God, who created all things by Jesus Christ: to the intent that now unto the principalities and powers in heavenly places might be known by the church the manifold wisdom of God, according to the eternal purpose which He purposed in Christ Jesus our Lord" (Ephesians 3:9-11).

Kenneth S. Wuest translates these two Scriptures in this manner:

These things, all of them, Jesus spoke in the forms of illustrations to the crowds, and apart from an illustration He spoke not even one thing to them, in order that it might be fulfilled that which was spoken through the intermediate agency of the prophet saying, "I will open my mouth in the forms of illustrations. I will utter things which have been kept secret from the time when the foundations of the universe are laid."[1]

He translates Ephesians 3:8-12 in these words:

To me, the one who is less than the least of all the saints, there was given grace, to the Gentiles to proclaim the good news of the incomprehensible wealth belonging to the Christ, and to bring to light what is the administration of the mystery which has been covered up from the beginning of the ages in the God who created all things, in order that there might

---

[1]Kenneth S. Wuest, *The New Testament: An Expanded Translation* (Grand Rapids, Michigan: Wm. B. Eerdmans Publishing Co., 1961).

be made known now to the principalities and powers in the heavenly places through the intermediate agency of the church the much variegated wisdom of God, according to the eternal purpose which He carried into effect in the Christ, Jesus our Lord, in whom we are having our freedom of speech and entree in perfect confidence through faith in Him" [See also I Cor. 2, Matt. 4: 11-12, and Matt. 13: 34-35].[2]

Some ancient authorities attribute the original quotation to Isaiah. However, we do not find it in this form in the book bearing his name in the Bible. This does not close the possibility that Isaiah was the author of it. It could have been brought forward by word of mouth, and it is possible that the writer of the Seventy-eighth Psalm obtained his ideas in this fashion. This Psalm says, "I will open my mouth in a parable: I will utter dark sayings of old, which we have heard and known and our fathers have told us. . . . . that the generation to come might know them, even the children which should be born; . . . that they might set their hope in God, . . . and might not be as their fathers, a stubborn and rebellious generation."

This ancient writer, whoever he might have been, was saying that God had mysteries that lay hidden since He laid down the foundations of the universe, and that these mysteries of God would be revealed only through thought projections (parables). This ancient writer was not aware of the person through whom these thought projections would come. Jesus laid claim to this right to speak for God, and He revealed to man these hidden mysteries of God through the thought projections He uttered. In Matthew 13:34-35, this claim is registered by Jesus.

Paul later declared in his letter to the Ephesians his qualifications to be used by God as a human instrument to reiterate these same revealed truths. He called these "mysteries," "the good news," "the Gospel of the Kingdom of God." Jesus unlocked these secrets of God and brought them to light for man to see through thought projections, and Paul said that he had been commissioned by Christ to rebroadcast them to all men.

These revelations (mysteries of God) lie within at least two areas of life. One area has to do with man's knowledge of God up to the time of Christ's life on earth, and the other area is found in man's new relationship with God (father-son relationship). The first revelation has much to do with the second. Let us look first at the

---

[2]*Ibid.*

revelations that shed new light concerning man's concept of God before Christ came to earth.

If one were able to read the entire Old Testament without a break—without putting it down before finishing it—not only would that person be weary physically, but also spiritually. He would have a hazy concept of God, and not a very attractive concept at that. If he were asked to describe the impressions of the characteristics of God he received from the Old Testament, and the reactions of the men of the Old Testament to God, the description would be rather drab and fearful. He would have seen a God who manifested great and fearful anger against His own chosen people; and this not without course as He tried to deal with a rebellious people. It would be a picture that we would not like to hang over our beds to see just before turning out the lights. He would be a God of power, justice, and even ruthlessness, especially in those actions when He directs the total destruction of a city or a nation.

We would find ourselves repelled by the forms of worship found in the Old Testament. The smell of burning animal flesh in the temple, the cry of dying animals being offered to God for the sins of the people, and the stench caused by the flowing blood from these sin offerings (attracting flies and other insects) does not offer a conducive atmosphere for worship. A trip to church in those days would not be one we would look forward to with much pleasure. It would be hard not to disassociate all this slaughter and sacrifice of animals from our concept of the God to Whom it was being offered. What a change in the atmosphere of worship we find around Jesus! Jesus paints a different picture of God as He gathers small children in his arms saying, "Forbid them not, for such is the Kingdom of God."

The picture of a kind, compassionate, and merciful God in the Old Testament is there, but it is overshadowed by other pictures of God we see painted in it. There are many compassionate pictures: "The Lord is my shepherd, I shall not want" (Psalm 23:1). But these pictures have a difficult time shining through to the casual reader of the Old Testament. A somewhat similar parallel can be found in the way historians write history. They spend their time recording the wars nations have fought, telling about the nations that have been destroyed, and saying very little about the great things done by man. Our historians have not painted a very pretty picture of the human race. The same observation can be made concerning man in the Old Testament.

When we turn from the Old Testament and begin to read the four Gospels that contain all the thought projections of Jesus, how quickly the atmosphere changes! We are quickly lifted out of the drabness and the harshness of worship as reflected in the Old Testament. The cry of dying animals is replaced with the laughter of children flocking around Jesus. The cry of the money changers of the temple gives way to the Sermon on the Mount. Love, forgiveness, services to God and man, the yielding of oneself to God—these are the new notes for the new songs of Zion. What brought this change of attitude in the minds of the people? This can be traced to the new—the mysteries concerning God that Jesus reveals through thought projection after thought projection, each revealing some new and wonderful thing about God that man had not known before.

God is revealed as a "Good Shepherd" who leaves ninety-nine sheep to go out into the stormy night to find one lost and rebellious sheep that needs to be saved from his own foolishness and folly. He lifts up the found sheep and brings him tenderly home in His arms. The people learn that God is like the father who loves his wayward son who has wasted his inheritance; the son returns home to be a servant, and instead of being received as a servant, the father restores him to his sonship with a royal dinner. Each new thought projection paints a new and wonderful picture of God!

God is no less powerful, but now men see God using His power to help man rise above weakness and sin. God is not less just, but His justice is immersed in His great love and compassion for men. This is why Jesus came to earth, to fulfill the demands of this justice. The love of God is now in the forefront, and one can understand better the need for this justice. A thought projection painted the picture for him of the good shepherd dying for his sheep. Each thought projection adds a little more to our knowledge of the true nature of God; each removes some of the shadows from His face; and what man sees makes his heart leap for joy, and the fear of God finds less of a lodging place in our minds. Each thought projection adds to our knowledge and understanding of God, and each makes Him become a more familiar figure to us; and what we see, we like. We can now approach death with more confidence, for we can say to Him when we meet face to face, "You are my Heavenly Father, I would recognize you anywhere, for I have seen you many times in the pictures your Son, Christ, my personal Saviour, painted for us in the hundreds of thought projections we found in the Bible."

These are some of those mysteries known only to the Heavenly Host since this universe was formed. Men had sought for these in the Old Testament, without too much success, but in the thought projections, Jesus opens the windows into heaven to reveal the face of the Heavenly Father, so that each man might know Him better. To know Him is to love Him, and what we see in Him makes us want to serve Him. Without the thought projections of Jesus, we would still be extremely limited in our knowledge of God.

There is another area in life to which the thought projections of Jesus make a direct contribution by their revelation of the hidden mysteries of God. This is the hidden mystery concerning man's eternal relationship with God. In the Old Testament, we learn of man's fall. He is separated from God by the sin barrier. Man rebelled against God and he was placed under the curse of sin.

God made a promise to man that a redeemer would be sent. Man seemed not to understand just what this meant. Systems of worship were worked out by man. Attempts were made by man to find ways to appease an angry God. Offerings and sacrifice became the main emphasis of contact between man and God. Various forms of worship rose and fell with each generation. The Jewish people, God's chosen people, were blessed as a nation as long as they walked within the will of God. This revelation seems to have been in keeping with their capacity to understand. It was a progressive revelation, but the people either were unwilling to conform to the restrictions placed on them or they preferred the ways of other people, for their history is one of revolt against God, forsaking His ways and His precepts. One idea had been kept alive, however, the idea of the coming of a Messiah. He would restore the nation and He would restore the reigning house of David. But when this Messiah did come, they were not ready to receive Him or to recognize Him as their Messiah. It was these people who could not be satisfied until He, Christ, was nailed to the Cross. Little did they know that by this very act, this same Christ, in dying at their hands, fulfilled the promises made to their forefathers and to them for a Messiah. This sacrifice was to be the last sacrifice God would require of man for his sin debt.

What have the thought projections to teach us about this great eternal mystery of salvation? All these new revelations concerning God brought to man by Christ through the use of thought projections were used of the Holy Spirit in presenting Christ as the Saviour of the world. *The greatest of all the hidden mysteries of God is the mystery of salvation.* How can God, the creator of all things and the maker of man himself, concern Himself with the saving of the human race, which has lived in rebellion since its own birth on earth? How can God, pure, holy and righteous, love someone so unlovable as sinful man? Why would God attempt to save man from his folly of sin at the cost of His own precious Son? How and why could God remain silent as His precious Son died on the cross of Calvary, because He atoned for the sins of man? What can God see in man that would keep Him from destroying all mankind and starting afresh with another race of men? The only answer to all these questions is found in one verse of Scripture spoken by Jesus Himself: "For God so loved the world, that He gave His only begotten Son, that whosoever believeth in Him should not perish, but have everlasting life" (John 3:16). Such love is beyond the ability of mortal man to understand. This is the greatest of all the hidden mysteries of God: The one hundred and fifty-one thought projections found in the Gospel of Matthew will help us to better understand this great mystery.

We learn from these thought projections that God is personally concerned with every lost sinner. Jesus tells us this by the use of many thought projections: The Lost Sheep, The Lost Coin, The Prodigal Son, and many other such thought projections.

We learn that salvation is a personal matter with God. "I have come to seek and save the lost." This is a personal search of God for every lost person in the world. God says that each person is of great value. Salvation is a personal transaction—man to God, and God to man. God is no longer projecting a program to recover a lost world, a lost nation in the world (Israel), nor even a lost family (Abraham's). God is reaching for the individual. Christ died on the cross to save one man. When these separate individuals are saved, they will give back to God—families, cities, nations, and large sections of the world. But the human race must return to God *one by one.*

This has always been the plan of God, since the foundation of the world was laid. Man lost this plan in his search for an easier one or confused this plan through the ages, and in his attempts to rediscover it, strayed even further.

Through the thought projections of Jesus we learn that salvation is a personal experience we have with God. We enter into a new relationship with God. We become sons, and He becomes our Eternal Father. This is an astounding revelation (mystery)—man becoming a member of God's family: This means that Christ is our elder brother, and that we are co-heirs with Him in all things (Rom. 8:17). No longer do we stand in fear and awe before God (Luke 1:74); we enter into His presence through our worship with gladness and confidence. We call upon Him in prayer as an expectant son who is not afraid to make a personal request of his father.

If the Christian could strip his mind of all the things he has learned about God through the thought projections of Jesus, it would impoverish him far more than he might think. He would find himself back in the age of paganism; he would be as misplaced theologically in this modern age as a stone ax in a modern electronic plant! And yet, we have many "theological stone axes" in our modern theological seminaries and churches. They have refused to examine these "hidden mysteries" of the Gospels!

8

Some Psychological Procedures Underlying the Thought Projection Method of Interpretation

How does one get another human being to react the way he wishes? What does it take to motivate an individual into doing certain things? We know that a fish cannot be driven from the rear to take a bait. If the fisherman is to get him into a frying pan, he must be coaxed into taking the bait by the fisherman. We know, too, that we can train animals to react to certain stimuli, but what about human beings?

Psychologists have been telling us for years that man reacts to a situation with instincts with which he came into this world, or with conditioned reflexes that respond to symbols that stimulate and motivate his behavior. Stimuli act upon reflexes learned or instinctual that lie within the nervous system of the body. These, in turn, motivate action. The degree of human response to stimuli is in direct ratio to the degree of that stimuli. Dr. George Crane in his book *Applied Psychology* says, "The more specific the stimulus, the more immediate will be the response, and this leads to an axiom of psychology, that stimuli of the first degree are more effective than stimuli of the second degree, while stimuli of the second degree are more effective than those of the third degree."[1]

Instincts (these could also be early conditioned reflex chains) are for self-preservation (fear, pain, hunger, etc.) and love (used in the broadest sense: parental, filial, and sexual drive). The number in these two groups will vary with the psychologist you are reading.

The habits or conditioned reflexes a person has are also many or

---

[1]George W. Crane, *Psychology Applied* (Evanston, Illinois: Northwestern University Press, 1937).

few in number—depending upon the psychologist speaking. The response to stimuli that motivates the will or the body to act follows the rules as set forth by Dr. Crane, and if we want a person to respond quickly to some action, we must choose symbols that will stimulate to a point of motivation the will of that person. The degree of this action and the quickness of his response will be determined by the degree of such stimulation. Response to a stimulus is also determined by the pattern to which this stimulus is associated.

If I had never tasted a malt candy bar, the thought or picture of a malt candy bar would have no appeal for me if suddenly I became very hungry. It would not stimulate nor motivate me to go into a store and buy one. It might as well be a piece of coal. But if I had eaten many such candy bars in the past, the very thought of past experience with such candy bars would set up a second-degree stimulus in my mind. The sight of the bar of candy on the store counter would be a first-degree stimulus. A symbol that is a stimulus must be related and associated with some experience in the past. The more closely the symbol is related to the experience, the stronger is its power to motivate. A child badly burned by an electric iron will react very quickly to that iron, but as the child grows older and sees her mother use the iron to make her favorite dress pretty, the reaction of fear to that iron or all other electric irons will fade gradually until she has no fear of one.

Dr. Crane makes a very striking statement regarding words as symbols used to cause motivation in people when he writes:

By means of words, therefore, we can symbolically dangle juicy beefsteaks, delicious peach shortcake, roses, automobiles, radios, silks, and satins—indeed, any object we have in mind, before our subjects. We can make them thirsty. We can discuss savoury viands before a group that wasn't hungry until we began talking, and in a few minutes have them so restless from hunger sensations that they can scarcely sit still. We can discuss sleep, relaxation, perfect repose, pleasantly flaccid muscles, and deep restful slumber until we have the listeners in an artificial sleep, or a natural one.

Words can make the tears flow; they can wrench a staid personality from its moorings, incite it to lofty endeavor and noble deeds, or lead it to a lynching party and human ignominy. Words can make men lend a helping hand directly or through the medium of their contributed dollars, or they can place bayonets in their grasp with which they viciously rip open the intestines of the same people to whom they previously lent a friendly hand. Words, as in the mouth of an Iago, can destroy the sweetest faith and pure love, or they can build the highest type of human trust and confidence out of originally casual acquaintanceship. Words can sculpture a beautiful manhood or womanhood out of a helpless bit of animate human flesh, or they may render it bestial and cruel. They may build a small company into a billion-dollar industry, or drive a great corporation into bankruptcy.

However, words are not effective stimuli unless in the personality on whom they are employed, habit systems are already developed which may be ignited by such stimuli. Like pulling the trigger on the rifle, no energy discharge results unless a cartridge (habit) is present to be acted upon. This fact is illustrated in the quotation: "Give not that which is holy unto the dogs, neither cast ye your pearls before swine, lest they trample them under their feet, and turn again and rend you" (Matt. 7:6b).[2]

Stimuli can be used to coax or to club a desired reaction. Clubbing is a stimulus of a promised punishment for not reacting in a desired manner. Jails, detention homes for children, and even armies are all symbols of clubbing stimuli.

The Old Testament is filled with this type of religious stimuli. The "thou shalt nots" of the Old Testament say to us, "God will punish you if you fail to keep these commandments." The very root word in the Hebrew for worship carries the idea of "awe" built on fear. This was not the approach God was trying to make to the human race, but this is the interpretation the people made of God's advances to them. Fear is still the "big stick" in some forms of Christianity. It is extremely difficult for any act stimulated and motivated by fear to become loving, nor does it produce in an individual a sense of joy or happiness. A child made to eat his supper by the threat of a spanking is not going to enjoy that meal—no matter what is on the table before him.

Coaxing is the method of achieving results by the stimulus of reward; i.e., the motivation that causes the individual to respond is the reward. This reward can be in the world of tangible things: money, property, a better job, etc., or it might be in the area of the emotions. Words of praise cost nothing, but a child will give up an hour of play to gain the praise of a parent for cleaning up the yard, or helping mother with the dishes. Even the words "thank you," though seldom heard in our modern world, work miracles for the person receiving them. They create an inner sense of well-being and even make the world a nicer place in which to live.

This is the approach of Jesus in His many thought projections. He does not move around in an atmosphere of burning sulphur, fire, and smoke from the pit of hell. He does not ignore the presence of

---

[2]*Ibid.*, pp. 34, 35.

those in the theological background of man, but He lives and breathes the atmosphere of the Heavenly Father; more love, compassion, and tenderness are in evidence in His messages. "Come, follow me and I will make you—good, fine; give you life full and complete, and make you one of my Father's children by forgiving your sins and by sharing His love with you." Christ approaches man from the front—coaxing and inviting him to follow Him for blessings man will gain and share with God, His Father. Never does he attempt to club or drive anyone into God's family.

Jesus used the thought projection method in His teaching and preaching to take his hearers out of their world of "things" into His world of the spirit, and to teach them spiritual truths missing from their lives. This was done by starting with third- and fourth-degree stimuli from where they were living, and by the use of "things" found in that sphere. By using word symbols, He converted these stimuli into first- and second-degree stimuli, thus creating the motivation for their acceptance of what He was teaching.

For example: The word "man" is at the extreme end of an emotional stimulus chain. If we want a person to react, to be motivated, to become involved with this word, "man," we will have to do something to bring the "man" from his extreme position into a closer relationship with that person by converting the word into first-degree stimulus. This "man," we say, "is a father"; this is a step closer, and we have gained a little more attention but not enough to get the desired reaction. We say, "This man is a father—your father; here is his picture." You are now employing a second-degree stimulus, but if you say, "Open that door," and there stands that person's father, whom he had not seen for years, and who had been reported lost at sea: This is a first-degree stimulus. The son reaches out for his father and they fall into each other's arms. This is the way Jesus uses the thought projection method on people.

Matthew recorded twenty-one narrative parables. These are thought projections of Jesus fully developed by Him into a story form or narrative. With two exceptions, each parable needed no explanation. The people seeking certain truths from Jesus found what they were seeking in these narratives. We believe that Jesus was not only teaching through these narrative thought projections, but He was training His disciples and others to draw their own stories from the one hundred and thirty pure thought projections and the twenty-one narrative thought projections found in twenty-two of the twenty-eight chapters of Matthew. He was saying to them, "Watch and listen closely to what I am saying and doing; later you do the same with the 'thought seed' I shall plant in your spiritual gardens." He was offering them His paint brush of words, and telling them to draw their own picture from the raw material He would give them.

A teacher of mathematics first explains a problem to the class on the blackboard, then problems are assigned to members of the class to work out for themselves. When they have mastered, or learned, the teaching technique they are ready to solve the problems in mathematics they will face in life later. We learn faster and more by doing a thing ourselves. A person must become involved himself before there is a learning situation. Jesus involved His listeners in the solution of their own problems by giving them the "do-it-yourselves" tools.

Jesus takes four figures of speech; using subjects common to the people of His day, and He identifies this subject with a spiritual truth He saw they needed to meet a certain emptiness or void in their lives. He says to them, "Place this figure of speech alongside of your need and study it carefully, and you will not only recognize the need but will also find the answer to it as you construct the picture for yourself."

The four figures of speech used by Jesus in these thought projections must be, and are, related to the basic meaning of the words in Greek and Hebrew for "parable." This word parable does not mean, "an earthly story with a heavenly meaning." The word "story" weakens this definition making it almost worthless to a student of the Bible. For the word "parable" suggests only one thought, "to place alongside of." To take a known factor or an accepted fact and place it beside an unknown one so that the unknown takes on the identity or characteristics of the known. This word does not place limitations on how this transference is done—by story or by the power of suggestion (stimuli). These figures of speech, as we have already noted, are: the proverb, the allegory, the simile, and the metaphor. I would suggest six laws governing the application of the thought projection principle in our search for the thought projections of Jesus found in the New Testament:

1. A thought projection used by Jesus will always contain something which is familiar to His hearers and within the range of their

experience. He spoke of fishermen and their nets, shepherds and their sheep, etc.

2. Each thought projection used by Jesus had a close relation in its basic nature and function to the spiritual truth Jesus was trying to convey. The lost sheep was a picture of a lost man. Man did not suddenly say to himself, "I am tired of God, I am going to leave His Kingdom." Sheep get lost by degrees, eating a blade of grass here, then there, until they find themselves lost from the flock and the shepherd.

3. There must be a transferable relationship of the thought projection to the spiritual truth under consideration. "I am the door." Doors were the only entrance into a home. They kept the unwanted out and protected those within. Jesus wanted to be that to His listeners. They would enter God's family through Him, and, in turn, He would be their protection, keeping out the evil one, and keeping in perfect safety, His own. "I am the bread of life" not, "I am a stone"; nor would He have said, "I am a grain of sand," but He did say, "I am the water of life." Each of these metaphors used by Jesus gives emphasis to a transferable characteristic from the object to Himself. Thus, "I am a grain of sand," would have had no such possible transferable spiritual truth.

4. Not only must the subject be well known to those to whom Jesus was speaking, but it had to be simple in its nature so that it would not be misunderstood. It must be simple enough so that it would be accepted without question, for in seeking to unravel an obscure figure of speech, the thought being illustrated would be lost in the process. The metaphor "I am the good shepherd" needed no explanation to any man of that day.

5. Every thought projection used by Jesus grew out of a personal need of the people. Jesus never used a narrative-type thought projection just to be telling a story to entertain the crowd or to pass a few idle moments. Each was spoken with an object in mind—to meet some need He saw in the lives of the people. "I am the light of the world." Blind people were everywhere in the Holy Land. The unbroken glare from the sun caused many people to lose their eyesight before they were thirty years of age. Blindness was a walking companion of every person of that day. The blind knew what He was saying. He would be their eyes. His light would shine through the darkness of their blindness.

6. A thought projection of Jesus dealt with just *one* thought. You cannot paint several pictures on the same small canvas without creating confusion. If a painting has more than one object, all other objects are there to give focal emphasis to one. A thought projection has one simple idea. Other ideas might appear, but they are there to support or to give sharpness to the one central point. When you pray, say, "Our Father." Everything in this the model prayer starts and ends with the two words "Our Father." The narrative thought projection of the Prodigal Son starts and ends, not with the son but with the father. The son is in the story to tell us about the great love, compassion, and the heart of forgiveness God the Father has for us, His wayward children. And yet, how often the son is kept in the spotlight of the story when it is used for a sermon or a devotional thought. The father is the hero, not the son.

7. All pure thought projections, like all narrative thought projections, have for their basic purpose, the revelation of knowledge concerning the nature of God. These were uttered by Jesus when He saw the need of the people to understand God better. They were unaware of what God was really like in nature, and did not know or understand God's love and concern for them and their personal problems. To say that God notices a fallen sparrow; that man's hairs were numbered and God knew when a man lost even one strand of his hair—this was refreshing, startling news to the man of the street in the days of our Lord! If God loved them as a human father loves his starving and hungry children, then they had hope—new hope—for they knew how far they would go to feed their own children; if God would go as far for them, they would have to change their attitude toward God. They could love, respect, and worship such a deity.

The average man in Christ's day had a drab and almost purposeless life. His life consisted of "What am I to eat?" "Where can I find shelter?" "How can I keep alive?" Jesus came and lifted men out of their hopelessness. To do this Jesus had to get man's attention and turn it into interest to motivate him into action that would restore in man his lost sonship.

Nature has provided safeguards for the human mind. Escape mechanisms have been built in us. When we find ourselves facing defeat, we keep ourselves going by extricating ourselves from such a situation by REVERIE. We recall the good things we once had or the good things we hope to have some day and these thoughts lift us out of our despondency. Jesus reminded His listeners that there are better things for them and that they can rise above their drabness by looking to the eternal things God offers to them.

Identification is another method of escape. Jesus offers to men an opportunity to lose themselves in Him, become a part of Him. His victory over the grave will be shared by us, and His Heavenly home will become ours too. These two methods of stimuli—and others—are used by Jesus to motivate people to do something about their spiritual needs, and the most effective method to involve the people into His program of human rehabilitation is the thought projection method.

Thus, the thought projection method (explained elsewhere in this volume) can be summed up in a few brief statements:

1. Thought projections (parables) are made up of one of four figures of speech: simile, metaphor, allegory, or proverb.

2. Each has one general theme (there may be a subdivision of this to give extra clarity to the main theme).

3. Each comes from a need Jesus saw in the lives of the people before Him.

4. Each demands an answer from those who hear it.

5. Jesus used many objects in these Thought Projections, but never one that was not familiar to His listeners. To the farmer, He talked of seed and soil; to the housewife he talked of lost coins and yeast.

6. Jesus takes an "obvious" fact to teach hidden truths.

7. A thought projection should never be taken out of context and forced to say something it does not say; nor should we fail to let it say what Jesus wanted it to say.

8. Narrative thought projections are simple stories that do their own explaining. We believe these were used by Jesus at first as object lessons, much as a mathematics teacher puts a problem on the blackboard, works it out for the class, and then says, "Work the others the same way." The listeners can take His pure thought projections and work out their own story from the seed Jesus plants in their minds. "I am the door," said Jesus (John 10:9), "now paint the story for yourself and see what is meant. What should I mean to you from this thought"? Their minds go to work at once, using the background from their own lives. "A door—we put doors

in houses to enter the house; in fact, this is the only way to get into the house without ruining a wall or the roof." Their minds do not stop there. "A door keeps out the thief at night. It is my protection. It also keeps my house from becoming a prison for me and my family. I can go in and out. Suppose I awaken at night and discover the house is on fire; the door is my measure of safety for me and my family. He says He will be that to me if I will let Him. He wants to be my spiritual door."

Yes, a thought projection does reveal a spiritual truth by putting what is known beside an unknown spiritual fact; what is more, a thought projection takes a second-degree stimulus and turns it into a first-degree one by forcing one to think for himself. Thus, man's emotions become involved, and emotions are the stimuli that trigger all our decisions. We must feel something before we will act upon it.

9

Classification of
the Thought Projections
in Matthew

In this chapter I have numbered the thought projections in the Gospel of Matthew in the order in which they appear, starting with the fourth chapter (there are no thought projections in the first three chapters). They are tabulated according to Scripture, subject, subject illustrated, figure of speech, and classification. There are two classifications: pure thought projections and narrative thought projections.

In addition to the first three chapters of Matthew, there are no thought projections in chapters 14, 27, and 28.

Of the one hundred fifty-one thought projections in Matthew, twenty-one are narratives and one hundred thirty are pure thought projections. The narrative thought projections break down to nine similes, five metaphors, six allegories, and one that is both a simile and an allegory. The pure thought projections break down to eighty-nine metaphors, nineteen similes, sixteen allegories, and six proverbs.

Thought Projection No.	Scripture (Matt.)	Subject (There are no thought projections in Matthew 1, 2, or 3)	Subject Illustrated	Figure of Speech	Classification
1.	4:4	Man does not live by bread alone	Man is more than physical being	Metaphor	Pure T.P.
2.	4:18-20	Fishers of men	Christ calls men to be soul winners	Metaphor	Pure T.P.
3.	5:3	The poverty of spirit	Man must recognize his own spiritual need	Metaphor	Pure T.P.
4.	5:4	The mourner	The concerned ones give comfort and are comforted in return	Metaphor	Pure T.P.
5.	5:5	The meek	The ones submissive to God are happy	Metaphor	Pure T.P.
6.	5:6	The hungry and thirsty	The physically healthy are hungry for physical food; spiritually healthy are hungry for the truths of God	Metaphor	Pure T.P.
7.	5:7	The merciful	The spirit of compassion is Christian	Metaphor	Pure T.P.
8.	5:8	The pure of heart	Sin-cleansed life	Metaphor	Pure T.P.
9.	5:9	The peacemaker	The Christian is one	Metaphor	Pure T.P.
10.	5:13	The salt of the earth	Influence (good) of the Christian	Metaphor	Pure T.P.
11.	5:14-16	The light of the world	Influence (good) of the Christian	Metaphor	Pure T.P.
12.	5:19	The way to smallness or greatness	Our attitude toward the laws of God	Metaphor	Pure T.P.

13.	5:20	Righteousness plus	Found in Christ only (Grace)	Metaphor	Pure T.P.
14.	5:48	The perfect ones	Complete surrender to the will of God	Metaphor	Pure T.P.
15.	6:1-4	Alms giving; false piety and hypocrisy	Hypocrisy in religion	Simile	Pure T.P.
16.	6:5-6	Prayer (location of public prayer)	False piety in religion (in prayer)	Simile	Pure T.P.
17.	6:11-15	Prayer structure (many words not necessary)	False piety in prayer	Simile	Pure T.P.
18.	6:16-18	Fasting in public	False piety	Simile	Pure T.P.
19.	6:19-20	Treasures in Heaven	A wise investment	Metaphor	Pure T.P.
20.	6:21	Where is your heart?	Motivations of life	Metaphor	Pure T.P.
21.	6:22-23	Eye trouble	Life motivated by what you see	Metaphor	Pure T.P.
22.	6:24	Two masters	Allegiances in life	Metaphor	Pure T.P.
23.	6:25-26	Let the birds teach you	Needless worry	Metaphor	Pure T.P.
24.	6:27	Worry cannot add to your height	The folly of worry	Metaphor	Pure T.P.
25.	6:28-29	Let the flowers teach you	God has physical laws for everything	Metaphor	Pure T.P.
26.	6:30	Let the grass teach you	God has laws for physical beauty	Metaphor	Pure T.P.
27.	6:31-34	Tomorrow's worry	Needless worry	Metaphor	Pure T.P.
28.	7:1-5	The beam in the eye	Moral judgment; censoriousness is wrong	Metaphor	Narrative
29.	7:6(a)	Giving holy things to dogs	Our responsibility for holy things	Allegory	Pure T.P.

Thought Projection No.	Scripture (Matt.)	Subject	Subject Illustrated	Figure of Speech	Classification
30.	7:6(b)	Casting pearls before swine	Our responsibility for holy things	Allegory	Pure T.P.
31.	7:7-12	Bread, fish, serpent	Prayer: tell God needs and trust Him	Metaphor	Narrative
32.	7:13-14	Two gates; two roads	Man must make choices; determine directions of life	Metaphor	Pure T.P.
33.	7:15-16(a)	Prophets: two kinds, true and false	Wolf not changed in nature by sheep skin	Metaphor	Pure T.P.
34.	7:16(b)	Fig trees; grape vines: two natures	The fruit will identify the tree	Metaphor	Pure T.P.
35.	7:17-20	Sound and sick trees; two natures or two conditions	Good fruit comes from good trees; a good life produces same	Metaphor	Pure T.P.
36.	7:21-23	Who are the true prophets, or who enters the Kingdom	The test of a Christian is in doing the will of Christ	Metaphor	Pure T.P.
37.	7:24-27	Two foundations: sand and rock	A good foundation is needed for life	Simile	Narrative
38.	8:5-13	Eating with Abraham and Jacob	Gentiles become a part of the promise	Metaphor	Pure T.P.
39.	8:18-20	Foxes' holes and birds' nests	Cost of discipleship	Metaphor	Pure T.P.
40.	8:21-22	Let the dead bury the dead	Christ must come first in your life	Allegory	Pure T.P.
41.	9:10-13	The well needs no physician	The self-righteous needs no saviour	Proverb	Pure T.P.

No.	Reference		Meaning	Type	
42.	9:14-15	You do not fast at a wedding	It is no sin for a Christian to be happy	Metaphor	Pure T.P.
43.	9:16	Do not put new patches on old clothes	Some new theological ideas cannot be put into old theology	Proverb	Pure T.P.
44.	9:17	Do not put new wine in old bottles	Danger of destroying the value of both	Proverb	Pure T.P.
45.	9:35-36	Shepherdless sheep	People, like sheep, need a shepherd	Simile	Pure T.P.
46.	9:37-38	Unharvested wheat will be lost	People, like wheat, must be harvested or they will be lost	Allegory	Pure T.P.
47.	10:5-7	The lost sheep of Israel	Israel went astray; needs message of Christ	Metaphor	Pure T.P.
48.	10:9-11	A laborer deserves to be fed	The Christian worker earns his pay	Proverb	Pure T.P.
49.	10:15	Cities reject Gospel	Cost of rejection is always destruction	Metaphor	Pure T.P.
50.	10:16(a)	Sheep sent among wolves	Dangers of the ministry	Simile	Pure T.P.
51.	10:16(b)	Wise as serpents; harmless as doves	Disciples must be wise, but gentle	Simile	Pure T.P.
52.	10:24-25	A teacher and his pupil	Pupil can expect the same response from the world accorded to the teacher	Metaphor	Pure T.P.
53.	10:24-25	The servant and his master	Each shall be treated alike by the world	Metaphor	Pure T.P.
54.	10:27-32	God's evaluation of a sparrow	God's evaluation of us	Metaphor	Pure T.P.
55.	10:34-39	Peace, war, and the sword	Christianity and evil are at war —total war	Metaphor	Pure T.P.

85

Thought Projection No.	Scripture (Matt.)	Subject	Subject Illustrated	Figure of Speech	Classification
56.	11:7-8	The shaking reed	Instability is not the mark of John the Baptist	Allegory	Pure T.P.
57.	11:8	A man in soft clothing	Clothes make the man	Metaphor	Pure T.P.
58.	11:15	Elias the prophet	Both had the same mission, but were not the same man	Metaphor	Pure T.P.
59.	11:16-19	Children playing weddings and funerals	Wisdom of action justifed of herself	Simile	Pure T.P.
60.	11:20-24	Cities judged	Punishment sure for those who reject Jesus	Metaphor	Pure T.P.
61.	11:28-30	The yoke of Jesus	It is easier to be a Christian than not to be	Allegory	Pure T.P.
62.	12:6-8	Something greater than the temple	Jesus is superior to organizations	Metaphor	Pure T.P.
63.	12:9-13	Sheep fall into the pit on Sunday (Sabbath)	Man is of more value than a holy day	Metaphor	Narrative (Contrast)
64.	12:23-28	A divided house will be destroyed	Good and evil cannot live together	Metaphor	Pure T.P.
65.	12:29	The thief and the householder	The stronger must overcome the weaker	Metaphor	Pure T.P.
66.	12:33	The tree is known by its fruit	Fruit must, and will, match the tree	Metaphor	Pure T.P.
67.	12:34	A brood of vipers	Men were evil because their acts were evil	Metaphor	Pure T.P.

86

No.	Reference	Title	Meaning	Figure	Type
68.	12:35	A good man and his treasure	From out of treasure comes that put in; be it good or evil	Metaphor	Pure T.P.
69.	12:36-37	Idle words reveal true character	We shall be judged by our idle words	Metaphor	Pure T.P.
70.	12:38-42	The sign of Jonah	The Resurrection of Jesus is this sign	Metaphor (Historical)	Pure T.P.
71.	12:42	The sign of Sheba	She was attracted by what she heard; believed what she saw	Metaphor (Historical)	Pure T.P.
72.	12:43-45	The danger of the empty house	A clean life is not enough; must be occupied with the right thing	Allegory	Narrative
73.	12:46-50	True brothers of Jesus	All Christians	Metaphor	Pure T.P.
74.	13:3-9,18-23	The sower	People, like soil, have power to reject the message of Christ	Allegory	Narrative
75.	13:10-12	Why did Jesus use parables	To reveal the hidden truths of God	Metaphor (Historical)	Pure T.P.
76.	13:13-17	Hearing and seeing not	What we see and hear needs to be interpreted	Metaphor	Pure T.P.
77.	13:24-30,36-42	Tares and wheat	Good and evil in church shall be separated in the end	Simile & Allegory	Narrative
78.	13:31-32	Mustard seed	Sin of abnormal growth	Simile	Narrative
79.	13:33	Leaven	Power of evil influence	Simile	Narrative
80.	13:34-36	Hidden things revealed	The use of the parabolic method	Metaphor	Pure T.P.
81.	13:43	Shine like the sun	The Christian shall shine	Simile	Pure T.P.
82.	13:44	The hidden treasure	Jesus hides Gospel in world (plants it)	Allegory	Narrative

Thought Projection No.	Scripture (Matt.)	Subject	Subject Illustrated	Figure of Speech	Classification
83.	13:45-46	The pearl merchant	Church is pearl of great price	Allegory	Narrative
84.	13:47-50	A fisherman's net and a catch of fish	Judgment day will be one of eternal separation	Simile	Narrative
85.	13:51-52	The instructed scribe	He uses the old and the new as source material	Simile	Pure T.P.
86.	13:57	A prophet without honor	Jesus rejected by His own; danger of the familiar (we underrate the familiar)	Proverb	Pure T.P.
		(There are no thought projections in Matthew 14)			
87.	15:7-9	Lip worship	Pharisees' traditions had covered over and submerged the laws of God; they had become slaves to tradition	Metaphor	Pure T.P.
88.	15:11, 15-20	Eating does not defile the body	The inner man is the real man	Metaphor	Pure T.P.
89.	15:12-13	God must plant if there is to be life	God will destroy that which He does not plant	Metaphor	Pure T.P.
90.	15:14	The blind leading the blind	The blind will destroy themselves and others	Metaphor	Pure T.P.
91.	15:22-28	Scraps belong to the dogs	God rewards faith	Metaphor	Pure T.P.
92.	15:24	Lost sheep of Israel	The lost people of Israel wanted to be saved	Metaphor	Pure T.P.
93.	16:1-4	Bad weather prophets	They could read the signs of the skies; but not the signs of the Creator	Metaphor (Historical)	Pure T.P.

No.	Reference		Meaning		
94.	16:12	The leaven of the Pharisees and the Saducees	The danger of false doctrines	Metaphor	Pure T.P.
95.	16:13-18	Peter the rock	Not Peter the man; but God the Eternal Rock	Allegory	Pure T.P.
96.	16:19	The keys to the Kingdom	The Gospel message	Allegory	Pure T.P.
97.	16:22-24	Peter is called Satan	Peter is Satan possessed at this time	Metaphor	Pure T.P.
98.	16:24-28	You must lose life to gain it	Victory in defeat	Metaphor	Pure T.P.
99.	17:10-13	The coming of Elias	John, a figure of Him	Allegory	Pure T.P.
100.	17:14-20	Mustard seed faith (quality versus quantity)	Quality, not quantity	Simile	Pure T.P.
101.	17:24-27	Who should pay taxes	The Christian is both a citizen of earth and of heaven; thus he has a dual duty	Metaphor	Pure T.P.
102.	18:2-3	Entrance into the Kingdom	Simple, childlike faith; complete acceptance	Simile	Pure T.P.
103.	18:4	Greatest in the Kingdom	Complete devotion such as a child gives a parent	Simile	Pure T.P.
104.	18:5-6	Stumbling blocks to children	The danger of causing a child to sin (fall)	Metaphor	Pure T.P.
105.	18:7-8	Cut off hand, foot	No cost too great to pay for salvation	Metaphor	Pure T.P.
106.	18:10-11	Angels and children	God protects His own	Metaphor	Pure T.P.
107.	18:12-14	The Lost sheep and the 99	God does not play percentages; loves all	Metaphor	Narrative
108.	18:18	Loosing and binding	God recognizes and honors action of the church	Metaphor	Pure T.P.
109.	18:21-22	70 × 70 is not 4900	Unlimited forgiveness	Metaphor	Pure T.P

89

Thought Projection No.	Scripture	Subject	Subject Illustrated	Figure of Speech	Classification
110.	18:23-35	The king and the unjust servant	Forgiveness	Simile	Narrative
111.	19:5-6	Two become one	Marriage	Metaphor	Pure T.P.
112.	19:10-12	To marry or not to marry; to divorce or not to divorce	Eunuchs	Metaphor	Pure T.P.
113.	19:13-15	The Kingdom belongs to children	All in the Kingdom must come in by childlike faith in Christ	Metaphor	Pure T.P.
114.	19:23-27	A camel and a needle's eye	Salvation is impossible outside of Christ; by grace not works	Metaphor	Pure T.P.
115.	19:30	The last shall be first	God's order of things or persons, not man's	Metaphor	Pure T.P.
116.	20:1-16	Laborers and the vineyard	Payment is to fidelity of opportunity	Simile	Narrative
117.	20:20-23	Drinking from the cup of Jesus	We are to share in the blessings and the sufferings of Jesus	Allegory	Pure T.P.
118.	20:24-28	To be great, one must be small	Ruler-servant relationship of world, not Kingdom method	Metaphor	Pure T.P.
119.	21:13	A den of thieves	God's house not a market; spiritual place	Metaphor	Pure T.P.
120.	21:16	Out of the mouths of babes	Adulthood does not assure one of wisdom	Proverb	Pure T.P.
121.	21:18-21	The cursed fig tree	Israel rejected because of lack of faithfulness	Allegory	Pure T.P.

No.	Reference	Title	Meaning	Type	Mode
122.	21:28-32	The two sons	Test of sonship obedience	Metaphor	Narrative
123.	21:33-41	The dishonest husbandman	Jesus takes away the Kingdom from Israel (leadership)	Allegory	Narrative
124.	21:42	The rejected cornerstone	Man's rejection can be God's final rejection	Allegory	Pure T.P.
125.	21:43	Kingdom taken away from Israel	Any nation can now become a Christian leader for God	Metaphor	Pure T.P.
126.	22:1-14	The king's wedding banquet	You cannot "gate-crash" God's Kingdom	Allegory	Narrative
127.	22:21-22	Dual citizenship and dual responsibility	Render unto God and Caesar what is due both	Metaphor	Pure T.P.
128.	22:29-33	The dead shall be like the angels	Earthly relationships and heavenly relationships are not the same	Simile	Pure T.P.
129.	23:1-15	The seat of Moses	The religious leaders were oppressing the people	Metaphor	Pure T.P.
130.	23:16-22	Which is greater, God or the altar	The religious leaders had changed the spiritual values for the people	Metaphor	Pure T.P.
131.	23:23-24	Straining at a gnat and swallowing a camel	Narrowness in religion can cause many to die (law bigger than the people)	Metaphor	Pure T.P.
132.	23:25-26	Clean outside; dirty inside	Hypocrisy; inner man is real self	Metaphor	Pure T.P.
133.	23:27-32	White sepulchres full of dead men	Physically alive but spiritually dead (theologically)	Simile	Pure T.P.
134.	23:33-36	The snakes of hell	They, like their fathers who killed the prophets, will kill Jesus	Metaphor	Pure T.P.

Thought Projection No.	Scripture	Subject	Subject Illustrated	Figure of Speech	Classification
135.	23:37-39	Jesus weeps over Jerusalem	The rejection of Jesus as their Saviour	Simile	Pure T.P.
136.	24:27	When the lightning begins to gather	The nature of Christ's return	Simile	Pure T.P.
137.	24:28	When the vultures begin to gather	The judgment of His return	Allegory	Pure T.P.
138.	24:31(a)	The four winds of earth	Angels to gather the elect from all parts of the earth: the Christians	Metaphor	Pure T.P.
139.	24:31(b)	The ends of heaven	Angels will also gather the elect who have died	Metaphor	Pure T.P.
140.	24:32-35	When the trees begin to bud	God works on a time schedule	Simile	Pure T.P.
141.	24:36-42	When the floods begin to come	Deals with the "when" of Christ's return to earth	Simile (Historical)	Narrative
142.	24:42-44	When the thief breaks in to steal	The Christian's responsibility regarding Christ's return	Metaphor	Pure T.P.
143.	24:45-51	When the steward is left on his own	The Christian is a steward of Christ's return	Metaphor	Pure T.P.
144.	25:1-13	The ten virgins	God's law of eternal segregation	Simile	Narrative
145.	25:14-30	The talents	God's eternal stockbrokers	Simile	Narrative
146.	25:31-46	Separation of sheep and goats	Your prejudgment is to be the final one	Simile	Pure T.P.
147.	26:26	This is my body (bread)	Symbol of body of Jesus given for us	Allegory	Pure T.P.

92

148.	26:27-29	This is my blood (wine)	Symbol of the blood of Christ offered for our sins	Allegory	Pure T.P.
149.	26:31	When the shepherd is smitten, sheep scatter	Disciples forsake Christ	Metaphor	Pure T.P.
150.	26:37-46	Let this cup pass	Christ Jesus saw the depth of the cost to redeem man; He drew back	Allegory	Pure T.P.
151.	26:52	To live by the sword is to die by it	The Kingdom of God does not use force, but the Message to fight evil in the world	Metaphor	Pure T.P.

(There are no thought projections in Matthew 27 and 28)

93

PART II:

Thought Projections in the Gospel of Matthew

10

Matthew 1, 2, and 3

Summary: Matthew 1, 2 and 3 relate the historical events concerning Jesus, from His birth to His entrance into His life's work. *There are no parables or thought projections in the first three chapters of the Gospel of Matthew.*

Matthew 1 opens with the genealogy of Jesus, starting with Abraham and ending with Joseph, the earthly foster father of Jesus. This covers the first seventeen verses of the chapter. Joseph is told of Mary's pregnancy by the Holy Spirit in a dream and accepts this as an act of God. He marries Mary but knows her not as a wife until after the child Jesus is born. This completes the first chapter.

Matthew 2 begins with the coming of the wise men from the east to Bethlehem. They had seen and followed His star. They came to King Herod, who instructed them to find the child and return to him with the news concerning his habitation. The wise men found Jesus, but they did not return to King Herod because of a warning from God. An angel of the Lord warned Joseph to take the child Jesus and flee into Egypt to escape the wrath of King Herod. Herod, at being defied, had all male children under two years of age killed in Bethlehem and in the regions near Bethlehem. Later, an angel instructed Joseph to return to Israel with the child Jesus, for King Herod had died. Fearing the wrath of the son of Herod, Archelaus, and being warned not to return to Bethlehem, Joseph went to a district of Galilee, to a town called Nazareth.

Matthew 3 records the preaching of John the Baptist and the people's response to his preaching of repentance. He declares the coming of the Messiah, and when Jesus approaches him and requests baptism, John declares Him to be the Promised One. Jesus is baptized by John in the River Jordan. The Spirit of God descends upon Jesus as he leaves the water after his baptism, and a voice out of heaven speaks, saying, "This is my beloved Son, in whom I am well pleased."

At this point Jesus enters into His public ministry. No longer will He enjoy the quiet life of a private citizen. He will now become the property of the public, the people. He lives for the next three years under the harsh glare of the fickle emotional moods of the people to whom He was sent of God to serve and save. The cross, ever before Him, becomes the object of His life and mission on earth. He did not come to earth to live, but to die, and in dying, makes it possible for men to live. This was His mission, and everything He did or said was secondary to this purpose. It is His death that gives meaning to everything He said or did on earth.

11

Matthew 4

Summary: Matthew 4 contains two THOUGHT PROJEC-
TIONS:
1. Man does not live by bread alone (Matt. 4:4) METAPHOR.
2. Fishers of men (Matt. 4:18-20) METAPHOR.

Matthew 4 opens with the temptations of Jesus. He had left the
crowds on the banks of the River Jordan. God had just declared
Jesus to be His own Son. This public act of baptism marked a
decided change in His life. He would never return to his home except
for short visits with his earthly family. This baptism marked a break
with the past and obscurity. Henceforth, he would be a public figure
until He was placed in the tomb of Joseph. He would appear only to
His disciples after that.

Jesus had sought the solitude of the desert for prayer and fasting.
Why? We do not know. He fasted and prayed for forty days, and at
the end of this time, Satan came to Him to tempt Him. This is the
background for the first of one hundred and fifty-one thought projections and parables in the Gospel of Matthew.

Thought Projection No. 1: Man does not live by bread alone
(Matt. 4:4).

"Man shall not live by bread alone, but by every word that pro-
ceedeth out of the Mouth of God." This metaphorical statement of
Jesus is a direct quotation from chapter 8, verse 3 of the book of
Deuteronomy. It came in answer to the temptation Satan threw at
Jesus. Jesus had just finished his fast of forty days. He was hungry.
Satan approached Him and suggested that since He was God's Son,
why not use the divine power at His disposal and turn some of the
stones at His feet into fresh bread? This would not have been a
problem for the Son of God: Satan never doubted that Jesus was the
Son of God. The text does not suggest this. "If Thou be the Son of
God," should be translated, "Since you are the Son of God, turn
these stones into bread."

Satan was trying to place Jesus in the same position politicians get into sometimes during an election when an opponent suggests that they do something that is good, something that they want to do and should do, but if they act upon this suggestion, the opponent assumes the credit for the act because he had suggested it. If the politician fails to carry out the good suggestion, he is blamed for not doing it. Satan was trying to "box" Jesus in with his suggestion.

Satan was trying to command an action of Jesus—a good act. We have no record in the New Testament of Jesus using His supernatural power to benefit Himself in any way. He only used this power to help others. Jesus was not going to start His earthly ministry to benefit Himself or by carrying out any suggestion made by Satan that could be thrown into His face or into the face of His disciples at some later date.

Jesus quoted Deuteronomy 8:3 to Satan. Moses, in this chapter was reminding the children of Israel that when they arrived in the Promised Land they were not to accept the blessings of God in the same spirit their fathers had accepted the blessings of God in the wilderness. Their fathers had accepted God's gifts without giving God the honor and glory due Him for His goodness. Moses said to them, "You will prosper, and get wealthy. You will be prone to say, 'Look what I have done,' and be lifted up in your own concern and forget all the blessings of God." They might be the ones to plant the seed after plowing the soil and cultivating the fields, but it is God who would send the rain to water their fields, and it would be God who would send the sun to shine and cause their seeds to burst into life, and it would be God who would protect the crops from danger until harvest. These things they must not forget when they come into the Land of Promise.

Jesus was also suggesting that life is more than physical food, more than clothes to wear to keep warm, and more than a house in which to live and be safe. Life was more than the reproduction of the human race. Man is more than a physical being—he is a spiritual being too. Neglect the body and it will die, but one can feed and care for the body and neglect the soul; then the soul will die in spite of the healthy body in which it resides.

Jesus had spent forty days and nights without food, but He had food not known to man. Jesus expressed this thought to His disciples after His conversation at the well of Jacob with the Samaritan woman (John 4). They did not understand what he meant when he tried to explain this experience at Jacob's well. They offered Him some of the food they had been sent to buy. He replied to their offer, "I have food to eat which you do not know." His disciples asked themselves, "Has anyone brought Him food?" Jesus continued, "My food is to do the will of Him who sent Me and to accomplish His work" (John 4:31-33).

Moses said that God had fed the children of Israel in the wilderness to create a spirit of humbleness in them, to create an attitude of appreciation in their hearts for the goodness and thoughtfulness of God. Moses charged them to never forget this. To remember this would be to have the continued blessings of God in the future, but to forget this would be to lose such blessings.

Thought Projection No. 2: Fishers of men (Matt. 4:18-21).

While Jesus was passing by the sea of Galilee, He saw two brothers, Simon, called Peter, and Andrew, his brother. They were busy fishing, casting their nets into the sea for fish. No doubt, Jesus paused to watch them for a while, saw something in them that He liked, and was moved to challenge them to leave their nets and their boats and follow Him: "Follow me, and I will make you fishers of men." The amazing thing about this scene is that these professional fishermen did not stop to argue or discuss terms of service before accepting His invitation. They did not make excuses that might have delayed their action or decision. The Scriptures say simply, "and straightway they left their nets and followed Him." This was truly amazing!

What is often overlooked by many newly born Christians and older Christians, too, is that Jesus did not send these two men out the next day to fish for men. He had said that he "would make them fishers of men." Jesus was saying, "I will train each of you to do this job and make you as successful in the art of catching men for me and the Heavenly Father as you were in catching fish for the market."

With salvation comes a desire to win others to Jesus, but very few Christians ever become soul winners, and not many Christians get beyond the "desire" to win others. They have not been trained to win others, nor do many know what the church expects of them. Herein lie two great sins of the church through the ages. The church has failed to train the newly won to Christ and to inform them what God expects of them. An army first trains its soldiers to fight before sending them into battle. The church should do no less.

Jesus spent three years training his disciples to become efficient fishers of men. The average church member today has had less than three minutes of such training. The pity of it all is that many ministers serving churches are well trained in every facet of religious work except this phase, the most important of them all! Many have never sat down face to face with a man and led him to know Jesus as a personal Saviour. The writer once heard a minister of a large church say to a group of pastors of similar churches, "Let us not kid ourselves about soul winning. We can stand behind a pulpit and talk about it, but we cannot sit down with a man and explain to him in a personal way." The others agreed that he was right.

"I will make you fishers of men." How does one become a successful fisherman? You may have "fisherman's luck," that is, cast a line into the water of a river or lake for the first time and pull out a record catch; this has been done, but one catch does not make you a professional fisherman.

Peter was a professional fisherman. He knew his job. Jesus was saying to him, "Peter, follow me and I will make you a professional fisher of men." Three years later, Peter emerged as the top man of his class!

A fisherman must know the nature and habits of the fish he wants to catch. He must know the kind of lure or bait that will attract the fish. He must know the water in which he fishes. He must know the tools of his profession—nets, boats, and so on. He must acquire the necessary skills in handling these tools. "Peter, you see it will take time for you to become a professional fisher of men. Are you willing to give me this time?"

Transfer this application to the new Christian and you have the answer to this thought projection.

Jesus promised to make these two men, Peter and Andrew, "fishers of men." Every Christian is given the same promise and can become a soul winner if he will let Christ direct him and use his life. "And they straightway left their nets and followed Him." This is the secret of these men; here is where most of us falter. We are not willing to turn loose of the "things" that would stand in our way and keep us from surrendering our lives to Him. When one is willing to let go and let God take control of everything in life, there is no limit to what God can do to and through that life. Peter the fisherman left his dirty boats and patched nets to become the second most respected man in the New Testament.

12

Matthew 5

Summary: Matthew 5 contains twelve THOUGHT PROJEC-
TIONS:
  3. The poverty of spirit (Matt. 5:3) METAPHOR.
  4. The mourner (Matt. 5:4) METAPHOR.
  5. The meek (Matt. 5:5) METAPHOR.
  6. The hungry and thirsty (Matt. 5:6) METAPHOR.
  7. The merciful (Matt. 5:7) METAPHOR
  8. The pure of heart (Matt. 5:8) METAPHOR.
  9. The peacemaker (Matt. 5:9) METAPHOR.
  10. The salt of the world (Matt. 5:13) METAPHOR.
  11. The light of the world (Matt. 5:14-16) METAPHOR.
  12. The way to smallness or greatness (Matt. 5:19) META-
PHOR.
  13. Righteousness plus (Matt. 5:20) METAPHOR.
  14. The perfect ones (Matt. 5:48) METAPHOR.

Matthew 5 opens with the introduction of the Sermon on the
Mount. Jesus begins this message with a series of beatitudes, and He
ends His message with a picture of a house being destroyed by a
storm. Jesus starts this message with only His disciples gathered
around Him, but concludes it with a great multitude of people before
Him. Jesus addressed Himself to His disciples concerning the characteristics that God expected to see in His children, but He ended this
message by placing a choice before the crowd regarding His Kingdom. Jesus was not instructing the disciples on how they might become Christians, but on how they were expected to live as Christians.
The requirements Jesus presented were too great for any man to
attain by himself, but they were expected of every "twice born" of
the Holy Spirit, of every Christian. Only the Christian could meet
these demands of the Kingdom of God presented here by Jesus. The
abiding Spirit of God makes this possible within the heart of the
Christian. These demands are impossible for the sinner, but are ex-

pected of the Christian. They do not open the door of the Kingdom
for men, but present portraits of those who have already gone into
the Kingdom.

The Sermon ends in chapter 7 with these words, ". . . the people
were astonished at His doctrine." Jesus had withdrawn Himself from
the crowd to be with His disciples for this period of instruction. The
crowd had intruded and had heard things designed only for the ears
of the disciples. It was not strange then for them to be "astonished"
at the things they had overheard. This is understandable, for they
were not prepared to meet the demands Jesus was making of those
who would become His followers. Only a Christian could understand
and appreciate what Jesus was saying. This is still true in our day, for
the world cannot understand the requirements Christ makes of His
children nor the demands the Christian makes upon himself.

In the first few verses of this chapter, Jesus throws out thought
projections with the rapidity of a modern antiaircraft gun. If we
keep in mind our original classification of thought projections (parables) as those forms of speech used by Jesus to reveal spiritual truths
through the processes of identification, association, or comparison,
this fifth chapter becomes a window into the mind of God for the
student of the New Testament.

We have already noticed that Jesus used the Beatitudes to intro-
duce His message. We classify seven of these as thought projections,
for they identify the life of a Christian with a particular characteristic
expected in the life of a Christian. Jesus is saying that a Christian will
be recognized by these characteristics. These are the marks of the
Christian. We do not classify the other two Beatitudes as thought
projections, for they are suggesting outside negative forces that will
be brought to play upon the life of the Christian to test and try him.

Thought Projection No. 3: The poverty of spirit (Matt. 5:3)
(Psalm 33).

The Beatitudes offer to the world a beautiful bouquet of spiritual
flowers. We do not like to disturb the continuity of thought suggested by this group of thought projections, because we believe they
ought to be considered as a single unit, but more is lost if we fail to
pluck them from their lovely background and examine each separately before we study them as a unit.

"Blessed [happy] are the poor in spirit, for theirs is the Kingdom of heaven." Anyone with normal intelligence knows that poverty does not offer happiness. If any person is happy in poverty, it will be not because of poverty but in spite of the circumstances surrounding his poverty. The people in Christ's time looked upon poverty as a spiritual penalty imposed upon the people by God, and they accepted wealth as a sign of God's approval. This was why the disciples seemed surprised at the statement made by Jesus when He said that it was almost impossible for a rich man to enter the Kingdom of God. The disciples asked Jesus, "Then who can enter the Kingdom of God if a rich man cannot?"

We believe that Jesus had in mind the words of the thirty-second Psalm. In the Psalm, the author pictures a man who has received forgiveness for his sins. He has been made aware of the poverty caused by sin in his own life, "When I declared not my sin, my body wasted away through my groanings all day long. For day and night thy hand was heavy upon me; my strength was dried up as by the heat of summer."

Throughout the entire earthly ministry of Jesus, He faced the self-satisfied, the religiously arrogant, and self-righteous religious leaders of the people. They had reached the pinnacle of spiritual perfection. Jesus could not teach them anything, nor could He give them a new revelation from God. They had all the answers before they met Him. All Jesus was doing for them was disturbing their religious vacuum. They were charged, commissioned, and ordained to perform, not enjoy, the performance. They did, however, enjoy the attention and respect their office demanded.

Jesus was saying, "Happy is the spiritual destitute, for he would recognize his own spiritual need, and any improvement in his spiritual state would make him happy." Jesus had something for such a person. He had a sonship to offer him, and a divine brotherhood with Himself. Christ knew that he could not save the righteous man, for such a person felt no need of salvation. This is why He said that He came not to the righteous but to the sinner. When man recognizes his spiritual bankruptcy, he is a candidate for all the rich graces Christ has for him, and when he receives this mercy and grace from God through Christ, his happiness is unlimited. This explains the great joy of a newborn Christian. His happiness comes from what he has received from God—complete forgiveness for all his sins and the gift of a new nature, an eternal nature!

Thought Projection No. 4: The mourner (Matt. 5:4) (Isaiah 61:2-3).

"Blessed [happy] are those who mourn, for they shall be comforted." This thought is also in Isaiah 61:2. Isaiah speaks of the promised Messiah who would come and give comfort to the suffering and the oppressed. He says that He would ". . . give them garland instead of ashes, the oil of gladness instead of mourning, the mantel of praise instead of a faint spirit; that they may be called oaks of righteousness, the planting of the Lord, that He may be glorified" (Isaiah 61:2-3).

Fine steels gets its temper from the fire. The great Christian gets his Christlike character through the fires of suffering for the sake of Christ. We gain our spiritual greatness from the shadows of life, for it is in these shadows that God's hand is most often sought and found by the Christian.

This is no "cry-baby" text. God does not promise to run to us at the first wail of hurt feelings. This word suggests mourning over the recognition of a great loss or a great need. The sinner mourns over his sinfulness and his lack of ability to change things in his life. He cries out to God and finds the comforting hands of God's forgiveness. He mourns over the need he sees in others and cries out to God for help, and God responds by meeting that need. The tears of compassion will not go unnoticed by God.

Thought Projection No. 5: The meek (Matt. 5:5) (Psalm 37:11).

"Blessed [happy] are the meek, for they shall inherit the earth." In Psalm 37:11, it says, "But the meek shall possess the land, and delight themselves in abundant prosperity." David begins this Psalm with, "Fret not thyself because of the wicked, be not envious of wrongdoers: For they will soon fade like grass, and wither like the green herb." This is a Psalm of contrast. The wicked seem to run over the righteous of God. The wicked seem to win at the expense of the righteous man. David is saying, "Do not let this upset you, for in the end, victory is yours. Commit your way to the Lord; trust in Him and He will act. 'He will bring forth your vindication as the light, and your right as the noonday' " (Psalm 37:6).

The meek shall inherit the earth. This is challenged by the foes of Christianity. They point out that the weak and meek are crushed by the strong. The strong control the world and shall always control the world. The meek and weak are killed off or become the servants of the strong.

Those who would defend this text would say in response, "The meek do inherit the earth. Look at the small ant, and where are the great beasts of the ages?" They would also point out that the strong men of history only reigned until the "weak" rose up and overthrew them. We believe both are in error in their application of this text. Jesus is reminding the disciples of the words of Isaiah in the sixth chapter where he speaks of the children of Israel "inheriting the land." They failed to do this in the early years after leaving Egypt. They were a rebellious people, and for many years gave Moses many heartaches. They failed to inherit this promised land for thirty-nine years and never did fully "inherit" all the land God had promised them. Their failure lay in their improper attitude toward God's leadership. They lacked "meekness"—submissiveness to the will and purpose of God.

Meekness is the attitude one has toward another. It has more to do with right relationships than it does with a "cowed," "crushed," or "dejected" personality. "As a man thinketh in his heart, so is he." If a man's heart is in right relationship with God, he is humble, submissive; and yet, he walks with his head erect, with the pride of Christ shining out from his life. He can look any man straight in the eye without feeling beneath or above that person. When man finds his right relationship with Christ, he will find also his right relationship with man.

Thought Projection No. 6: The hungry and thirsty (Matt. 5:6) (Isaiah 55:1,2).

"Blessed [happy] are they that hunger and thirst for righteousness, for they shall be satisfied." Jesus was echoing the words of Isaiah, "Ho, every one who thirsts, come to the water; and he who has no money, come buy and eat: Come, buy wine and milk without money and without price. Why do you spend your money for that which is not bread, and your labor for that which does not satisfy? Hearken diligently to me, and eat what is good" (Isaiah 55:1,2).

The human body has a built-in hunger gauge that will notify its brain when the body needs food and water. Without this gauge, the body would die of starvation or dehydration. When there is a deficiency of water or food in the body, the brain tells the body what to do about this need. When the body lacks the fuel it requires for healthy function, an alarm is sounded by this gauge, and the brain puts the body to work rebuilding what it needs.

In this text, Jesus uses the two metaphors "thirst" and "hunger" to describe the healthy and growing Christian. He will possess a natural hunger and thirst for spiritual food and drink. When a person is converted into a child of God, the Holy Spirit is placed into that life. That newborn Christian must feed and water his spiritual nature if he is to have normal, healthful growth. The Holy Spirit is our spiritual gauge. He will sound the alarm when we need an intake of spiritual food. Ignoring these warnings will bring the same destructive results to our spiritual nature as those that come to the body when the warnings for physical food are ignored. Each day of neglect weakens the warning system, and the time comes when this system is of no value to the body. Death is the ultimate result of this neglect. The Christian, neglecting the need of spiritual food, will also have the same negative response. He will not be separated from Christ in respect to salvation, but there will be no power of Christian influence left in that life. He will be among the "living dead" on earth.

When God created the first man, He formed him so that man could respond to a spiritual stimulus. This stimulus comes from God himself. Man's soul-spiritual nature is never satisfied with a response from any other source. Man and God were to have communion each with the other. Man, the only created thing to have such a built-in system of communication, was so endowed so that he could have communication (fellowship) with God. Man's sinfulness has caused his communication system with God to become maladjusted in such a way that he cannot communicate with God. Man was unable to make the necessary correction in his system to restore contact with God. God sought out man by sending His Son, Christ Jesus, Who came to earth and made the adjustment in man so that this communication with God could be restored. We call this adjustment "regeneration," "conversion," or the "new birth." Jesus used the tools of the cross of Calvary and the open tomb of Gethsemane to repair the broken line of communication between God and man. Now, once again, the Holy Spirit could travel from God into the heart of man. The spiritual gauge could once again function in man (the Christian), permitting him to grow and develop into the spiritual man he should be.

"Blessed are those who hunger and thirst for righteousness, for they shall be satisfied." Happy is the man who has had his spiritual gauge (nature) restored so that he can respond to the spirit of God that lives within his life. This spirit bears witness with man's spirit that he is the son of God (Romans 8:16), and he knows that this spirit will cause him to seek more and more the things of God (righteousness). As a normal healthy child is happy, so will a normal healthy Christian be happy; but he will also be always hungry and thirsty for more spiritual food (see also John 4:14, John 6:48-59).

Thought Projection No. 7: The merciful (Matt. 5:7).

"Blessed [happy] are the merciful, for they shall obtain mercy." This beatitude is not based upon any quotation from the Old Testament. Jesus is making a simple statement regarding the attitude of a Christian toward his fellowman. If the Christian is in tune with the heart of Christ, he will have compassion when he looks upon a fellow being in distress. His heart will respond to the other's need. When Jesus saw the crowd "as sheep without a shepherd" (Matt. 9:36), He had compassion and concern for them. It is this same compassion that causes a Christian doctor to forego a lucrative practice and the comforts of his native land to go and serve in the hot jungles in Africa for small material rewards, and it is the same compassion that sends some of our finest young people to serve as missionaries and ministers in countries around the world.

This mercy is more than a feeling of concern, for it demands a response to this concern. Jesus is saying that the street of mercy is a two-way street. The person rendering mercy will also be the recipient of mercy. If this mercy is not returned from the one receiving it, God himself will render in kind His mercy to the merciful one who shares his own with a person in need. It is not strange that wherever Christ is preached, hospitals spring up, children's homes are established, care is provided for the poor, the needy, and the aged. These are "side benefits" of Christianity.

Thought Projection No. 8: The pure of heart (Matt. 5:5-8) (Psalm 24:3,4).

"Blessed [happy] are the pure in heart, for they shall see God." Jesus was speaking from the background of the twenty-fourth Psalm. "Who will ascend the hill of the Lord? And who shall stand in His holy place? He who has clean hands and a pure heart, who does not lift up his soul to what is false, and does not swear deceitfully." The heart used in this text is the seat of the affections and the mind, the inner man. Jesus once spoke about His disciples as being "clean" (John 15:3). He spoke to the scholar Nicodemus in the third chapter of John's Gospel, saying that he must be born again, made a new man, a new creature. The "pure in heart" in the New Testament are those who have been "washed in the blood of the Lamb"; the ones who have been redeemed by the death of Christ on the Cross of Calvary.

Sin has built a barrier between man and God. Christ removed this partition by His death and resurrection, so that man and God might again have fellowship. But one must travel to Calvary before he can enter into this divine state. It is at Calvary that man exchanges his righteousness for the righteousness of Christ. It is Christ's righteousness that cleanses the heart of man, makes him "pure of heart," and it becomes a permanent state once this fellowship is established. Paul speaks of this in his letter to the Romans: "We are more than conquerors through him who loved us. For I am persuaded that neither death, nor life, nor angels, nor principalities, nor things present, nor height, nor depth, nor anything else in all creation, will be able to separate us from the love of God in Christ Jesus our Lord" (Romans 8:37-39).

Thought Projection No. 9: "Blessed are the peacemakers" (Matt. 5:9).

"Blessed [happy] are the peacemakers, for they shall be called sons of God." The Christian is a "peacemaker." He is more than a man of peace because he helps others to become peaceful. The sinner is at war with God. Man stands in disobedience and is living outside the grace of God. The Christian brings men and God together so that they can become reconciled to God. Man and God, again, live in peace. His action is that of a peacemaker.

The Christian is living in peace with God. This is a peace the world cannot understand. The Romans could not understand how the early Christians could be burned at the stake and be fed to the lions with a song on their lips and peace in their hearts. Paul before his own transformation of regeneration did not understand how Stephen could ask God's forgiveness for those stoning him to death. Later, Paul speaks of this peace of his life as something beyond human understanding.

"Blessed [happy] are the peacemakers, for they are called the Sons of God." This peaceful characteristic is the mark of the Sons of God. He breathes the spirit of peace wherever he might be. This is his nature. This has nothing to do with his attitude toward military service. Some of the greatest military leaders of the ages have been devout Christians.

Thought Projection No. 10: The salt of the earth (Matt. 5:13).

"Ye are the salt of the earth; but if salt has lost its taste, how shall its saltiness be restored? It is no longer good for anything except to be thrown out and trodden underfoot by men." We leave the Beatitudes in verse twelve, but find that Jesus continues His usage of thought projections with five more metaphors in the remaining verses of this chapter. "Ye are the salt of the earth," is the first of these.

Many theories have been suggested concerning the meaning of this thought projection. No metaphor can be understood without a consideration of the time and place it was spoken. We must ask ourselves, "What did salt mean to the people to whom Jesus was speaking?" When Jesus said to the people, "Ye are the salt of the earth," what did this mean to those people?—not to us today.

Dr. G. Campbell Morgan sums up the meaning of this statement, and this writer must agree with this brilliant scholar in the accuracy of his interpretation when he says, "Salt is not antiseptic, but aseptic. Antiseptic is something which is against poison, and which tends to cure. Aseptic is something which is devoid of poison in itself. Salt never cures corruption. It prevents the spread of corruptions. If meat is tainted and corrupt, salt will not make it untainted and pure. But salt in the neighborhood will prevent the spread of corruption to that which otherwise would become tainted."[1]

One should guard against a "world grand tour" on the word "salt," for it does offer some challenging views for the theologian with an imaginative mind. Salt was precious in the days of Christ, salt was used for money in China, salt was and is a necessary substance for life—plant, animal, or man. Each of these ideas can provoke thought stimulation for sermons or devotional messages to any Bible student, but did Jesus have any of these ideas in mind when He said, "Ye are the salt of the earth"? We think not.

The value of salt then and, also, today is to be found not in the smallness of a grain of salt, but in its nature when grains of salt associate themselves with other grains of a like nature. When they do become associated with other grains of salt, they take on the peculiar characteristic of influencing all things they touch. One grain of salt has very little influence to exercise upon any object it might come in contact with, but let a pound of salt be sprinkled on a piece of meat, for example, and its "influence" will have an effect for many months on that meat or on anyone attempting to use the meat.

One Christian in a sinful community will not necessarily "save" that community, nor will several Christians; but they will act as a restrainer to the spreading evil in that community. In restraining the evil influence with their good influence, the Christians will help make a better community. They will perhaps help influence others to consider the claims of Christ, causing transgressors to even accept the Christian concepts they represent.

During World War II, those of us who served in Africa were required to take a medicine called "Atabrine." This medicine did not possess the properties to cure malaria, but it could keep a person from becoming a victim of the malaria germ as long as he would take this medicine. It was aseptic and not antiseptic. It could not cure malaria, but it would keep the malaria germs from spreading among the soldiers and from weakening our war effort in Africa. Christians can be to their community what these atabrine pills were to our war effort in Africa. The greater the number of Christians in a community, the greater should be the moral and spiritual influence for Christ in that community and the harder for the forces of evil to destroy the moral and spiritual fiber of that community.

---

[1]G. C. Morgan, *The Parables and Metaphors of Our Lord* (Old Tappan, N.J.: Fleming H. Revell Co., n.d.), p. 18.

From the lives of eleven of the twelve disciples to whom Jesus was speaking has flowed through the ages a restraining influence for good in our world. This restraining influence shall continue until Christ returns for His own. Some people and some religious groups do lose their "saltiness"—their aseptic value—but when they do, they soon also lose their influence for good; they cease to have spiritual or moral value. You will find such nations, religious denominations, or individuals resting upon the spiritual junk heaps of history. "If salt has lost its saltiness [taste], how shall its saltiness be restored? It is no longer good for anything except to be thrown out and trodden under foot of men."

Thought Projection No. 11: The light of the world (Matt. 5:14-16).

"Ye are the light of the world." In the metaphor of salt, Jesus was pointing out the Christian's moral influence upon others. The Christian protects his society by being salt and by not transmitting the negatives of life; thus, that society is improved both in its morals and in its spiritual fiber. Here Jesus is speaking of how the positive spiritual influence of the Christian is to spread abroad: He will shine.

The object of light is to destroy darkness. It replaces darkness with light. This light reveals the danger hidden in darkness. It makes possible the avoidance of dangers darkness covers up. It is the job of the Christian to shine, to illumine this world. We do it as an individual (candle), or as a group or a unit (church). We shine as individuals like a candle so that man might read, or together we shine so that the righteousness of God can be seen afar by the traveler seeking safety and peace from a long journey.

Jesus once said, "I am the light of the world" (John 8:12). Now he is saying that "Ye are the light of the world." It is a light transferred from Christ as the flame of a match transfers itself to a candle. Nothing is taken away from one light as it is transferred to another. So it is with the Christian. One candle can only radiate so far, but if it lights a hundred candles, the light from the hundred candles can be seen by many people for a great distance. Today, we measure the density of light by "candle power."

Jesus tells us why we are "lighted." We are to shine so that men may see the truth. We shine not to be seen ourselves; our light, rather, is to be the object of attention. "You do not," said Jesus "light a lamp or candle and put either under a bushel, but you put it on a stand for all to see." One of two things will happen if a lighted candle is put under a bushel basket: The bushel basket will put out the candle, or the candle will set the bushel basket on fire and both will be lost.

We are to shine so that "men might see our good works and glorify the Father who is in heaven." We do not endorse some of the thoughts proposed by Dr. Leslie Weatherhead in his book *The Christian Agnostic*, but we support the idea he suggests in this statement: "One of the hindrances in the church at present is that it is cluttered up with well meaning, spiritually anemic people who have never taken Christ seriously, and do not even intend to do so, and who, through years of churchgoing, have developed such a thick armor against the shafts of Jesus that His most searching and scathing words neither challenge nor touch them. The trouble is that not entering His Kingdom themselves, they stop others, for assuredly no one wants to be like them. . . . 'Come and be like us,' they cry. But the man in the street says in his heart, 'From being like you, may your God deliver me.' "[2]

This is not what Jesus means. Perhaps, if Jesus were speaking today to our generation of churchgoers, He would modify this metaphor by saying something like this: "Ye should be the green light for men, not red. Too many professed Christians do stop men from seeking the Kingdom; they see those Christians' light, but it is red or yellow, and man has a right to question the wisdom of their direction."

The test of the light in our lives can be easily made. Do our lives, the light from our lives, produce good works that glorify God, Our Heavenly Father?

Thought Projection No. 12: The way to smallness or greatness (Matt. 5:19).

"Whoever then relaxes one of the least of these commandments and teaches men so shall be called least in the Kingdom of Heaven; but he who does them and teaches them shall be called great in the Kingdom of Heaven." The word translated "relaxes" (breaks) is the word used to slack off the ropes of a tent to let it sag. This is done

---

[2]Dr. Leslie Weatherhead, *The Christian Agnostic* (New York: Abingdon Press, 1966), pp. 176, 177.

when the tent is about to get wet or be taken down. A tight tent will pull itself (its pegs) out of the ground when it becomes wet.

Jesus says that the sign of smallness in the Kingdom is seen in those people who teach men to be slack with the laws and teachings of God's word. The Old Testament was the only sacred word for the Christian at the time of this statement of Jesus. We believe that the sacred word applies to the words He spoke, the words recorded later by holy men, which became our New Testament.

Smallness in the Kingdom of heaven means that one is loose in his practice of the Words of God. He does not take them very seriously in his own life. The second way to become small in the Kingdom of heaven is to teach others to also become loose in their application of God's laws and truths. We might become famous in the world for our "unusual" interpretations of God's word, but Christ says that this is a good way to shrink in the Kingdom.

To be great in God's Kingdom is to live the laws of God and to make the revealed truths of God a part of our daily living. To increase our spiritual stature is to teach others the importance of believing and living these truths of God in their lives. How small is the Christian? What is his attitude toward the word of God? If he is loose with it in practice and in his teaching of it to others, mark him as a small man in the Kingdom. But if the Christian is living these eternal truths of God and teaching others their true value, that man is a great man in the Kingdom of heaven. Our size in the Kingdom is measured by the Word of God.

Thought Projection No. 13: Righteousness plus (Matt. 5:20).

"For I tell you, unless your righteousness shall exceed that of the scribes and the Pharisees, you will never enter the Kingdom of heaven." "Shall exceed" means to overflow like a river overflowing its banks at flood time. Jesus was saying that to enter into the Kingdom of heaven, one had to have righteousness exceeding that of the scribes, a select but small group of teachers of the law, and righteousness exceeding that of the Pharisees—the separate ones, the orthodox priests. Was Jesus throwing up an impossible barrier into His Kingdom, for who among the average citizenry could meet this requirement? Jesus was demanding righteousness plus!

This was true, but Jesus also was offering them this righteousness plus. His righteousness was to be their righteousness. He would replace their own self-righteousness with His own righteousness. When they possessed His righteousness through their expressed faith and acceptance of Him as Saviour and Lord of their lives, they would have this superior righteousness that far exceeds the self-righteousness of the scribes and the Pharisees. This is what Jesus was saying. These men claimed their righteousness from the law, in their ability to keep the law; but Jesus said that this was not enough. The law was to lead them to Him. The law was to be a schoolmaster, but they erred in making the law the saviour. This is why they rejected Jesus and why they felt no need for Him. But the Kingdom of God was entered into only by men of faith, faith in Christ as the redeemer promised by God. Such men had committed themselves into His divine grace and love. Salvation was not of works but of grace alone, grace plus nothing.

Thought Projection No. 14: The perfect ones (Matt. 5:48).

"You, therefore, must be perfect, as your heavenly Father is perfect." Jesus has been talking about the Christian plus over against the strict requirements of the Jewish law. He says that these laws are not to be ignored, broken, or modified. They are the starting point to a more personal and devout devotion toward God and man. The Christian life is to be a "plus" life. Jesus then brings all this to a conclusion by saying, "You therefore, must be perfect, as your heavenly Father is perfect." This is the highest form of commitment, a striving for a total surrender to the will of God. The word translated "perfect" (*telos*) means "end" or "goal." This is the goal for your life. To this end you are striving. You are reaching up, striving daily to become more perfect in your union with God the Father. It has nothing to do with sinless perfection; this is not possible on earth for man. Man can set his spiritual sights on becoming more and more like Christ by striving daily to live within the will of God for himself. The principle of cybernetics rests in this word for the Christian—the goal, striving stimulus. It is this image that keeps him reaching toward the Godly idea brought to earth by Jesus.

13

Matthew 6

Summary: Matthew 6 contains thirteen THOUGHT PROJEC-
TIONS:

15. Alms giving; false piety and hypocrisy (Matt. 6:1-4) SIMILE.

16. Prayer location: false piety and hypocrisy (Matt. 6:5,6) SIM-
ILE.

17. Prayer structure: false piety and hypocrisy (Matt. 6:11-15)
SIMILE.

18. Fasting in public: false piety and hypocrisy (Matt. 6:16-18)
SIMILE.

19. Treasures in Heaven (Matt. 6:19,20) METAPHOR.

20. Where is your heart? (Matt. 6:21) METAPHOR.

21. Eye trouble (Matt. 6:22,23) METAPHOR.

22. Two masters (Matt. 6:24) METAPHOR.

23. Let the birds teach you (Matt. 6:25,26) METAPHOR.

24. Worry cannot add to your height (Matt. 6:27) META-
PHOR.

25. Let the flowers teach you (Matt. 6:28,29) METAPHOR.

26. Let the grass teach you (Matt. 6:30) METAPHOR.

27. Tomorrow's worry (Matt. 6:31,34) METAPHOR.

Chapter 6 is literally a gold mine filled with unmined thought
projections of Jesus. We find thirteen spiritual nuggets from the
mind of Christ to enrich the life of anyone who will gather them up.
There are two general classes of spiritual nuggets to be found in this
chapter. In verses one to eighteen, the four thought projections of
Jesus deal with the general subject of hypocrisy or false piety. In
verses nineteen to thirty-four, the nine thought projections deal with
motivations of life.

Jesus in this chapter examines some misdirected spiritual principles brought over into the daily lives of the people. He places His
finger on some very religious sensitive areas: alms giving, prayer,
fasting, spiritual motivations, worry, and so on. Jesus was not dis-

couraging activities in some of these areas; rather He was aiming at the misdirection of the people's energies. They were "spinning their religious wheels" without traction and were reaping lives of spiritual emptiness. He is pointing out to the people the hypocrisy of their actions and the lack of proper motivation. They were guilty of a psychocybernetic error, and this had to be corrected before their lives could measure up to what God was expecting of them. Applied religion in the moral life of man comes from the spiritual pattern man has within himself. If this is not in proper focus with the will of God, neither will be the actions or the religious expressions of man.

What is often overlooked by the casual reader of the New Testament is that many of the great truths enunciated by Jesus have not only spiritual significance, but also values for man in nonreligious spheres. This is true in the thought projections found in this chapter. Their true value can be demonstrated in the social and business life of a community or in the life of an individual practicing them. Each should be examined with this in mind. A teacher was speaking here as well as a spiritual leader.

"Beware of practicing your piety before men in order to be seen by them; for then you will have no regard from your Father who is in Heaven." Jesus opens this chapter with this warning. He illustrates what he is saying by the use of three illustrations. He pictures a parade. It is a one-man parade. The man has a group of trumpeters to precede him as he marches up to the temple with a gift. He wants everybody to recognize his generosity.

The second illustration is a man at prayer. This man has chosen his place of prayer carefully. He wants to be sure people know what he is doing. He, too, wants the spotlight of public attention properly focused upon him.

The third illustration concerns itself with the hypocrisy of fasting. Again, fasting was done to get the attention of others. The motive was self-centered.

Thought Projection No. 15: Alms giving; false piety and hypocrisy (Matt. 6:1-4).

"Thus when you give alms, sound no trumpet before you, as the hypocrites do in the synagogues and in the streets that they may be praised by men." The value of a gift is not in its intrinsic value or even in the act of giving. What is in the heart of the giver? What motivated this gift? These two questions determine the true value of any gift, be it made to man or God. Jesus was challenging the people to look beyond the gift and into the heart of the one making the gift.

Jesus was not condemning a gift made in public. He was condemning the motive behind the gift, if it was made to catch the attention of the public or made to elicit the praise of the public. We have several examples of these two forms of giving in the New Testament.

Jesus was standing with his disciples by the receptacle for gifts at the temple. A wealthy man passed by, paused to get the attention of the crowd, and then dropped a large sum into the receptacle. He knew that he was applauded, both by the temple priests and by the people standing near. Jesus said, "He has just received his reward for his gift. He gave for this purpose and he was paid off, there is not further praise due him by God. God has let him receive it from men because this was the way he wanted it."

A very poor woman also passed by the same receptacle and deposited her gift. She did not hide it (out of shame), but few paid attention to her or her gift, for they knew at a glance her gift would not enrich the temple treasury, nor cause any excitement in the heart of the treasurer of the temple when he counted the money. For this she cared not, for her gift was given out of an abundance of love even if it came from a purse of poverty. She had nothing left; this mite was her all.

Jesus looked both at her gift and into her heart. The size of her gift was measured by the size of her heart. He said to His disciples, "Of the two gifts just made, the woman's gift was the larger. Her reward will be great from the Heavenly Father for she gave her all to Him. Her praise will be from God, not man. The man gave out of an abundance, but he gave from a heart of poverty-smallness. He gave to gain the attention of man and for the praise of man, but she gave to God out of love for God." Real giving for any cause can be measured not by the amount of money given by an individual but by the amount left in the hands of the giver after the gift is made. It is an act of false piety and of hypocrisy to give to a religious cause if the gift is made not to honor God but to bring honor to the giver himself. Man, too often, is concerned only with the amount he is giving; he ought to be more concerned with the motive for making the gift. This seems to be the burden of this thought projection of Jesus.

Thought Projection No. 16: Prayer location: false piety and hypocrisy (Matt. 6:5,6).

"And when you pray, you must not be like the hypocrites; for they love to stand and pray in the synagogues and at the street corners, that they may be seen of men. Truly I say unto you, they have their reward." What is the true posture of prayer? Jesus was not condemning standing, nor was he recommending a kneeling position. Some people feel that they cannot "get through to God" unless they are kneeling; others feel that they must stand to pray. The key to prayer posture is found in the phrases of Jesus, "to be seen of men," and "they love to stand." The emphasis is on the words "stand" and "seen." Hypocrites love to stand in the synagogues and at the street corner (where more people could observe their actions) and pray. Hypocrites stood to pray because they could get more attention from men by standing. Hypocrites were more concerned with what men thought of their prayer life than they were with communion with God in prayer. They were upstaging God, stealing the spotlight from God. They were the focal point of the prayer—not God.

Prayer posture or body position in prayer should reflect one's own training and religious background. If one has been conditioned to pray kneeling, he will feel more in a proper prayer mood when he kneels than when he is standing. The only value in the position of the body when one prays is found in the effect it has upon the mind of the one praying. The motive of prayer can be discerned by the position of the one praying. If public prayers are offered to gain the attention and applause of the crowd, then any position one assumes in public to pray is an act of hypocrisy.

Thought Projection No. 17: Prayer structure: false piety and hypocrisy (Matt. 6:7-15).

"And in praying do not heap up empty phrases as the Gentiles do; for they think that they will be heard for their many words. Do not be like them, for your Father knows what you need before you ask him." Jesus here shifts his attention from the Jewish hypocrites to the attempts of the Gentiles to catch God's ear with their prayer structure—the length and content of their prayers. Jesus does not call these people "hypocrites," but merely points out the weakness of their approach to their God in prayer. "Do not heap up empty phrases." A prayer should have the proper content—meaningful substance—if it is to be an effective prayer.

Jesus was not suggesting in the next fifteen verses a prayer form to be used by the Christians in the years ahead. Nor was he saying that man should limit the length of his prayers. He was not saying that a prayer had to have perfect organization, beauty of words and thoughts, or pleasant sounds that please the listener. Prayer is more than the grouping of words to form a religious prayer cadence. While all these things may have their place in public prayer, they can all be present and still not be an acceptable prayer to God.

Sincerity and the spirit of humbleness should mark the prayer life of the true worshipper. These things will give meaning to his prayer, but without them, prayer becomes merely spoken words. One should lose himself in the depth of sincerity and humbleness as he reaches out toward God in prayer. God's attention is captured by this spirit of self-emptiness, and God responds by filling the worshipper with the awareness of His presence.

Thought Projection No. 18: Fasting in public: false piety and hypocrisy (Matt. 6:16-18).

"And when you fast, do not look dismal, like the hypocrites, for they disfigure their faces that their fasting may be seen of men. Truly, I say to you, they have their reward." Jesus adds a fourth dimension to the picture he was drawing of the religious hypocrite. Here was a group of religious leaders parading their piety before men in the form of "downgrading" the physical, their bodies. They would paint or mar their faces and deny their bodies the food required for the day. All this done in the name of religion. They disfigured their faces to inform the public that they were fasting. These men were not on a low-calorie diet to get a slim figure, nor were the facial mud-packs there to improve their beauty. Both were used to gain the admiration of men for what they were doing in the name of religion.

Jesus was not condemning either practice. He was tearing the false mask of piety from their faces to expose their real motive—to get glory for themselves. They would get the nod of admiration, not God for whom they were fasting; their motive was not to honor God. Of them it would be said: "What wonderful religious men these are; they disfigure their faces and starve their bodies for their God." The worshipper and not the one worshipped receives the honor. But an even greater sin is that the actions elicit this response from the nonbeliever: "What a cruel, selfish, and heartless God these people must have, if he demands that his children should thus suffer." This sort of thing does not attract men to God but, rather, drives them away.

Jesus said, "When you do these things, retire and do them in secret. I will see you and understand what you are doing and I will reward you for doing it."

In the rest of this chapter, Jesus deals with the motivations of life. Perhaps Jesus read the question in the minds of His listeners, "Why do men become hypocrites in their religious lives and in the expressions of their religious selves before men?" In the following seven thought projections of Jesus, we have the answer to this question; it rests in what motivates man.

Thought Projection No. 19: Treasures in Heaven (Matt. 6:19, 20).

"Do not lay up for yourselves treasures on earth, where moth and rust consume and where thieves break in and steal, but lay up for yourselves treasures in heaven, where neither moth nor rust consumes and where thieves do not break in and steal." We will separate for our study the twenty-first verse from these two verses, because it contains another thought projection aside from the one suggested in verses nineteen and twenty. The first two verses deal with the folly of spending life in gathering things that easily perish or things you can quickly lose. If the drive in life is to gather and store the goods of this world, how can one be sure that the world will not take them from you and that life itself is not wasted or lost in the process?

The people in the days of Christ could not rush down to the corner bank on Monday morning and deposit part of their weekly wage. They could not invest in bonds and stocks. Cloth with threads of gold and silver interwoven could be bought, not for wear but for their value, redeemable at a later date. Gold and silver could also be bought and hidden in the earth. All this was good, that is, until you go to recover your gold, only to find that a thief had dug it up for himself; or go to the storage place of your expensive garments to find that the moths have been entertaining their guests at your expense; or that rust had played havoc with the metal in the garments or in the coins buried.

Jesus is not condemning the practice of saving, nor the practice of providing for future years. He is saying, however, that there is more to life than storing up to have security for old age. If one is living this life so that he can have a better life later, one should be sure that he is saving the right things that he will need for that life to come. Life is more than food, shelter, and clothing. If we spend our lives trying to secure these things in the present so that we might have them in the future, we might be putting the wrong thing in the wrong bank.

It has been wisely said that we cannot take the physical things with us when we depart from this world, nor can we carry across death the money to which we gave our lives to acquire. The medium of exchange in this world is not the medium of exchange in the next world. The only investment we can carry with us across death is that which we have made in the personalities of others. A person might invest or give a milion dollars to a Christian college. The money will remain on earth, but the lives touched by what the money provided will be the return from that investment awaiting the giver beyond the grave. Jesus is saying that an eternal investment is a much better one to make on earth than an earthly one. The former investment is safe, but the latter is never safe.

Thought Projection No. 20: Where is your heart? (Matt. 6:21).

"For where your treasure is, there will your heart be also." In the two verses before this one, Jesus indicated two dangers regarding what you did with the reward for your labors. You might invest your savings from your labor in something that might be lost in time by the work of the elements (rust), by the action of nonhuman life (insects), or by man himself (thieves). He also pointed out the danger of depositing your savings in the wrong place. "Why place your life's savings," asks Jesus, "where thieves, moths, or rust can rob you?

"Where your treasure is, there will be your heart." If you should ask a person, "Where is your heart?" he would respond, "On the left side of my chest." Jesus would correct him by saying, "Your heart is there, but your interest in life is where you have placed your possessions. If you place all your life's savings in a farm, you interest will be in that farm, its rainfall, its productivity, its safety from the forces of nature and man, and with everything connected with it."

The reason why many people are not concerned with the life after death is that they have placed nothing in God's eternal bank. They might be wealthy while they are alive, but they become paupers the second they breathe their last breath on this earth. "Where your treasure is there will your heart be."

Man's possessions become a magnet around which his whole life revolves. If he fills his life with things of the world and starves his soul of the spiritual things the soul needs, his mind centers on and is controlled by the things of the world. Just as the spirit-filled life is reflected outwardly and guided by spiritual interests, so is the life that is controlled by the nonspiritual. The life we live reflects the thing to which we are dedicated. Not only are our interests reflected in our actions, but they will mold our vocabulary (a professional baseball player will have his own nomenclature, as will an engineer, and so on), the way we think, and even the way we dress. Our choice of friends will also reflect our interests in life.

If Jesus would have said, "Your self-image is the driving force in your life," His listeners would not have understood, but this is what he was saying when he said, "Where your treasure is there will be your heart." If you live for the dollar, your life becomes motivated by the dollar mark, and you will think, eat, and sleep planning and scheming about how to make and collect more dollars. If your heart could be photographed, it would appear as a dollar mark.

Thought Projection No. 21: Eye trouble (Matt. 6:22,23).

"The eye is the lamp of the body. So, if your eye is sound, your whole body will be full of light; but if the eye is not sound, your whole body will be full of darkness. If then, the light in you is darkness, how great is the darkness." Jesus was speaking to people who knew the terror of blindness. The sun's glare, the dust, and insects became allies in the destruction of their vision. Many of the people in that area of the world were either blind or in some final stage of blindness before the age of thirty. The people to whom Jesus was speaking were reminded of this fact every time they walked the streets of their towns and cities.

Jesus here has jumped from the danger of a life lived for those things that perish or are easily lost, to the thought of blindness—the loss of vision. Not all could earn enough to have money to bury and be stolen or to have cloth that moths might eat (for they wore daily all the cloth they had, and they had nothing to fear from moths), but all had eyes and all were faced with the possible loss of vision. This danger was real to them.

Jesus says that the eyes are the passages for light into the soul of man. If something happens to these eyes, no light will penetrate the darkness within. Great becomes the darkness that lives within such a person. Two words used by Jesus are very interesting. The word "single" or "sound" means that the light rays can enter into the eye and strike the retina in the right position—not too soon, not too late, nor at the wrong angle. If this condition does not exist, if the eye is "unsound," three common defects result: nearsightedness (myopia), farsightedness (hyperopia), or astigmatism; the eyes simply do not convey things rightly or bring the true character of what they are transmitting to the brain. If the eye is so damaged that it can not transmit any light rays, the mind must live in darkness and all is night within.

Man must be careful in what he carries into his mind through the eye. If he fills his mind with the ugly, the undesirable, and the filth of the world, the mind will not only receive it—it has to receive it —but it will become it. The mind is like a computer, it can only record and feed back upon demand that which it has received. It will respond to the "programming." It does not make its program, but it develops the one the operator feeds into it.

Jesus is saying here that man might not be able to control the actions of others; that is, the thief who steals his wealth, and so on, but he can control that which might and can steal his life and soul. He alone can control the things that go into his life. The "sound" eye produces the sound life, but the "unsound" eye will be the father of a darkened life.

Thought Projection No. 22: Two masters (Matt. 6:24).

"No man can serve two masters; for either he will hate the one and love the other, or he will be devoted to the one and despise the other. You cannot serve God and mammon." If Jesus were using modern expressions of our day (He was using a modern expression of that day), He would have said something like this: "A man cannot play ball on two football teams in the same game. He cannot represent two schools at the same time on the baseball diamond. He has to choose the team and the school he wants to represent." No one would challenge nor attempt to prove Him wrong.

A man cannot serve two masters at the same time. To do so would be to give each divided loyalties. No man can have two masters ordering him around. Such a person would soon become a patient in some mental hospital. And yet, how many Christians today are trying to live in the world for the world and at the same time live in the Kingdom of God for the glory of God. The results of this? Spiritual shipwrecks floating onto the religious beaches of theology, ready to be picked up and redeposited upon another beach with the rise and fall of every tide.

Jesus was saying in the language of our day, "You must recognize the impossible position you would be in if you were forced to take orders in the business world from two bosses who are in competition with each other. Be as practical in your religious life and apply the same logic into the spiritual world as you do in your business. You cannot serve God and mammon." The word "mammon" comes from the Greek word for "wealth or money" and is a personification of wealth. If your life is given over to the obtaining of money, money or things that money will buy become the driving motivation of your life; God and religion become secondary.

Thought Projection No. 23: Let the birds teach you (Matt. 6:25-26).

"Therefore I bid you put away anxious thoughts about food and drink to keep you alive, and clothes to cover your body. Surely life is more than food, the body more than clothes. Look at the birds of the air; they do not sow and reap and store in barns, yet your heavenly Father feeds them." One should be careful not to read into the Scripture something not there. Jesus is not saying that man should be like the birds—not work or save something for the days ahead when he cannot work. He is not saying that man is to let others provide for his daily needs. He is not saying that man should not look at the uncertain future or try to provide for himself and his loved ones.

Jesus is saying that we can learn a lesson from the birds about worrying. A bird learns to adjust himself to the seasons and to trust nature to provide for his daily needs. He might eat fresh grass seeds or blades of grass in the spring and berries in the fall. He might migrate south in the winter and north in the spring.

Birds do work for their food. They have to hunt for it, flying down to it. Although they do not plow the fields, they sow many seeds in their droppings of waste. The bee flies many miles to get the nectar to feed himself and to produce his honey. The bird does what he can and leaves the rest to nature. He knows that nature produces an overabundance, far more than he can eat in his lifetime.

So Jesus says to His listeners, "If God provides so abundantly for a small bird that has little market value, what of you, the most valuable possession the Heavenly Father has on earth, do you think for a second that God would not take care of your needs, too?" Thus to worry means we question the goodness of God. The bird does not wait for the worm to be brought to him by an angel; neither should we wait for an angel to feed us, for God will bless our efforts to feed ourselves from the abundance of God, which is to be found all around us here on earth; that is, if we will reach out for it.

Thought Projection No. 24: Worry cannot add to your height (Matt. 6:27).

"And which of you by being anxious can add one cubit to his span of life?" Sandwiched between the thought projection of the birds and the lilies is this gem-thought. To properly approach this diamond in the rough, one needs to strip from it all the negatives surrounding it. Jesus did not say, "One cannot add length to his life nor to his height." A man is promised a longer life if he gives proper respect and love to his parents, and also if he lives a certain type of life. One can add to his height by proper exercise. These things do not stand in contradiction to this Scripture. Jesus is saying that worry and anxiety will not add to the length of life. Worry will not cause your body to add an extra cubit. Jesus is saying, "This is not the procedure of adding height nor length to your life." This is all that He is saying. He could have continued by saying, "Worry will not add to the mental ability to meet life, but prayer, worship, Bible study, and service will add to the spiritual stature of a Christian."

There is some question among scholars as to the exact meaning of the words "add one cubit to his life span." "Life span" is also translated "height." The meaning Jesus is trying to convey can be applied to both ideas—WORRY ADDS NOTHING TO LIFE, SO WHY WORRY? Worry will take away from both length of life and physical health. This is an unquestionable fact of modern medicine.

Thought Projection No. 25: Let the flowers teach you (Matt. 6:28,29).

"And why are you anxious about clothing? Consider the lilies of the field, how they grow; they neither toil nor spin; yet I tell you, even Solomon in all his glory was not arrayed like one of these." This thought projection ought to be studied carefully by the women of America: It contains some beauty secrets often neglected by them.

Jesus had pointed out the folly of spending one's life worrying about his food. A man must have food to live, but "man does not live by bread alone." Jesus said (Matt. 4:4). Worrying about food will not feed one, but when he does the best he can do and will trust God for the results, God will supply all his needs.

Jesus now turns to the worry men have about their clothes. Again, we ought to remove the negatives from around these lilies as we did from the birds. Jesus is not saying that men ought not to concern themselves about what they are to wear in the morning or at dinner tonight. He is not saying that a man ought not to make himself attractive as he can, within his means. He is not saying that there is virtue in ugliness, holiness in drabness, or spiritual merit in the unlovable. We believe that Jesus would have taken the opposite position. He would say to all his children, "Be as beautiful and as handsome as you can within your income, for you do it to the glory of your Heavenly Father." It is natural and normal for nature to produce things of beauty—a sunset, snow on a mountain turned into gold by the rays of a rising or setting sun, a rose kissed into radiant beauty by the soft spring breeze, or the blaze of color from the flowers of spring after being awakened from their winter sleep. God is a God of beauty, and He does not suddenly become a God of negatives when He looks at the human race. He would say through the voice of Christ, "Look at the lilies and learn their beauty secret, and become like them."

A lily takes the things it finds in its present environment and turns these into things of beauty, and by doing this, it changes its own ugly environment into beauty. It does not resist its environment but yields to it and lives to change it; thus, its surroundings become like itself. It rises above the muck and the filth of the swamp, raising its head toward the sun from whence comes its strength, and, in turn, it shares in the warmth and beauty of the sun that changes it into a thing of beauty to be admired by all who pass that way. The job of the lily is to be beautiful where it is and to get the ingredients for this beauty from where it is. It does not spend its time worrying because it is not somewhere else or something else.

Jesus says to us, "If I will do this to a seed buried in the mud of a swamp, do you think I would do anything less for you? If I want my lilies to be beautifully clothed so that they will bring glory and honor to me, do you think I am less anxious to clothe you so that you might do the same?"

Jesus is looking beyond the cut of the suit or the texture or fiber of the dress on the Christian. He is looking at the outward beauty of the life of His children. The Christian's beauty will come from the way he responds and uses the environment in which he finds himself at all times. It is our job to change that environment by using what it offers to us under the warmth of the spirit of the Son of God so that we may develop spiritual beauty within ourselves. Worry will not produce this beauty. Learn this secret from the lilies.

Thought Projection No. 26: Let the grass teach you (Matt. 6:30).

"But if God so clothe the grass of the field, which today is alive, and tomorrow is thrown into the oven, will he not much more clothe you, O men of little faith." This is a continuation of the thought of the lilies. Only Jesus changes the metaphor from lilies to grass. Before He was speaking of the beauty of the lilies, but here he is speaking of the brevity of the life span of grass. He is saying, "If God goes to all the trouble it takes to cause the grass to cover the fields—spreads the seeds, sends the rain, puts the necessary minerals in the ground, and brings it to life with the warm rays of a spring sun—all this for a few months of beauty after which the grass is cut and burned: How much more would the Father be willing to invest in your life which has a longer span than grass? O ye of limited faith. You have so little faith in the plan and purpose of God for your lives." This is not a question of the quantity of their faith, but the quality of that faith. Faith in God in Jesus' time was quite thin. A large quantity of thin-quality (poor) faith does not add up to very much in God's eyes.

Much can be said today concerning the so-called New Theology. It has grown out of the environment of men who possess thin-quality faith in the Bible. Jesus would say of them as he said of the men of His day, "O ye men of poor quality faith, the more you possess, the weaker is your faith in Me and in my Holy Word."

Thought Projection No. 27: Tomorrow's worry (Matt. 6:31,34).

"Let the day's own trouble be sufficient for the day." Jesus could have said, "Let each day do its own worrying," for this is the substance of the last two verses of this chapter. Jesus here is summing up what he has been saying: "This is my conclusion," Jesus says, "do not worry about what will happen tomorrow; let each day do its own worrying. You will find that each day will have enough problems for you to handle without your having to borrow from the next day. If you do this, you will be so busy solving your problems that you will find no time to worry about them."

An old Negro man in the deep South was once asked by the man who was his employer, "Sam, you have worked for me for several years. Tell me something. I have never seen you unhappy or worried about anything. What is your secret for the happiness you seem to possess. I do not have it myself, and I have more of the good of this world than you."

The old man stopped, took time to think, then smiling replied, "I suppose it is this way, boss. You see, when I get worried about something, I just stop my work and go take a nap. When I awake, I have forgotten what was worrying me and I am happy again." We might not be able to follow this simple formula for worry, but we can try the one Jesus offers us in this chapter.

14

Matthew 7

Summary: Matthew 7 contains ten THOUGHT PROJEC-TIONS:

28. The beam in the eye (Matt. 7:1-5) METAPHOR; NARRATIVE.

29. Giving holy things to dogs (Matt. 7:6a) ALLEGORY.

30. Casting pearls before swine (Matt. 7:6b) ALLEGORY.

31. Bread, fish, serpent (Matt. 7:7-12) METAPHOR; NARRATIVE.

32. Two gates; two roads (Matt. 7:13,14) METAPHOR.

33. Prophets: two kinds, true and false (Matt. 7:15,16a) METAPHOR.

34. Fig trees, grape vines: two natures (Matt. 7:16b) METAPHOR.

35. Sound and sick trees: Two natures or two conditions (Matt. 7:17-20) METAPHOR.

36. Who are the true prophets, or who enters the Kingdom? (Matt. 7:21-23) METAPHOR.

37. Two foundations: sand and rock (Matt. 7:24-27) SIMILE; NARRATIVE.

Chapter 7 is the continuation and conclusion of the Sermon on the Mount. It is made up of ten thought projections of Jesus. They deal with the subjects of judging one another, responsibility of the Christian for holy things, prayer, choices in life, the danger of false prophets, the rejection of religious workers at the judgment of God, and the two kinds of foundations of life. The crowd is left with the shattering sounds of a house being smashed by a storm— their house, the house of the foolish builders. "And when Jesus finished these sayings, the crowds were astonished at his teaching, for He taught them as one who had authority, and not as their scribes."

Thought Projection No. 28: The beam in the eye (Matt. 7:1-5).

"Judge not, that you be not judged. For with the judgment you pronounce you will be judged, and the measure you give will be the measure you get." Jesus follows with the graphic story of a man with a huge beam protruding from his eye trying to remove a speck of sawdust from the eye of another. What a ridiculous sight! Jesus was suggesting to them that it would be no less amusing, no less impossible for a Christian to attempt to remove a moral speck of evil from the life of another when this well-meaning Christian has a log of the same substance overshadowing his own life.

When one becomes the judge of a brother, he must in turn expect to be the object of the same kind of judgment he renders to the other. The degree of judgment he himself makes of others will in turn be the degree of judgment he can expect from others. There is no profit in acting as a judge of other Christians. Jesus emphasizes that man is not a qualified judge of other men. His own weaknesses and sins disqualify him in this area.

Thought Projection No. 29: Giving holy things to dogs (Matt. 7:6a)

"Do not give to dogs that which is holy." Jesus shifts His thought pattern from the judging of other Christians to more important functions of the Christian. The Christian is not to concern himself about the character of his Christian brother; he stands or falls before God and not man. Jesus says, however, that the Christian should be alert to those who have no respect nor regard for the divine things of God. The word for dog here is one used when one speaks of the wild scavenger dogs that lived on the garbage of the city. They were satisfied to get the food not fit for human consumption. Their sense of value was conditioned by what they had to eat. To them, food was food, for they could not distinguish between a costly piece of choice beef and a cheap cut. It would be a waste to throw them choice cuts of meat instead of the cheap cuts. These dogs were interested in quantity and not quality of food.

Jesus is warning that such men would not appreciate nor receive the precious gift of the Bread of Life. They would place no value on the Cross of Calvary. They would be satisfied with the cheap things in life, in religion. This principle was proved when the Saviour

Himself was nailed to a cruel cross. Many people today place no value on the Gospel Message of Christ. It has neither meaning nor value for them.

Paul warns the Christians at Corinth (I Cor. 11:17-34) about the danger of the misuse of the Lord's Supper. He said that some of them were dead and others sick because of their misuse and wrong applications of the ordinance of the Lord's Supper. Their sin was in "not discerning the body of Christ." Every non-Christian who takes the Lord's Supper is guilty of this sin, for only a Christian can really understand the full meaning of what is meant by this ordinance.

Should the Gospel be given to a person who is under heavy influence of an alcoholic drink or some form of narcotics? Is such a person capable of discerning the value of what he is hearing? Should one wait until the other is sober enough to understand what is being said to him? What about the hardened, indifferent non-Christian who is hostile to Christianity? These are questions each of us must face as we deal with such persons. It seems that Jesus is talking about any person who cannot, or will not recognize spiritual values when they are presented in the Gospel message. The Gospel is never to be forced upon the unwilling mind. Each must accept or reject it himself, but each must know the value of what is being presented if the Gospel is to have an opportunity to speak for itself. If this is missing, the seed is cast upon "stony soil" and has no chance to bring forth life. It is wasted seed that could have been sown upon fertile ground later and could have brought forth a manyfold crop; now it will bring forth nothing.

Thought Projection No. 30: Casting pearls before swine (Matt. 7:6b).

"Do not throw your pearls before swine, lest they trample them underfoot and turn and attack you." This is but another side of the same coin. On one side we see the picture of the waste of holy things upon scavenger dogs; here we have the picture of precious pearls being cast to swine.

Swine are not capable of determining the value of precious jewels. They are concerned only with something to eat. They live to eat and eat to live and anything that does not feed the body is not wanted. The swine was thought to be the lowest form of animal life to the hearers of Jesus, and pearls were considered the highest order of precious jewels. The folly of wasting the most precious of things upon the lowest form of life is the picture Jesus is painting. What makes it even more unacceptable is the waste: The pearls were not appreciated, nor did they perform the service for which they were intended. The swine were not satisfied nor fed, and the pearls were lost in the mud of the pigsty. A total loss was suffered by both the swine and their owner!

Jesus warns that the swine, in their disappointment, would turn upon the giver of pearls and attempt to kill him. The swine wanted corn, not pearls. It associates its failure to be fed with the man offering pearls, and turns on him.

The pearl of this metaphor, like the holy things in the metaphor of the dogs, is the Gospel message of Christ, the "Good News" of God, the new life that God was offering to men, as found in Christ Jesus. Men were eager to eat the bread Jesus offered them and even follow Him if He would use His divine power to restore the earthly kingdom of Israel, but they had no desire to follow or accept the spiritual and moral offerings He was making. They wanted "corn" not spiritual "crowns." They wanted their physical cravings satisfied, and they were not seeking the spiritual gifts He came bearing. They ate the bread and fish He offered, but when these ran out and the supply stopped, they turned and nailed Him to the cross.

We should not waste our energies upon those whose hearts are so hard that they cannot see, nor do they want to see, the precious words of life we bear. There are many who are hungry for the message, and it is to these we should turn. The Gospel is not to be cheapened by forcing it upon those who do not want or value it.

Thought Projection No. 31: Bread, fish, serpent (Matt. 7:7-12).

"Ask, and it shall be given you; seek and ye shall find; knock, and it will be opened to you." Ask . . . seek . . . knock . . . are three key words that find their answer in three actions of God.

It has been suggested that we ask something of another who is near us. "Will you give me that knife?" We seek out a person from whom we want a favor, whose whereabouts is unknown, as perhaps in another room of the building. "John, I have searched for you all over the building. Now I have found you." But when the location of the person from whom we seek the knife is known to us we go to him. John is in his bedroom, I knock on his door and say, "May I come in, John? I want to borrow a knife from you." John recognizes my voice as a friend's voice and opens the door and lets me in; I borrow the knife because he has opened the door to me.

There are times when we feel so close to God that we just say to Him, "Will you tell me what to do about this problem?" There are other times when we are not aware of His presence—the world of business, the world of things has come between us—and we withdraw from the world and seek his face through prayer and the study of His Holy Word. We then again feel His presence. Many times in life we feel that a locked door stands between us and God. We have shut him out; we then humbly knock on this door and say, "Father, it is I. Will you open the door and let me enter and have communion with you again? I am sorry for my neglect of you." We ask . . . seek . . . find . . . not the three steps we must take to find God, but three different methods of approach, each depending upon the circumstances. The important thing about all three methods is not in the method used, but in the glorious fact that God will hear and respond. He will let us find Him, and He will open the door when He hears our voice crying out to Him.

He then tops off this cake with the icing: "If you earthly fathers will not give your own children a rock when they ask for bread; nor a serpent when they ask for a fish, do you think your Heavenly Father would do any less?" You should expect God to be a better provider for His children than a man is for his own children. We should make our requests known to God and then trust God to give us the answer we need. He will give us the best answer.

Thought Projection No. 32: Two gates; two roads (Matt. 7:13, 14).

"Enter by the narrow gate; for the gate is wide and the way is easy that leadeth to destruction, and those who enter by it are many. For the gate is narrow and the way is hard that leads to life, and those who find it are few." Jesus thus turns from the subject of prayer to the two choices placed before all men.

Jesus never created the illusion that the peoples of the world would all join the heavenly crowd and that the gatekeepers of heaven would be overworked letting the people in. He did not picture a worldwide movement into Christian ranks. In fact, He took the opposite view. He warns in this metaphor of the narrow gate and says that the crowds would not gate-crash the heavenly portals.

The gate into the Kingdom is narrow, but the road becomes wider and more beautiful as you travel it day-by-day. The gate to destruction is wide, but the road leading from it becomes more narrow and dangerous each day spent upon it, and less attractive to the traveler. No dying sinner looks back upon his life and says, "What a wonderful life I have lived." His cry is one of despair and a plea for a chance to relive it.

America is a nation of many and great churches, but on any given Sunday in the year—Easter notwithstanding—there will be more people outside the churches, by many times, than will be found in them. For each million to be found in houses of worship in the world, there will be a hundred million who are not.

The test of a life is not its beginning but its end, its final destination. But the end of a life is determined by the entrance gate one takes first in this world. Jesus says that "my gate is narrow and many will not seek it nor enter it," but the smallness of the crowd does not certify its importance—the majority is not right in this instance. If we "follow the crowd" it will be to destruction. Do not let the crowd make your choice of life; make the choice with the end in view.

Thought Projection No. 33: Prophets: two kinds, true and false (Matt. 7:15,16a).

"Beware of false prophets who come to you in sheep's clothing but inwardly are ravenous wolves. You will know them by their fruits." Jesus steps down from the crowd to individuals who would mislead the crowds. "Take your eyes off the crowd now and look at the ones leading them astray." This is the emphasis Jesus is giving to the people from verse 15 to 22. There are some tests people ought to make regarding their spiritual leaders. If a wolf could place upon himself the fresh skin of a sheep, he could go among a flock of sheep and do great damage before being discovered by the shepherd. He would look like the rest of the sheep and even smell like one, but he would not have the appetite of a sheep nor the disposition of one. He would still be a wolf by nature.

This is the picture Jesus is painting. The test of a wolf is his nature. He does not become a sheep because he is wearing the skin of a sheep; nor is a prophet a man of God because he is wearing the clothes of a prophet. It takes more than "holy" cloth to make a man a priest. Jesus said that there is a test you can apply to all such men: "What kind of fruit do you find in their lives." The spirit of Christ in the life of any man will be manifested by the kind of Christian fruit borne by his life. A prophet's life speaks louder than his words. The ultimate fruit of every Christian life is to produce other Christians. A Christless life cannot do this.

Thought Projection No. 34: Fig trees, grapevines: two natures (Matt. 7:16b).

"Do men gather grapes of thorns, or figs of thistles?" Jesus illustrates what he has been saying about the test of a prophet by directing His listeners' attention to some hard facts of nature. One does not expect a grape to grow on a thorn tree. The grape has a different nature from the nature of a thorn tree. Neither would you expect to find figs growing on a thistle bush. The nature of a fig is not that of a thistle bush. There is nothing startling in these statements, but man seems unable to carry this simple logic from his daily life over into the moral and spiritual world. The morals and the spiritual life of a man come from the nature of that man. The kind of man he is, is found in the fruits of his life. You are not passing "moral judgment" on another, but you are classifying the species—thistle or fig, grape or thorn. What is the nature of the prophet? You have a right to ask this question and to seek an answer.

Jesus warns us to be careful of the crowd we are in. Look at the leader: Does his life give proof of divine leadership or does he give the lie to the life he professes to have? This does not take the trained mind of a theologian to discern—any boy on a farm knows the difference between figs and thistles, grapes and thorns.

Thought Projection No. 35: Sound and sick trees; two natures or two conditions (Matt. 7:17-20).

"A sound tree can not bear evil fruit, nor can a bad tree bear good fruit. Every tree that does not bear good fruit is cut down and thrown into the fire. Thus you will know them by their fruits."

The metaphors used by Jesus in verse sixteen were ones of contrast—figs and thistles, grapes and thorns. The unlike cannot grow on like stock. Here Jesus talks about a tree, the nature of a tree that produces fruit of little or no value. An unsound (diseased) tree can not bear healthy fruit. A germ gotten into a tree will cause a blight that spreads through its branches and into the fruit itself. The tree will slowly wither until it is dead. The owner of the land knows all this, and when he discovers such a tree, he cuts it down lest it spread its disease to other trees.

The Christian is spiritually healthy because of his spiritual birth. He should produce good fruit. The test of his life will be seen in this fruit. The unregenerate cannot produce healthy fruit; his nature is possessed with the disease of sin; it spreads into his whole life and any fruit from that life must be unsound.

There is a warning here for the Christian who nurtures even the smallest sin within his life. This sin can grow and corrupt the life and in turn affect the quality of fruit from that life. Paul seemed to have one great fear; he was afraid that God might toss him on the "scrap pile" of life and no longer use him as His voice. This ought to be the fear of every Christian. A pastor once told of a member of his church who came to him with the news that he was giving up his Bible class. This teacher was a Ph.D., a professor in one of our state universities. He said, "I am going to retire now from service. I have taught long enough." This pastor replied, "Suppose the Lord should do the same to you?" Within a month, they buried that professor. It would have been more tragic for a person to have lived for many years without the power to bear fruit than to die; so death it was. Death was the better of two choices.

"Every tree that bears not good fruit is cut down and thrown into the fire." (Matt. 7:19) This could mean physical death or it could mean the death of influence, or both.

Thought Projection No. 36. Who are the true prophets, or who enters the Kingdom? (Matt. 7:21-23).

"Not everyone that saith unto me, Lord, Lord, shall enter into the Kingdom of Heaven; . . . And then will I profess unto them, I never knew you; depart from me, ye that work iniquity." Verses 21 to 23 might be questioned regarding their classification by the author as a thought projection or as a metaphor. But Jesus qualifies this as a metaphor by the use of the word "evildoers." These were the people who had spent their lives in mission work. They had preached in the name of Jesus, had cast out demons in His name, and had done mighty works in His name. We are led to ask, as did the disciple regarding those who could be saved, "If the wealthy man could not enter into the Kingdom of God who could?" If such people mentioned by Jesus were classified as "evildoers," who, then, are the "righteous ones"? It must be remembered that Jesus once said that of all the prophets John was the greatest, but the smallest Christian (weakest) was greater than John the Baptist. The Christian has one quality not possessed by other non-Christian religious workers. This is a spiritual new birth.

These workers of righteousness used the name of Jesus their deeds to perform, but they lacked the spirit of Christ within their own lives. "Depart from me ye evildoers, I never knew you." If they were not known by Jesus, they could not have known Jesus. They knew his name but not the person of the name: It is not enough to do good, even in the name of Christ; it must be done by Him through us. The key to these verses is "Not everyone who says to me 'Lord, Lord' shall enter the Kingdom of heaven, but he who does the will of my Father in heaven." One cannot do the will of the Father without knowing the Father. One cannot know the Heavenly Father without knowing Jesus, for no man can come to the Father without Christ.

These people claim Christ as their source of power without having a claim on Christ. They were using Christ, but Christ was not using them. They gathered the glory that belonged to Him for themselves. They were living outside of the will of Christ and, thus, outside of the will of God.

Thought Projection No. 37: Two foundations: sand and rock (Matt. 7:24-27).

"Everyone then who hears these words of mine and does them will be like the wise men who built his house upon the rock." Jesus sums up his entire Sermon on the Mount by a beautiful wordscape. He draws a picture of two men. Each selects a building site. Each selects his building material with care and each builds the strongest house he can. Each seems to be satisfied with what he has done and each moves into his house. Then things begin to happen. A storm comes to test these two houses. The wind blows against each, the rain lashes out against each, there are flashes of lightning and roars of thunder. One house stands serenely aloof from it all. The owner sits calmly listening to the howl of the storm. His mind is free from fear. He has faith in his house for it is built well. He had built it with such a storm in mind. His foundation was of rock.

The second man begins to feel his house tremble slightly at first, and then, second by second, with increased force. The wind and rain were not causing the trembling, for the movement was from below. His foundation begins to melt away with each rain drop; then with a great crash, the house collapses upon the owner and all is lost. Jesus concludes with these words: "Great was the fall of it." He adds nothing to the story, draws no conclusions for His listeners, for His introduction is his conclusion. "Everyone then who hears these words of mine and does them will be like the wise man who built his house upon the rock . . ." It is the foundation of the building that gives safety to the house. One should be sure of the foundation upon which he is building his life. God's word is the sure foundation: "Every one that hears these words of mine and does them . . ."

15

Matthew 8

Summary: Mathew 8 contains three THOUGHT PROJEC-
TIONS:

38. Eating with Abraham and Jacob (Matt. 8:5-13) META-
PHOR.

39. Foxes' holes and birds' nests (Matt. 8:18-20) METAPHOR.

40. Let the dead bury the dead (Matt. 8:21-22) ALLEGORY.

Chapter 8 finds Jesus departing from the mountain side upon the completion of the Sermon on the Mount. He meets a leper who asks Jesus to have mercy upon him and cure him. Jesus cures the leper. He enters Capernaum and cures a centurion's servant at the urgent request of the centurion. This is the foundation for the first thought projection in this chapter. Then Jesus cures Peter's mother-in-law. Because of the press of the crowd, Jesus decides to cross over the sea. A scribe comes to Him and offers to follow Him anywhere, providing the background for the second thought projection. Another would-be disciple comes to Jesus, saying that he, too, would follow Him anywhere. This is the background for the third thought projection.

The chapter continues with a dramatic storm at sea and Jesus calming the storm and sea with a miracle. He meets two demoniacs who lived in the land of the Gadarenes. They were so dangerous that men were afraid to pass their way. As Jesus approaches the men possessed by demons, the demons cry out to Jesus to leave them alone. Jesus casts out the demons from these two men and into a herd of swine who are feeding near the sea. The swine rush down into the sea and are drowned. The people of that country ask Jesus to leave their land, even though Jesus had changed two of their unfit citizens into normal and productive citizens.

More important than the miracles performed in this chapter by Jesus are the three thought projections He uttered. The miracles He performed benefited only three people, who have long passed off the stage of life, but the truths Jesus reveals here are eternal ones.

Thought Projection No. 38: Eating with Abraham and Jacob (Matt. 8:5-13).

"I tell you, many will come from east and west and sit at table with Abraham, Isaac, and Jacob in the Kingdom of Heaven while the sons of the Kingdom will be thrown into the outer darkness; there men will weep and gnash their teeth." The man who approached Jesus in behalf of his sick servant was not a son of Abraham. He did not enjoy the fruits of God's promise to Abraham. He had no religious right to come to Jesus. His only qualification was a personal responsibility he felt for another's need. He did not justify his coming except to say his servant needed Jesus. "Lord, my servant is lying paralyzed at home, in terrible distress." This was all that the centurion said to Jesus. Jesus replied, "I will come and heal him."

"Master, I am a man of authority and have soldiers under me who will obey quickly every command I issue. But I am not worthy to have you enter my home. If you will just say the word, my servant will be cured." This man was not demanding miracles before he would believe in Jesus. He was saying "I believe" before the miracle. This man's faith was not limited to what he could see Jesus do, but he trusted in the ability of Jesus to perform a miracle even by remote control.

Jesus was so impressed with the centurion's quality of faith that he turned to the crowd and to His own disciples and said, "I tell you, many will come from east and west and sit at table with Abraham, Isaac, and Jacob in the Kingdom of Heaven while the sons of the Kingdom will be thrown into the outer darkness; there men will weep and gnash their teeth."

What happened here demands that we study this centurion himself. He was a person with authority in a country where such authority meant something. His authority rested in Rome itself. He spoke for Rome. And yet, his approach to Jesus was not made to impress Jesus with his community status. We believe that his reason was just the opposite. He was magnifying the great gap that he felt existed between him and Jesus. He was nothing—unworthy to have Jesus enter his home, even on a mission of mercy.

Jesus looked beyond his words into his heart and saw the great depth of sincerity and was moved by it. Here was a man, a Roman soldier, without the theological background of the Pharisees, Scribes, or Sadducees, but who had a more complete faith in Him than they did. He was a hated and despised Roman soldier—the enemy—and yet, Jesus said He had not seen any greater faith exercised in Himself than was being demonstrated by this man. It was the man's faith in Jesus that caught the attention of Jesus.

What Jesus said to the crowd and to His disciples must have shocked them all. In substance Jesus said: "The promise was given to Abraham and was to be shared with all his descendants. God gave this promise to Abraham because of his great faith in God to redeem it in due season. This promise was renewed to Isaac and to Jacob, whose name was changed to Israel. I came as the fulfillment of this promise, but my own receive Me not. They will not trust Me, they lack the faith of Abraham. Faith is the key into the Kingdom of Heaven. They will not use it. It is growing rusty for lack of use. This man, a hated Roman, comes and takes this neglected key and uses it, not in behalf of himself but for another who is in great suffering. I am saying to you that henceforth my promise to Abraham is now open to all men who will exercise faith in Me."

Jesus is saying that the descendants of Abraham had forfeited the promise because of their lack of faith. The promise was given in reward for faith and now it was lost for lack of faith. Jesus is saying that rejection of Him is a rejection by Him. Henceforth, those that reject Him—Jew or non-Jew—would be cast out into outer darkness. The ones who walk in faith walk in light but those who reject Christ must walk in darkness.

This centurion did not know Jewish theology concerning the Promised One but he eagerly accepted Jesus on "face value." What he saw in Jesus challenged him to accept whatever Jesus was, and thus he identified himself with Jesus by exercising faith in Him. The promise of Abraham is now replaced by an individual personal faith in the Lord Jesus Christ; it has been opened to all men of all ages of all races.

Thought Projection No. 39: Foxes' holes and birds' nests (Matt. 8:18-20).

"Foxes have holes and birds of the air have nests; but the Son of man has nowhere to lay his head." The many miracles performed by Jesus drew great crowds of people. Many came for many reasons, but some wanted at once to join the "band-wagon," and ride with Jesus over the sea of popularity. Jesus was always eager to accept anyone coming to Him in a spirit of sincerity, but he had no patience for the publicity seekers.

Just as Jesus is boarding a ship to cross the sea, a scribe rushes up to Him and says, "Teacher, I will follow you wherever you go." Instead of saying to him, "Welcome my friend, glad to have you aboard," Jesus says to him, "Foxes have holes and birds of the air have nests; but the Son of man has nowhere to lay his head." This was enough for the young scribe. He was not willing to follow a person, though he was performing miracles, who could not even claim a bed nor a room in which to sleep. He was seeking glory and fame, not obscurity and poverty. He quickly loses himself in the crowd and we hear no more of him. We can not help wonder if he did not later join the crowd that helped bring Jesus to Calvary.

Jesus never said that it would be easy to follow him. He never said that it would be without cost. He did say that He would supply all our needs—that is all! Jesus says, "For a man to gain his life he must lose it." When a life is lost in Christ, real discipleship results. Man's true reward is being identified with Christ. Jesus sums this up for us in what he says to his own disciples who return after a successful mission trip, rejoicing, happy, and pleased that they had been able to exercise power and authority over evil spirits. Jesus says, "A greater cause for rejoicing is in knowing that your names are to be found in the book of life—that you belong to me and the Father." This is what really counts for man.

Thought Projection No. 40: Let the dead bury the dead (Matt. 8:21,22).

The dust stirred up by the rapid retreat of the scribe who had offered himself in the service of Jesus had hardly settled when there appeared a would-be neophyte who said, "Let me go and bury my father, then I will come and follow You anywhere." Jesus replied, "Follow me, and leave the dead to bury their own dead." Now this was a shocking thing to say: What could have prompted this outburst by Jesus? Again Jesus recognized the insincerity that lay behind this man's offer. He wanted to follow Jesus, but to do so on his own conditions and at the time of his own choosing. Jesus would have no part of this kind of agreement. Jesus saw what was in the heart of this man; He looked beyond the words he mouthed, and what He saw He did not like.

The father could have been in good health, and the son, who was perhaps the oldest, might have had the responsibility of caring for his father until his death. He might have meant that when this responsibility was discharged he would be in a position to assume the one of following Jesus. He would be a "backup reserve," but still getting all the honor that might fall to any follower of Jesus. He did not want to be left out.

Or his father could have just died. It could take several days for the final burial. When this job was over and the mourning period past, then he would catch up with Jesus and the rest of the disciples and become a follower of Jesus. Either one of these things could have been possible, but what Jesus saw were not these circumstances or problems, but the insincerity of the man who was offering his service. He, too, is quickly swallowed up by the crowd and we hear no more of him.

There could be something else in the statement of Jesus, "Let the dead bury the dead." You ask, "How can the dead bury the dead?" Was Jesus trying to tell them that men would be born, live, and die without any interest in Him or spiritual things? Would they be the "living dead," living and dying and burying the spiritual dead, as they were themselves? This is not the important thing in life—to live and to die; the important thing for God's children is that they give themselves in proclaiming the message of the Kingdom of God—the words of life, the Gospel, the good news. Nothing else ranks in importance to this task, and nothing should stand between us and our responsibility to proclaim Jesus. Let the "living dead" go about their business of burying themselves, but let the children of God share their message of hope with all men.

16

Matthew 9

Summary: Matthew 9 contains six THOUGHT PROJECTIONS:

41. The well need no physician (Matt. 9:10-13) PROVERB.

42. You do not fast at a wedding (Matt. 9:14,15) METAPHOR.

43. Do not put new patches on old clothes (Matt. 9:16) PROVERB.

44. Do not put new wine in old bottles (Matt. 9:17) PROVERB.

45. Shepherdless sheep (Matt. 9:36) SIMILE.

46. Unharvested wheat will be lost (Matt. 9:37,38) ALLEGORY.

Chapter 9 of Matthew begins at the point where Jesus has cured the two demoniacs in the country of the Gadarenes and is asked to leave their country. Jesus bows to their wishes and gets into a boat to return to his own country. He is met by a group of men carrying a paralytic. When Jesus sees their faith, He forgives the paralytic of his sins. When questioned by persons in the crowd concerning His authority or right to do this, Jesus asks and answers a question. "Is it easier to cure his body than to cure his soul?" Then Jesus says to the paralytic, "Take up your bed and go home." The man rises and obeys Jesus.

Thought Projection No. 41: The well need no physician (Matt. 9:10-13).

Jesus passes a man called Matthew collecting taxes. He calls to him to "Follow Me," and Matthew gets up without a question and follows Jesus. Later, while Jesus is at dinner with other tax collectors and sinners, some Pharisees see Him. They turn on the disciples of Jesus and ask, "Why does your teacher eat with tax collectors and

146

sinners?" Jesus responds in behalf of His disciples by offering them
a thought projection to mull over in their minds. "Those who are
well have no need of a physician, but those who are sick. Go and
learn what this means, 'I desire mercy and not sacrifice.' For I came
not to call the righteous, but sinners."

Jesus says, "Here is a known proverb. Study it carefully and make
an application." Jesus is quoting from Hosea 6:6. "For I desired mercy
and not sacrifice; and the knowledge of God more than burnt offerings." Hosea here is crying unto the people to turn unto the Lord
to be healed. God had smitten them, but he said that if they would
return to Him, he would bind up their wounds and heal them. God
was more concerned in a "healing" ministry than he was in a "punishing" ministry. God was more concerned with saving than in punishing and destroying the disobedient. God wanted the people in
the days of Hosea to know of His abundant mercy—to share it and
in the knowledge of Him.

A doctor has to go to the sick and dying or they must come to
him if his knowledge and skill are to be used in their behalf. The
healthy have no need for medical treatment and will not go to a
physician. Pain is nature's alarm clock to call attention to a need for
medical service. Fever warns man that something is wrong with the
body; an enemy of the body is at work trying to destroy it. Without
such advance notice given, death could and would capture all of us
without a battle.

Jesus says to these Pharisees, "Go back and study this sixth chapter of Hosea, then you will understand why I am eating with these
men." Hosea says, "O Ephraim, what shall I do unto thee? O Judah,
what shall I do unto thee? For your goodness is as a morning cloud,
and as the early dew it goeth away. Therefore have I hewed them
by the prophets; I have slain them by the words of my mouth; and
thy judgments are as the light that goeth forth. For I desired mercy
and not sacrifice; and the knowledge of God more than burnt offerings" (Hos. 6:4-6).

The physician was trying to make the sick aware of their sickness
that would lead to death. God was winding up the alarm clock,
awakening them to their desperate need of a physician. "You ask me
why I am eating with sinners?" responds Jesus. The sinners needed
Jesus and His forgiveness: He was where he belonged. He was "seeking and saving sinners." Jesus then says, "For I came, not to call the

righteous, but sinners." This includes us all, "all have sinned" (Romans 3:23).

Thought Projection No. 42: You do not fast at a wedding (Matt. 9:14,15).

". . . Can the children of the bridechamber mourn, as long as the bridegroom is with them? But the days will come, when the bridegroom shall be taken from them, and then shall they fast." The disciples of John (the Baptist) come to Jesus. They are puzzled, for they never had it so good with John. He is an ascetic by practice and this meant that they too are ascetics. The question they ask is "Why do not your disciples practice being ascetics?" They thought that this was the mark of the religionist. Self-denial was the way of life for such men, a mark of their dedication.

We do not believe that these disciples were being critical of Jesus nor of his disciples. They had not been schooled to think one could enjoy a dedicated form of religion. They were asking, "Were they wrong themselves or did the error lie with Jesus and His disciples?" They wanted the right answer and came to the right source for it, Jesus. And He gave it to them, but Jesus did more than that. He lifted religion out of the shadows of life, gave it a new dimension. Happiness is no sin and one can enjoy it here on earth. The keynote is "rejoicing." The long-faced Christian is out of place around Jesus. What Christ puts into the heart drives out the shadows, the heartache, the fears; these are replaced with love, compassion, and His divine presence in the person of the Holy Spirit.

Jesus says, "They will mourn when the bridegroom is taken away from them. Then it will be the time for them to cry and be unhappy!" Jesus will never be absent from His children. His victory over the grave and death, His ascension back to the Father, and the sending of His Holy Spirit to abide within every child of God, means Christ will never be separated from us. (Romans 8:38,39).

These disciples of John the Baptist came with troubled minds, but went away with a new message about the Christ. He said that he came seeking the sinner so that He might save him, but in giving him a new life, he gave him a life of abundance. This was not only a religion of forgiveness, but one that offered a life filled with eternal happiness and joy: The bridegroom will never forsake the bride! God and man are to be on an eternal honeymoon.

Thought Projection No. 43: Do not put new patches on old clothes (Matt. 9:16).

"No one puts a piece of unshrunk cloth on an old garment for the patch tears away the garment, and a worse tear is made." The people of Jesus' day knew nothing about preshrunk material. They knew that one could not patch an old garment with a piece of new cloth, for after the first washing of that garment, the new material would shrink and tear itself loose from the old garment, thus ripping away at the cloth to which it was sewed. The hole, then, would be larger and the garment could no longer be used.

John's disciples and the Pharisees raised questions about the new religious pattern Jesus was developing: Eating dinner with sinners instead of ostracizing such persons; enjoying religion instead of fasting and punishing oneself. This simply did not fit into their religious mold. Jesus came not to punish the sinner but to save him from his sins. He was proclaiming the Gospel of good news, a message of the love of God not His wrath.

Jesus did not come to patch an old tire nor to give it a retread. He was offering men a new tire. He did not come to patch the old moral shirt worn by men, but to give them a new one. His Gospel was not a supplement to their theology, growing out of the old. He did not come to destroy the old with the new, nor to limit the new by handicapping it with the old. Both would be lost if these things were attempted. The "New Creature" would be the result of this new theology. The old would be saved and used as the background to understand the new, and the new would clarify the old.

Thought Projection No. 44: Do not put new wine in old bottles (Matt. 9:17).

Jesus gives special emphasis to this point by using a second thought projection to further illustrate the truth He is trying to present. "Neither is new wine put into old wineskins; if it is, the skins burst, and the wine is spilled, and the skins are destroyed; but new wine is put into fresh wineskins, and so both are preserved." This truth was demonstrated to these people many times during their life time. This was nothing new to them. It brought to their attention, however, a new truth that has not been generally accepted by theologians through the ages.

Christianity is not an extension of Judaism. Christianity was born in the theology of Judaism, but it is not its child. The concept of God found in the Old Testament is not the concept that Christ wanted in the New Testament. The Old Testament offers many blessings to mankind. There are still many riches to be enjoyed by the reader, but the New Testament message would destroy these concepts if the Gospel message were forced into the mold of the Old Testament; so would the values of the New Testament be wrecked if we were to force the Old Testament pattern upon the Gospel of the New Testament. Each has a contribution to make to the knowledge of man concerning God.

Jewish leadership rejected the overtures of Christ, because He refused to be forced into their concept of the promised Messiah. His life, message, and attitude did not measure up to nor fit into their theological mold. For this, they released their anger and hatred against Him and were not satisfied until they saw Him hanging from the cross.

Jesus did not come to destroy the law nor the promise made to Israel. He came to fulfill both and to move the old into a new relationship with God. He offered a new contract to all men to replace the one offered to Abraham and his children. He did not want the new contract to be lost in the confused theological wineskins of the past.

Jesus was interrupted in this series of thought projections by a ruler of the people who came to Him, asking that He go with him to his home, for his daughter had just died. Jesus rises and leaves with him at once, but on the way a woman suffering from an active hemorrhage touches the fringe of His garment. Jesus turns to her, saying, "Take heart, daughter; your faith has made you well." He presses on through the crowds and enters the ruler's home; He takes the child's hand and restores her to life. As He is leaving, two blind men beseech Jesus to restore their sight. "According to your faith be it done to you," and it is done. A dumb demoniac is brought to Jesus, and Jesus casts out the demon and restores his speech.

To all these visible manifestations of the power of Jesus to heal, the Pharisees respond by charging, "He casts out demons by the prince of demons." Later Jesus will answer this charge. He continues his working of miracles in their cities and villages, and in response to what he sees and feels, Jesus gives the two final thought projections in this chapter.

Thought Projection No. 45: Shepherdless sheep (Matt. 9:36).

"When he saw the crowds, he had compassion for them, for they were harassed and helpless, like sheep without a shepherd." When merchants see a crowd, they see only customers; politicians see only votes; generals see only soldiers. Jesus sees a crowd and senses their needs, their problems, and their yearnings for something better. He sees them as sheep without a shepherd to carry them to the feeding grounds, to water, and to shelter. What He saw filled His own heart, the Divine heart of God Himself with deep compassion.

The phrase "helpless like sheep without a shepherd" tells us much about the nature of man. People, like sheep, need a shepherd. Sheep will perish without a shepherd. They cannot protect themselves, cannot find their own food, and when frightened they will follow the other over a cliff, even to their own death. They are the most helpless of God's animals. They need a shepherd. They need one if they are to grow, to be healthy, and to produce good wool or meat.

Man needs a spiritual shepherd. He was made to need one. He cannot handle all the problems he will face in life without spiritual help. He cannot grow and develop a wholesome personality without outside help. Jesus saw all this, and His heart went out to the people with heartfelt compassion.

This verse opens a window into the heart of God. If Christ is concerned with the needs and the problems of man, so is God. If Christ has compassion and understanding of man, so has God. It is amazing to think that God cares for us poor, lost, wandering, rebellious sheep, yet, He cares for us.

Thought Projection No. 46: Unharvested wheat will be lost (Matt. 9:37,38).

Jesus saw men as shepherdless sheep, but he uses still another figure of speech to describe what he saw. He says, "The harvest is plentiful, but the laborers are few; pray therefore the Lord of the harvest to send out laborers into His harvest." Matthew closes the ninth chapter with this thought projection.

The unharvested wheat represents values to be lost. Jesus knows of the work of the farmer, the cost of fencing the field, the cost of the land, the cost of the seed, and the work it takes to cultivate a field. He knows that the farmer has a major investment in that wheat. Everything the farmer has done points to this one event—the harvest. If the wheat cannot be brought into the barns, it will be lost, and all the farmer has invested in bringing this crop up to this harvest will also be lost.

The investment that nature (God) has made in that wheat will also be lost. The work of the sun to kiss into life the seed and to impart some of its energy to it to give it life and growth will be wasted. The moisture from the cloud gathered by nature from the oceans of the world and brought to this farm will be wasted—lost.

What about the hungry mouths of the world needing every grain of wheat in that field? Productive land is limited and some of the world's population will starve without the bread this field could yield. This land has done its job well, but many will starve in spite of its yield, unless someone harvests the crop.

Jesus saw people as unharvested wheat. He saw man as an investment made by God, the world, and man himself. God wants that unharvested wheat; the world needs that unharvested wheat. The wheat must be harvested or it will be lost. There is only one thing lacking—men to harvest, to bring in the wheat before it is spoiled in the field.

Jesus does not ask us to pray for the wheat (the lost), but for men to become laborers to harvest this wheat. God is already concerned about the lost in the world. This has been demonstrated by the sending of His son Jesus to die for man. Christ has expressed his great concern by offering Himself to pay for the sins of man. This sacrifice is not enough to get the wheat into God's barns; God needs laborers to go among the wheat fields and gather the wheat: For unharvested wheat is lost; unwon men are lost.

17

Matthew 10

Summary: Matthew 10 contains nine THOUGHT PROJEC-
TIONS:

47. The lost sheep of Israel (Matt. 10:5-7) METAPHOR.
48. A laborer deserves to be fed (Matt. 10:9-11) PROVERB.
49. Cities that reject the Gospel (Matt. 10:15) METAPHOR.
50. Sheep sent among wolves (Matt. 10:16a) SIMILE.
51. Wise as serpents; harmless as doves (Matt. 10:16b) SIMILE.
52. A teacher and his pupil (Matt. 10:24,25) METAPHOR.
53. The servant and his master (Matt. 10:24,25) METAPHOR.
54. God's evaluation of a sparrow (Matt. 10:29-31) META-
PHOR.
55. Peace, war, and the sword (Matt. 10:34-39) METAPHOR.

Chapter 10 begins with Jesus calling his disciples together and
instructing them as to what to expect when they go out to preach.
We have recorded here in Matthew, for the first time, the list containing the names of the twelve disciples. Jesus charges them not to
go among the Gentiles, but only to the lost sheep of Israel. They
are given power to heal the sick, raise the dead, and preach the
Gospel. They are to take no extra clothes nor money with them.
Nor are they to receive any money. They are to accept offered hos-
pitality, however. They may not be well received by some people,
but they are to remember that even Jesus was rejected by many.
They are to be fearless, for God will supply them with their defense
when one is needed. In these instructions are to be found eight
thought projections. These need to be considered in the light of the
mission upon which they are departing.

Thought Projection No. 47: The lost sheep of Israel (Matt.
10:5,6).

"Go nowhere among the Gentiles and enter no town of the
Samaritans, but go rather to the lost sheep of the house of Israel."

153

This was the first "solo" flight of the disciples. Jesus sent them to their own people, who had the proper background for the message they were bearing. They had some contact points with those to whom they were to speak. They were going on a "home-mission tour"; to their own people who could think and speak their own language.

The "lost sheep of the house of Israel" is not referring to animals (sheep) owned by the Israelites, but to the Israelites who had acted like sheep in leaving the sheepfold of God and the Shepherd. They were God's people. The word "household" indicates the relationship that existed between God and Israel. In the tenth chapter of John's Gospel, Jesus refers to them as the "sheep that would not hear nor follow His voice." They were sheep in rebellion and in revolt. They were strays and had become lost sheep.

Christ came first to His own sheep, trying to reclaim them for the Father. He also sent His disciples to these lost sheep of Israel first and He spent three years trying to involve them in His program of redemption. "He came to his own, but His own received Him not." What heartbreaking words these were to God the Father, who sent His Son to find and save His lost sheep.

This does not suggest that these disciples are to go to only a few lost sheep that might just have happened to be lost. All are lost. None is righteous, no not one . . . all have sinned and come short of the glory of God. All men, Gentiles and Israelites alike, need to be found, for we are all lost sheep.

Thought Projection No. 48: A laborer deserves to be fed (Matt. 10:9-11).

"Provide neither gold, nor silver, nor brass in your purses . . . For the workman is worthy of his meat." The disciples being sent out by Jesus are told by Jesus not to take any money or extra clothes. They were to expect those to whom they gave themselves in service for their personal care. "For the laborer deserves his food." This is not charity. The people receive a service and the disciples, in turn, receive compensation for that service. The city where they were to preach would receive a special needful service from these men in the name of God. For a city to receive this service from the disciples and not return some form of remuneration (food and lodging) would be for that city or community to be the recipients of charity.

The metaphor "laborers" gives dignity to the service of the Christian worker. He is not to be a charity case, nor to feel that he is one. He is rendering a service to man for God. He is God's mouthpiece. He is a "sent one" from God. He has received his commission from God. Too often the men called of God to administer spiritual things on earth are looked upon by men of other professions as "nonproductive" individuals in the community. Since their contributions to community life cannot be measured in sales made, crops harvested, products manufactured and sold for a profit, operations performed, and so on, they are, at times, the object of jokes regarding their hours spent in work—"a one-day working week."

A blessing is promised those who recognize the position of the disciple in the community. These blessings come in many forms. The presence of a man of God in a home, even for a short time, can pay spiritual dividends in the lives touched, far out of proportion to the hours spent. What would happen in any American city if all the ministers and their families would leave that city together at one given time? What would happen to a country if all the Christian teachers in public schools and in our universities should all leave the country? Only eternity can reveal the true worth to our nation of these men and women called by God to serve Him in some professional capacity. It has been the influence of such people that has made our country the great nation it is. "A laborer deserves his food."

Thought Projection No. 49: Cities that reject the Gospel (Matt. 10:15).

"And if any one will not receive you or listen to your words, shake off the dust from your feet as you leave that house or town. Truly, I say to you, it shall be more tolerable on the day of judgment for the land of Sodom and Gomorrah than for that town." Jesus is reaching back into the history of the Jewish people to make his comparison, using a figure of speech that no one might misunderstand. The events concerning God's dealing with these two wicked cities are recorded in the tenth chapter of Genesis. God saved Lot and his two daughters, and almost saved Lot's wife before destroying these twin cities with fire, but then Lot's wife disobeyed God by looking back, and she was lost. God destroyed those two cities without mercy because of their sinfulness. Jesus said the same treatment could be expected of every city, nation, or individual rejecting the Gospel.

God did not destroy Sodom and Gomorrah without warning. Men refused to listen. Lot's own sons-in-law laughed at him when he tried to warn them of the coming wrath of God: A prophet of doom and of God's wrath against sin is never popular; he is more often an object of mockery and contempt. Christ says that a turning away from God's Word will not go unnoticed by God, and on the day of judgment, God will pour out His wrath on those that reject his offers of love and compassion. Sin must be forgiven or it will be punished. Man chooses what he shall receive. God offers all men two choices; He will respect the choice made by man.

Thought Projection No. 50: Sheep sent among wolves (Matt. 10:16a).

"Behold, I send you out as sheep in the midst of wolves; . . . " Wolves are the natural enemies of the sheep. A sheep is without defense when it is attacked by a pack of wolves. It is not the natural thing to pasture sheep in the middle of a wolf pack. And yet Jesus says, "I am sending you into a situation that is like a pack of wolves, one filled with the same danger. You will be attacked by these wolves and they will do all they can, use every resource they have, to bring destruction upon you and the work you will attempt in My name."

These wolves were the natural enemy to truth—God's truth about Himself as revealed by Jesus Christ. These human wolves were the natural enemy to the people, for they were withholding spiritual truths the people needed, causing the people to perish, because truth was denied them by their religious leaders.

A sheep has not the natural defenses possessed by other animals. A bird has flight as a defense mechanism; a snake has his poison; a lion has great strength: Each has something that nature provided for his defense—except the sheep. A sheep needs a shepherd. He looks to the shepherd for his protection; without a shepherd, sheep can be scattered and destroyed by wolves.

Jesus sends His disciples out as sheep. He is to be their defense. He has committed them to the Father's care. To attempt a defense for themselves within themselves would be to fail. It is true that they were being sent among wolves, but they were not without a shepherd. They were as sheep depending on the shepherd. They will lose their fear of the wolves, because this fear is lost in the awareness of their divine mission and His divine presence: God's children will always work among the wolves of the world. The wolves spared not the Son of God, Jesus Christ, nor will they grow weary in attacking the followers of Christ. Safety for the sheep lies within the sheltering will of the Good Shepherd. Wolves cannot touch the sheep that pasture within His will during their lifetime.

Thought Projection No. 51: Wise as serpents; harmless as doves (Matt. 10:16b).

"Be wise as serpents and innocent as doves." Jesus here is expressing the attitude He wants these disciples to maintain as they go as sheep among the wolves of the world. The disciple of Jesus, in any age, is to possess and use the wisdom of the serpent, not his poison. There is a vast difference between the two. Wisdom is not limited to the just. The wicked often use more wisdom—good common sense—to attain their evil designs than many Christians do. Too often Christians leave thier business-wisdom at the bank or store when they take up the business of the Kingdom of God. The author once knew a banker who refused to cooperate with his church in building a new house of worship, using for his argument, "What was good enough for my parents should be good enough for us today." It mattered not that the building was a fire hazard and inadequate to meet the present growth of the community. He directed his bank to spend many thousands of dollars modernizing the bank building to meet demands of increased growth, but he would not see the same need for his church.

Our world is in a great period of change. The average church will be the last institution in the nation to recognize changes which ought to be made in methods and procedures to keep pace with a changing society. The gospel will not be changed—only methods of presenting it to this changing world. "It is estimated that human knowledge doubled between A.D. 1 and 1750 and again between 1750 and 1900. Then it accelerated to rocket pace, doubling again by 1950, and again in ten years, 1950 to 1960. It should be double again by 1968, which means that the amount of gain in those eight years will be sixteen times what it was between A.D. 1 and 1950."[1] Jesus is

---

[1] Davis, Keith, and Blomstrom, Robert L., *Business and Its Environment* (New York: McGraw Hill Book Company, 1966), p. 5.

saying to the Christian, "Keep abreast of the world in presenting my message." It is no sin to use that same brain you are using for the glory of man, for the glory of God.

"Harmless as doves," is not to suggest "helpless" as a dove. A Christian worker who is not "wise," who does not possess wisdom, is not harmless; he is dangerous to the Kingdom of God and to man to whom he is giving his service. The dove is not a bird of war. It is considered the bird of peace and has become the emblem of peace. The dove has been wrongly cast in this roll. A dove is not a bird of peace; it is a bird of communication. From its family has come the carrier pigeon. Noah used the dove to discover if the flood had subsided, and it was the dove that returned with the message that the flood was over. It is a bird that is submissive to training by man and is one of the few birds of the air that is willing to become a servant of man. A dove is not a weakling among the fowls of the air. It will give its life in carrying out a mission and fighting for its young. The modern church today could use a great deal more of the wisdom of the serpent and the submissive will of the dove than it now possesses. Herein lies the secret of victory for the church as it lives in the world of wolves.

Thought Projection No. 52: A teacher and his pupil (Matt. 10:24,25).

"The disciple is not above his master, nor the servant above his lord. It is enough for the disciple that he be as his master, and the servant as his lord. If they have called the master of the house Beelzebub, how much more shall they call them of his household?" There are two figures of speech in these verses. We deal with the first of these two. A disciple is not above his teacher (master). The word "disciple" means a "learner." Students would separate themselves into groups under a teacher who would impart his knowledge and experiences to them. They would become identified with him. Paul had Gamaliel for his teacher before Paul found Christ. If a teacher is persecuted for what he believes and teaches, so will his disciples be persecuted. They will share in his knowledge and will also share in his persecution or any misunderstanding of him. The disciples were to share in the misunderstandings concerning Jesus and any persecution He might receive. They would not be exempt because they were merely his students. Teacher and pupil share alike in all things.

Thought Projection No. 53: The servant and his master (Matt. 10:24,25).

The other comparison, the other figure of speech, in these verses is the one comparing a servant to his master or lord: "Nor a servant above his master; it is enough for the disciple to be like his teacher, and the servant like his master. If they have called the master of the house Beelzebub, how much more will they malign those of his household." Just as the pupil shares in the criticism of his teacher so will a servant be blamed for anything the master of the house might do. Again, it is a matter of identification.

It is interesting to note that verses fourteen to twenty-four picture the persecution that is to come to the disciples in the years ahead; and it did come to them. After painting this picture of their persecution, Jesus says the pupil or the servant would suffer the same fate as his teacher or master. Jesus had not yet suffered these things Himself. They came to Him later. The disciples soon had a demonstration of what was to come to them.

With this relationship in suffering of pupil and teacher, servant and master, is an even greater relationship—that of the teacher sharing with his pupil his mind and his experiences, and by this sharing transplanting a part of himself to the pupil. The pupil experiences a transfer of a personality into his own personality. Although the relationship of the servant and master is not this close, there is the identification of ownership and of responsibility of the welfare of the other. Each is responsible for the other.

The Christian has this type of relationship with Christ. "Let this mind be in you that was also in Christ," said Paul. Jesus would have clarified this by saying something like this: "Since we have this kind of relationship—pupil and teacher, servant and master—the world will treat you as they would treat me. If they persecute me, they will you also. Glory in these things, for they testify of our relationship."

Jesus said a very wonderful thing when He said, "It is enough for the disciple to be like his teacher and the servant to be like his master." What more could a Christian ask than to be like HIM?

Thought Projection No. 54: God's evaluation of a sparrow (Matt. 10:29-31).

"Are not two sparrows sold for a penny? And not one of them will fall to the ground without your Father's will. But even the hairs of your head are all numbered. Fear not, therefore; you are of more value than many sparrows." How much is one sparrow worth? When Jesus spoke these words you could buy one for the smallest of Roman coins, equal to half a cent. If you bought four sparrows a fifth was given free. Nothing else could you find to buy or sell that would be worth less than a sparrow. If it were, it would not be worth selling. Jesus deliberately makes this extreme comparison.

Man's real value is found in his relationship with God. If God is interested and concerned over the fall of a single sparrow, how much greater is His concern for one of His children. If the death of a sparrow goes not unnoticed by God, how much greater is the value of man for whom His Son died?

If man has no value in God's sight, man has no value—period. He would be just another animal to die and to return to dust and to remain as dust for ages and eternity. God has raised man to the very highest possible position by making it possible for man to have communion and fellowship with Himself. God added further value to man when He offered His own Son, Christ Jesus, to become a sin offering to remove the partition thrown up between God and man by the sin in the human race. Because of this sin offering by Christ, man is now offered sonship in the Kingdom of God.

Jesus says to us, "If God cared for sparrows like that, what have we to fear from such a God?" Man can trust this kind of God; he can know that God's plans and purposes for his life cannot be wrong for him to follow. The disciples were being sent as sheep among vicious wolves, but Jesus says to them, "Fear not, you are of great value to me; be not afraid of what they will do to you; do your job well and trust God to supply all your needs for each occasion."

Thought Projection No. 55: Peace, war, and the sword (Matt. 10:34-39).

"Do not think that I have come to bring peace on earth; I have not come to bring peace, but a sword." Jesus uses this same figure of speech in Luke 21:24. Upon that occasion His disciples respond by saying, "Lord, behold, here are two swords." Jesus Himself responds with, "It is enough."

"Enough, Lord? Two swords against the Roman Army? Two swords enough to overcome a hostile world, and enough, Lord, to overcome these hostile people here before us bent on destroying you and us?"

Jesus knew that they had missed the point He was trying to make, and He concludes the conversation on this matter by saying, "It is enough on *this matter*, you have failed to understand what I have been talking about. You do not comprehend the nature of My Kingdom, nor its resources of power—the Holy Spirit, nor its method of conquest." He knew that they would understand all this later, but it was beyond the range of their experiences at the moment.

Jesus was using this figure of speech to say that He was sending them on a "diesive" mission. As a sword cuts apart, so will the Gospel message cut families apart. A husband will not receive it, but his wife or children will. Friends will be separated by this message. One will accept it, but his friend will reject it and thus these friends are cut asunder. Nations will be also separated by this message. History has proven the accuracy of these words of Jesus. The final division will come at the final judgment. Each man will be judged by the message of Christ.

Jesus is saying that the Christian enters his Kingdom to do battle as a soldier. Paul echoes this through his letters. He tells us to put on the "whole armour of God." Every Christian is a soldier, good or bad, and every Christian is on duty; he might be slack or alert, but he is on duty.

Peter also misunderstands the meaning of the sword when he takes up the sword of steel to defend his Saviour in the garden. He thinks he is doing the right thing. Jesus quickly steps in and says to him, "Those who live by the sword—this method of conquest—will die—be conquered themselves—by the sword." He is saying that our sword will not be made of steel, sharpened to a razor's edge nor be wielded by a strong arm, but it will be the Word of God, wielded by the Holy Spirit working in and through the Christian and blessed of God to the conversion of these who yield to its thrust. Skill must be learned by the Christian, both in knowledge of the sword (Word of God) and how to use it in the battle against sin in this world. We are at war with the forces of evil; it is God's war, and we are God's soldiers, and He will give any victory we might gain.

18

Matthew 11

Summary: Matthew 11 contains six THOUGHT PROJEC-
TIONS:
  56. The shaking reed (Matt. 11:7,8) ALLEGORY.
  57. A man in soft clothing (Matt. 11:8) METAPHOR.
  58. Elias the Prophet (Matt. 11:11-15) METAPHOR.
  59. Children playing weddings and funerals (Matt. 11:16-19)
SIMILE.
  60. Cities judged (Matt. 11:20-24) METAPHOR.
  61. The yoke of Jesus (Matt. 11:28-30) ALLEGORY.

In chapter 11, Jesus, having finished the instructions to His disciples and having sent them out on their mission, takes to the road
Himself. He goes into the towns and cities to preach to the people.
He meets first a group of John's disciples who come from John bearing a question. John wants to know if Jesus is the Promised One
of the Old Testament. John wants assurance that he has not wasted
his effort in announcing Jesus as the Messiah, or misunderstood the
leadership of the Holy Spirit. We do not believe it was a question of
doubting the identity of Jesus on the part of John as it was one of
reassurance for himself and his disciples. Jesus simply says to John's
disciples, "Go tell John what you have seen and heard about Me."
Jesus knew these reports would answer John's question. These reports
would satisfy John.

Jesus then gives his own personal opinion of John. He held John
in the highest regard as a prophet and as an individual. Jesus must
have read something in the attitude of the crowd regarding John
and himself, for He upbraids the people for their vacillating religious
evaluations. They did not like John's approach to religion nor that
of Jesus. The chapter closes with one of the few recorded prayers of
Jesus. There are six thought projections of Jesus in this chapter.
Three deal with John the Baptist and the others with the people
themselves.

162

Each of the following three thought projections is part of a picture of words painted by Jesus of the character of John the Baptist. Each has a direct contribution to make within its own right to the Kingdom of God that might go unnoticed—like a desert flower blooming in the spring with no traveler to see or admire its beauty —if we did not frame each in a separate frame. They should be hung in a "cluster"; for each to appear at its best, it should be viewed in association with the others.

Thought Projection No. 56: The shaking reed (Matt. 11:7,8).

"As they went away, Jesus began to speak to the crowds concerning John. 'What did you go out in the wilderness to behold? A reed shaken by the wind?' " John the Baptist was in prison and he was soon to lose his life. It all came about because of the foolish whim of a woman and her daughter. John did not know this, nor that the mission for which he was born was ended. He had prepared the way for the Messiah. The "Forerunner" had finished his course. Now he found himself in a cold, damp, lonely cell. He began to reflect upon the success or failure of his life's work. Was he born to die in a dungeon like this?

"Are you he who is to come or shall we look for another?" This question he sent to Jesus is not necessarily a question born of a shaken faith in Jesus, but one coming from a perplexed state of mind. He wanted his own convictions reaffirmed again. It would be like a wife asking her husband, "Do you love me?" She knows that he does, but she wants to hear him say it again and to have reaffirmed something that she knows is true in her heart.

Jesus seizes upon this opportunity to express publicly His own personal opinion of John the Baptist, His cousin in the flesh. Jesus accomplishes this by the use of contrasts. He asks a series of questions so phrased as to demand a negative answer. Jesus knew the mind of His audience and He made them give the right answer to His questions. Notice the first of these:

"What did you go out into the wilderness to behold?"—"to see?" Here, Jesus must have paused to let the question sink deeply into their minds; then he continues, "A reed shaken by the wind?" A shaking reed was a common sight to the people to whom He was speaking and it would have taken more than a shaking reed to cause the crowds to leave their cities and seek out John the preacher. They were too selfish to leave their businesses, their pleasures, and the comfort of their homes just to watch the wind blowing over some reed on the bank of a river. John the Baptist had emptied their town with his preaching.

The reeds to which Jesus was referring grew in the Jordan valley and were beautiful things to see. Tall, slender, and graceful, they were caressed into graceful movements by the soft winds from the desert. They grew to the height of twenty feet or more, and because of their slenderness and height they became an easy victim to any breeze that came near them. Even a whisper of a breeze would cause them to bend in its direction, but they would change direction just as quickly if a breeze a little stronger blew in the opposite direction. They would vacillate from breeze to breeze, from one direction to another.

Jesus had read in their faces a reflection of their thinking concerning John and his question. "Are we to understand," they might have suggested by their attitude, "that your own forerunner—your advance publicity agent—is now not even sure you are the person he thought you to be? If he cannot be sure of you, how do you expect us to accept what you say about yourself?" If John was a vacillating person, lacking stability in his own theology and opinions concerning Jesus, this could have serious repercussions and could seriously undermine the future program of the Kingdom of God that Jesus was establishing on earth.

Jesus led them to find their own answer to their doubts out of their experiences with John the Baptist. They had seen John in action, had heard his sermons, and had seen the results of both. They knew John before they knew Jesus. Jesus was suggesting this to the people: "What kind of man made you do and feel the things John's preaching made many of you do? What kind of man would it take to get the kind of response you made? You would not have gone out to the river bank to watch vacillating reeds swaying in the breeze, nor a man with that kind of character or life. You have passed judgment upon the stability of John by your past actions. You were right about him. He is a man with a sincere, honest, and stable character. Of all the prophets of history, John is the greatest." Nothing was left for them to say. Silence was their only reply. Any other answer would have been to bring into question their own lack of ability to evaluate the character of a person. They were not about to publicly do this. Their personal pride was at stake now in this matter. Their silence was more eloquent in approving the stability of John's character than a speech given in John's behalf. Jesus did not dignify their doubts about John by offering any answer himself.

Thought Projection No. 57. A man in soft clothing (Matt. 11:8).

"Why then did you go out? To see a man clothed in soft raiment? Behold, those who wear soft raiment are in king's houses." Jesus left the rest of His statement unspoken. He wanted them to supply it. They knew and He knew that such men would not be found in the dungeon, but in the king's palace. John was in a dungeon, a guest of the judicial and not the social arm of the king.

In chapter 3 of Matthew we have a picture painted of the dress of John the Baptist. In verse 4 it says, "Now John wore a garment of camel's hair and a leather girdle around the waist; and his food was locusts and wild honey." His dress was that of the frontier, and his spirit was that of a prophet with a message of urgency. Both his appearance and his message demanded and got attention. He was "Mr. Ruggedness" himself. He was a man you could not ignore—a man's man. The crowd knew all this, for they had seen and heard him, and to see and hear him was to be impressed by him. No, they did not need to be told all this by Jesus, for they already had the answer to His question etched in their minds.

Jesus could have added, "No, you did not go out to see an effeminately dressed person who hangs around the king's court as a part of the background for the king. You pass such men on your streets with a look of scorn. No one can respect such men." John was in the king's palace when he sent his question to Jesus, but in the basement dungeon and not at the banquet table. He was there because of his refusal to compromise with sin; he rested in the dungeon instead.

The demands of the Kingdom of God in that age, and in every age since, has no place for the vacillating, the weak-kneed person; rather they call for the strong and courageous and for those who are willing to dare for the cause of Christ! Jesus says to all who would follow Him, "Count the cost before you start!" It cost John his head and his life, but he gained an eternal crown of glory. Jesus said John was the greatest of all the prophets of all ages.

Thought Projection No. 58: Elias the prophet (Matt. 11:11-15).

"And if you are willing to accept it, he [John] is Elijah who is to come." John is Elijah! What is the meaning of this statement? Has Elias (Elijah) returned to earth in the form of John (reincarnation)? These questions must have been mirrored in the faces of the hearers of Jesus to have caused Him to make the statement and to continue with the words, "He who has ears to hear, let him hear." Again we have a figure of speech being used by Jesus to drive home His point and to teach an important lesson.

Jesus was quoting from the book of Malachi, chapter four, verses five and six. "Behold I will send you Elijah the prophet before the great and terrible day of the Lord comes. And he will turn the hearts of fathers to their children and the hearts of children to their fathers, lest I come and smite the land with a curse." These are the last words to be found in the Old Testament. You turn from them to the first verse in Matthew. The Old Testament closes with a promise that Elijah the prophet is to come before the great day, the great dreadful day of the Lord. He was to come to prepare the way for that day. Jesus calls His forerunner, John, that man.

Jesus had just said that John was the greatest of all the prophets, even over Elijah himself, and He adds more confusion to the fire burning in their minds by adding, "The least in the kingdom of God was even greater than John," the greatest of all the prophets. Jesus was not trying to confuse the people but to give emphasis to several great truths.

Jesus is saying that a Christian has more status in the Kingdom of God than a prophet. The sharer of the grace of Christ is better than a mouthpiece of God (prophet) who lived under the old contract that God had with man through His servant Abraham. The grace that makes a person a Christian is the fulfillment of the promise made to Abraham. The one having the fulfilled promise is better off than the one having only the promise. Marriage is better than an engagement to be married: The Christian has been united to God through Christ. The cross (death of Christ) and the resurrection are all part of the ceremony that brings man and God back together. Everything before Calvary is merely the engagement period.

Jesus is also saying that John is closing the books on God's old contract with man. No longer will anyone come to God by the "way of the promise." The last sale has been consummated in John. The old stock certificate has been recalled and a new one has been issued. The seal of the new is Calvary and the empty tomb; the old was sealed with the law of Moses and the promise of Abraham. Each has its place in the plan of God. God's plan for the salvation of the races is complete in Christ. Nothing can bring man and God into a closer relationship than the grace of Christ that comes by the way of Calvary.

Jesus identifies John the Baptist with Elijah the prophet, not as to persons but as to their work. When the priests approach John to inquire who he is (John 1:19-24), John denies that he is Christ (the promised Messiah) or Elias. "Who are you?"

"I am not the Christ," he confesses.

And they ask him, "What then? are you Elijah?"

And he says, "I am not." "Are you the prophet?" His answer is no. They then say to him, "Who are you? Let us have an answer for those who sent us. What do you say about yourself?"

"I am the voice of one crying in the wilderness, make straight the way of the Lord, as the prophet Isaiah said."

It was the work of Elijah that John was doing. This is the comparison being made. This is the identification of the two men by the same name. We use this figure of speech even today. We say of a speaker, "He is going to be another Billy Graham." Everyone knows what is meant by this, and no one expects the two persons to be one, or one the projection of the other at some later date.

In the ages of the Old Testament when God wanted to speak to man, he visited His spirit upon an individual to speak for Him. We called that man a "prophet." God's spirit rested upon that one until the message was given. If there was a job to be performed, God's spirit was given to an individual so that it might be completed for God. When the job was finished or the message delivered, the spirit of God was recalled by God until such occasions arose again that required God to speak to man. John was the last to be used in this capacity. After Calvary and the empty tomb, and after Christ ascended back to the Heavenly Father, the Holy Spirit takes up his residence in the heart of every believer—every child of God—and is to remain with that one until he is delivered safely to the Father after death. This is the new order of things. "And if you are willing to accept it, he is Elijah who is to come. He who has ears to hear, let him hear."

Thought Projection No. 59: Children playing weddings and funerals (Matt. 11:16-19).

"But whereunto shall I liken this generation? It is like unto children sitting in the markets, and calling unto their fellows, . . . But wisdom is justified of her children." Jesus is testing the crowd's reaction to the ministry of John and to Himself. He uses a common-place thing seen every day on their streets to do this. A picture of children playing in the streets.

How many times have we watched children playing the part of adults. It seems that it was just as common for the children of the day of Christ as it is in our day for children to playact funerals and weddings. These things seem to impress children more than anything they see adults do. Jesus says to them, "You are acting like the children playing in the market place: some want to play 'wedding," some playing the part of the musicians; but the others refuse to dance as they do at weddings. So the game is changed to a 'funeral.' Some of the children are the funeral musicians and play funeral dirges, but no one mourns."

John came, preaching a somber gospel and calling people to ascetic life, but they said of him that he was too demanding. They would not follow him because of the demands he made of self-discipline. They could not enjoy the things of the world and be disciples of John. Jesus came, preaching a life of abundance and joy. He was charged—by the same people who condemned John—of being too light-hearted, too human; a "gluttonous man" and a "wine-bibber."

Jesus says to them, "You are acting like children." They were as unstable as the children playing in the streets of their cities. They did not know what they wanted. They were quite sure about what they did not want. They did not want what John had to offer them, nor what Jesus was offering.

"Yet wisdom is justified by her deeds." Wisdom knows the necessity for mourning. There is a time to mourn and there is a time to laugh, and there is a time when laughter is out of place and crying is an embarrassment to those around you. The occasion dictates our emotional reactions. The juvenile, because he is a juvenile, lacks the wisdom to discern proper action on certain occasions. It is a sign of maturity to react properly. The response we make to a situation reflects upon the wisdom, or lack of it, of the person making it. These people were acting like children to John and Jesus, because they were juveniles in their theology regarding Jesus. Their actions were telling the world of their own limitation in this field. "Yet wisdom is justified by her deeds." The deed reveals the wisdom exercised in the performance. Laughter is the sign of happiness; it can also be the visible sign of a person not sure of himself who attempts to cover this up by laughter. He is not even aware of this uncontrolled display of emotions.

Thought Projection No. 60: Cities judged (Matt 11:20-24).

"Then began he to upbraid the cities wherein most of his mighty works were done, because they repented not: Woe unto thee. . . . But I say unto you, That it shall be more tolerable for the land of Sodom in the day of judgment, than for thee." Jesus turns the people's attention back to their own history, back to the wrath of God poured out on the two cities of sin, Tyre and Sidon. They were so wicked that Abraham could not find five righteous men in them to save. Jesus indicated that these two cities were so sinful and that the outcry against them so great that God's wrath had to be poured out upon them (Genesis, chapters 18 and 19). Jesus said that if the people of Tyre and Sidon had been given the same opportunity to hear his message that he was now sharing with them, they would have repented and turned back to God. He concludes that the punishment of the cities of Chorazin, Bethsaida, and Capernaum will be far greater than the punishment of Tyre and Sidon.

Several things are suggested here by Jesus. Greater the revelation and the opportunity, greater will be the demands upon those who are thus blessed. Each age is to be judged by God in the light of its knowledge and opportunity. There will be judgment on all peoples, but the degree of reward or punishment shall be determined by opportunity and knowledge possessed by them.

Great as the acts of sin of these Old Testament cities were—and they were great enough for God to give them His personal attention and, as a result of His inspection, to destroy both cities—even greater is the sin of a city, nation, or individual that rejects the Saviour. This is the greatest of all sins. "But I tell you, that it shall be more tolerable on the day of judgment for the land of Sodom than for you." (Sidon and Sodom are names of the same city with different spelling).

There is to be a judgment of individuals, nations, and cities. Each of these really has two judgments. The physical body of a sinful person will be penalized for the sins committed in his lifetime. Sin in the life of a nation will weaken and destroy that nation in the end, and a city can and will destroy itself by its sin. In addition there will be a judgment of all three at the end of the ages. Each will be reviewed and judged by God himself.

Thought Projection No. 61: The Yoke of Jesus (Matt. 11:28-30).

"Take my yoke upon you, and learn from me; for I am gentle and lowly in heart, and you will find rest for your souls. For my yoke is easy, and my burden is light." The people of that day were familiar with this figure of speech. The "yoke" was the instrument used to yoke two oxen together to form a team capable of pulling heavy loads. This was a wooden instrument cut to fit around the neck of an oxen and fastened with a leather strap. Each yoke was made to be used on two oxen. As each oxen strained against his part of the yoke, the other also strained against his. Thus the yoke helped the other share in the total "pulling power" of both.

The people were yoked to the law and to their religious rituals. If one was to fulfill all that was required of him, he would have little freedom for himself. They had become "religious slaves," victims to their own "yokes." Jesus spoke out and would continue to speak out against their leaders for overburdening the people with these religious rituals and laws, until his death on the cross. The anger he engendered by His frankness in this area hastened the day of His crucifixion. He charged the leaders of not only overloading the people with their religious demands, but of refusing to lift a finger to help the people carry their burdens.

"Yoke yourself to me," says Jesus. "Learn of me," you will discover that my yoke is easier for you to carry than the ones with which you are now struggling. Compared to the sin burden you are now carrying alone, my load of grace is easy and light to carry. The yoke of Jesus was easier to bear because Jesus was sharing the load with them.

Notice the words used by Jesus in verse 28: "Come to me," a generous and gentle invitation. "Do you have a burden, would you like for me to share it with you? Then come to me with it . . . 'I will give you rest.'" He will remove the burden, or share its weight until you get to your destination. The difference between a Christian carrying a burden (say, blindness) and a non-Christian carrying the same burden is found in this area—Christ does not restore the sight, but He shares the burden of blindness with the blind. The blind Christian does not live nor walk in blindness alone, he has the presence of Christ sharing it with him. The sinner has no such "yoke-partner."

"Learn of me"—the amazing fact is that Christ is willing to reveal Himself to mortal man, to share Himself with the creatures of His own handiwork, and to let man know him. What we learn of Christ is even more amazing. We find that He loves us in spite of our sins and weakness, and that He is always concerned about us. He is quick to forgive and slow to anger, and His Mercy is unlimited . . . "Learn of me" . . . "and you will find rest for your souls." Jesus offers rest and peace from the struggle with sin. Jesus offers freedom from the fear caused by the rebellion we have had in our hearts. Rest and peace—eternal peace—for we know that we are His through all eternity: What a privilege to be yoked with the Son of God, Christ Jesus the Saviour.

19

Matthew 12

Summary: Matthew 12 contains twelve THOUGHT PRO-
JECTIONS:

62. Something greater than the temple (Matt. 12:6-8) META-
PHOR.

63. Sheep fall into the pit on Sunday (Matt. 12:9-13) META-
PHOR; NARRATIVE (Contrast).

64. A divided house will be destroyed (Matt. 12:25-28) META-
PHOR.

65. The thief and the householder (Matt. 12:29) METAPHOR.

66. The tree is known by its fruit (Matt. 12:33) METAPHOR.

67. A brood of vipers (Matt. 12:34) METAPHOR.

68. A good man and his treasure (Matt. 12:35) METAPHOR.

69. Idle words reveal real character (Matt. 12:36,37) META-
PHOR.

70. The sign of Jonah (Matt. 12:38-41) METAPHOR (Historical).

71. The sign of the queen of Sheba (Matt. 12:42) . . . META-
PHOR (Historical).

72. The danger of the empty house (Matt. 12:43-45) ALLE-
GORY; NARRATIVE.

73. True brothers of Jesus (Matt. 12:46-50) METAPHOR.

Chapter 12 opens with Jesus and His disciples walking through a
grain field on the Sabbath. The disciples pluck and eat the raw
grain as they walk through the field. This act was all that the
enemies of Jesus needed to launch their campaign, which did not
let up until they saw Him die on the cross of Calvary. Henceforth,
they would weigh Him against their interpretation of their laws.
They could not find any other weakness in Him; His acts, conduct,
and teaching were beyond their ability to discredit—but breaches of
their traditions by Him were something else. This was what they had
been waiting and searching for, a weakness: The law was to be His

Achilles heel. The twelve thought projections found in this chapter are counterattacks of Jesus, some new concepts concerning the value of man himself, and man's right relationships to religious traditions, customs, and laws for all the ages to come. These principles enunciated by Jesus are still alive today in our society. They are eternal in nature.

Thought Projection No. 62: Something greater than the temple (Matt. 12:6-8).

"I tell you, something greater than the temple is here. And if you had known what this means, 'I desire mercy, and not sacrifice,' you would not have condemned the guiltless."

Jesus continues, "For the Son of man is Lord of the Sabbath." The quotation within Matthew 12:6-8, comes from Hosea 6:6.

Was Jesus referring to Himself here or to His works? The use of the neuter form (*tov iepou meisov estiv wde*) suggests that Jesus was referring to His work of redemption (the total work), or to Himself in His relationship to His mission of redemption as was conceived by the Heavenly Father—God—and being carried out by Jesus. Either one could be correct and neither overshadows the importance of the other. He could have meant that His program and Himself were of more importance than the Jewish laws, traditions, the Sabbath, or their temple.

If Jesus is answering the charges that His disciples are breaking the law of the Sabbath by eating grain in the field, He is implying that the health of the disciples is necessary to carry on His program and that their health takes precedence above their law concerning the Sabbath.

Jesus could have also used the neuter form of the word "something" in referring to Himself as being "Lord of all things." These men were working under His orders and He was assuming responsibility for their action. Since He was also the "Lord of the Sabbath" and these men were working under His orders, they were not in violation of a lesser or lower law which is superseded by a higher one. The metaphor used by Jesus, "something" or "someone," relates itself by usage to the authority that Jesus possessed by His divine nature, "All authority in Heaven and on earth has been given to me" (Matt. 28:18). It did not come from the codified law of Moses, nor from the many interpretations made of this law which, in turn, became laws in themselves that, in turn, changed some of the applications of the law of Moses. Jesus is Lord of all things—the law and the Sabbath included.

Jesus refers them back to Hosea and quotes Hosea 6:6, "For I desire steadfast love and not sacrifice, the knowledge of God rather than burnt offering." The temple they were so eager to defend against the abuses of Jesus had digressed in its worship of God—from a place where men came to gain knowledge of God and have inspiring fellowship with the Eternal God, to a religious slaughter house. Early sacrifices, made freely to express love and devotion to God, had become a lucrative business for the treasurer of the temple and a burden on the people. These offerings were offered as payment for sins and not as expressions of love and devotion to God. Services of love were turned into duties to be performed so as to avoid punishment. Offerings now became the means of buying off the "wrath of God." It was not strange, then, that Jesus, in righteous indignation, turned on the men in the temple and drove them out, saying, "You made my Father's house a place for thieves—it is supposed to be a place of prayer. You have turned it into a house of merchandise (Matt. 21:13).

"I would rather have your love without your sacrifice, than have your sacrifice without your love. I would rather have my house resound with the proclaimed truths about God, than filled with the smoke from your blindly offered sacrifices, made to appease my Father's anger. You do not know nor understand the Heavenly Father's nature." Said Jesus, these people had lost the true concept of the nature of God. "Things," "places," and "days" had replaced personal fellowship with God; animal blood had replaced love, and a codified law and the temple had become more important than the people for whom these things were created. They were more important than the people who came seeking from them knowledge of God. It was against such things that Jesus rebelled. Man, for whom He came to seek and to save, had been lost to the external things of religion; he had lost his values. Jesus would restore to men this lost value, and for this He would be put to death!

Jesus here is declaring that man is more important than a religious law, a religious house, or a religious day. If man has to choose between these and a personal relationship with God, Jesus is saying, he must choose that of the higher authority. Jesus is that authority for man today. He was saying that He had the authority to change the emphasis on certain traditional religious values. He brings the values of man to the forefront and relegates to a place of lesser importance all things religious which devaluate him. Man is no longer to be a slave to religious laws but is free to use these laws to develop his spiritual growth. After declaring this new concept in religion, Jesus henceforth practices it to the consternation of the religious leaders of His day.

Thought Projection No. 63: Sheep fall into the pit on Sunday (Sabbath) (Matt. 12:9-13).

Jesus enters the synagogue and sees a man with a withered hand. He is asked this question by someone, "Is it lawful to heal on the sabbath?" Again, they were attempting to attack Jesus on the battle-ground of Law and Tradition. Jesus does not fall into their trap, however, but asks them a question, "What man of you, if he has one sheep and it falls into a pit on the Sabbath, will not lay hold of it and lift it out?"

There were two schools of thought among the Pharisees on this point. One said if the sheep was in danger—had fallen into a pit on the Sabbath—one might pull it out without desecrating the Sabbath. That is, if it were his own sheep; but if it were not, it could not be done without breaking the law dealing with the Sabbath.

The second school of thought said not to remove the sheep from the pit on the Sabbath, but you could feed and water it, if it meant saving the life of the sheep. Either action taken would have meant some work on the Sabbath. These two positions were ignored by those questioning Jesus about healing the man with the withered hand.

"What man of you?"—the very wording of the question by Jesus had them caught in their own trap. Each man knew that he would pull HIS OWN sheep out of a pit. He would not pull out the sheep of a neighbour or a stranger, but no man would fail to rescue his own sheep. They would be acting on a selfish motive, and feel justi-fied by it. Jesus was acting on an unselfish motive. He came to rescue all lost sheep, those inside and outside of the sheepfold of Abraham. He was acting within the interpretation of their own laws—rescuing his own sheep.

Jesus throws another question at them that sealed their lips. "How much more valuable is man than a sheep?" "If you risk breaking a law to save a single sheep that belongs to you and costs only a few dollars, how much more ought you be willing to do to rescue or help a human being that has great value?"

The next statement made by Jesus is in keeping with His new emphasis that man is more important to God than a day, building, or a religious law. "So it is lawful to do good on the Sabbath." Notice, Jesus is not saying it is good to worship, but to perform acts of goodness toward man.

Thought Projection No. 64: A divided house will be destroyed (Matt. 12:25-28).

Having failed to discredit Jesus for healing and doing good on the Sabbath and seeing the increase of His influence among the people, the Pharisees challenged the source of His curative power. They said that He was performing miracles; this they could not deny, but they said that He was using the power and authority of Beelzebub, the prince of demons. Jesus answers this charge with another thought projection, "Every kingdom divided against itself is laid waste, and no city or house divided against itself will stand; and if Satan casts out Satan, he is divided against himself; how then will his kingdom stand? And if I cast out demons by Beelzebub, by whom do your sons cast them out? Therefore they shall be your judges."

Having failed to discredit Jesus for healing and doing good on the Sabbath and seeing the increase of His influence among the people, the Pharisees challenged the source of His curative power. They said that He was performing miracles; this they could not deny, but they said that He was using the power and authority of Beelzebub, the prince of demons. Jesus answers this charge with another thought projection, "Every kingdom divided against itself is laid waste, and no city or house divided against itself will stand; and if Satan casts out Satan, he is divided against himself; how then will his kingdom stand? And if I cast out demons by Beelzebub, by whom do your sons cast them out? Therefore they shall be your judges."

They knew that a family divided would destroy itself. A nation divided against itself would also destroy itself. Evil doing good would soon destroy (itself) evil, and Good would replace it. Good and Evil cannot live together. Satan and Christ cannot work together.

This was simple logic, and Jesus was saying that their charge would not hold water nor stand up in any court of law.

Jesus asks them another question, "If I am casting out demons—doing good with all my miracles—by what authority are your children doing them? The charge you are making against me must be also made against them. We shall let them judge what you say." They were again pressed into an untenable position. They all taught and believed that all good came from God, evil from Satan. Jesus was doing good; so were their sons, and they could not discredit Him by questioning His source of power without bringing into question the good He was doing. When they did this, they also brought under suspicion the good works of their sons.

Thought Projection No. 65: The thief and the householder (Matt. 12:29).

Jesus brings another thought projection into play in His defense against their charge that He was using Satan's power to perform His miracles by asking, "Or how can one enter a strong man's house and plunder his goods, unless he first binds the strong man? Then indeed he may plunder his house." Jesus is pointing out a very obvious fact: When a thief enters a man's house, he first binds the man and then he is free to plunder the house without any interference from the owner. To do this, the thief must be stronger than the man he overcomes.

If Satan's spirit is being used by Jesus to do good, who overcomes whom? If Jesus is using the power of God to perform His miracles—overcoming the evil spirit in people—then this power must be greater than Satan's power. To accept this fact—and his miracles were testimony—was to accept Him as the Son of God. In this discussion, Jesus introduces the unpardonable sin.

These two thought projections, as well as the first two in the chapter, combined with the seriousness of the Pharisees' charge that He was working hand in hand with Satan, lead us to conclude that Jesus considered the unpardonable sin the act "of giving credit to the spirit of Satan for the good works of Christ." They were giving Satan credit for the work of the Holy Spirit, and God would not forgive them for doing this. This is, indeed, a serious charge by Jesus.

They were "casting"—the root meaning of the word—reflections upon the Holy Spirit of God by associating Him and His actions with Satan. This insult would not be forgiven.

This could be expanded by saying that "unbelief" led them to do this and that "unbelief" is the unpardonable sin. To do this would be to err. The unbeliever is already lost because of his lack of committed faith to and in Christ. This lack of faith in Christ will and can lead a person into many destructive ways, but unbelief can be overcome by exercising faith in Christ. All believers were unbelievers at one time. We do not believe that unbelief is THE UNPARDONABLE SIN as suggested in I John 5:15,16. These two verses are more in keeping with the most-accepted theory of the unpardonable sin. We believe that there are two unpardonable sins suggested in the New Testament. These are the two. Each is different from the other but each has the same final results—eternal lostness.

Thought Projection No. 66: The tree is known by its fruit (Matt. 12:33).

"Either make the tree good, and its fruit good; or make the tree bad, and its fruit bad; for the tree is known by its fruit." Jesus is still answering His critics who charged Him with working His miracles through and by the power of Beelzebub, the prince of demons. He has made the point that a divided kingdom will destroy itself, and that a thief has to overcome the houseowner before plundering his house. Both of these thought projections of Jesus say to them, "If I am evil doing good, evil is at war with itself, and evil will in the end destroy itself. If I am good and overcoming evil, then I must be stronger than evil, and I have brought the Kingdom of God among you."

In this new thought projection, Jesus stresses a simple truth of nature. A healthy tree brings forth healthy fruit. A sick tree will not produce healthy fruit. You judge the health of a tree by the kind of fruit it produces. The state of health of a tree is to be found in the type fruit it produces. Evil cannot come from a pure heart, nor purity come from an evil life. This fact of nature is known to all of the people who live near the soil. Jesus is asking them to apply the same logic to Himself and to His work, "Let my work tell you the kind of person I am." Jesus knew that they would not do this. He is saying, "Eat of my fruit—how does it taste? If it is good, say so, but if it is not good, do not be afraid to say so. I am willing to rest my case on the kind of fruit my life is producing. All I am asking of you is to be honest and tell me what kind of fruit you see in me. Make the tree either good or bad, but please match the tree with the fruit, the fruit with the tree." That was all that Jesus was asking them to do.

If Jesus were speaking in the language of our day, he would have said something like this, "A tree does not have a split personality. If the fruit of a tree is good and edible, you must conclude that the tree is good. If you should approach a tree with questions in your mind concerning the quality of the tree and the nature of its fruit, the fruit you pluck from that tree will give you the answers you seek. It will also tell you the state of health of the tree. Make up your minds by what is seen in the nature of the fruit."

A Godly nature produces Godly acts. A Christlike life is expected to produce Christlike fruits from that life. A sinful nature must and will produce a sinful life filled with acts of sin. This is why the new birth is necessary for every sinner. You cannot grow righteous fruit on an unrighteous tree.

Thought Projection No. 67: A brood of vipers (Matt. 12:34).

"You brood of vipers! How can you speak good, when you are evil? For out of the abundance of the heart the mouth speaks." Jesus is saying the same thing in this verse that he said in verse 33, but is using a different metaphor to drive home His point. Just as the nature of a tree is revealed by its fruits, one can recognize a snake by its nature. No one will confuse a snake with a dog. What a man says tells others what he is inside. From out of our backgrounds will come our lives. Peter's speech gave him away as being a Galilean. A person reared in one of the southern states of the United States cannot hide this fact when he is traveling in a northern section of the country.

"O generation of vipers—you offspring (generation) of snakes— you have the same kind of poison fangs possessed by your parents. When you open your mouth to speak, death and evil come forth." This is what Jesus is saying to them.

This is true of all men until they have had a personal experience with Christ. This is why all men must be "born again" (John 3:7). We all need the spiritual nature that comes only from God through Christ Jesus His Son. The non-Christian cannot claim membership in the Kingdom of God until he is born into the Kingdom. He can only enter into the Kingdom of God through a new nature. If the old nature is not changed, he will not "fit" into the Kingdom, even if he can get into it. This new nature produces the Christian life. A non-Christian might attempt to imitate this type of life, but he cannot possess it, for it only grows out of a Christ-imparted nature. It cannot be put on, but it is an outgrowth of the implanted spiritual nature.

Thought Projection No. 68: A good man and his treasure (Matt. 12:35).

"The good man out of his good treasure brings forth good, and the evil man out of his evil treasure brings forth evil." Again, Jesus is emphasizing that the outward man is the man the world sees, and that the exterior is but an expression of the inner man. Jesus makes a comparison of two men. One man fills his treasure box with the good things of life. Each day he puts something good into his treasure (life). When the time comes for him to withdraw some of these things, he can withdraw only that which he placed in the treasure. The second man puts only evil things in his treasure. When he finds himself in need of this reserve, which he has set aside for this occasion, he can only get from his treasure that which he has put into it before the emergency arose.

Put Satan and sin into your life, and evil will be the nature of your withdrawals, but if you put Christ and his righteousness into your life, goodness is the nature of what comes out. God did not build into man an automatic filtering plant for his moral and spiritual output. Man will pump out of life only what he has pumped into his life. Fill life full of hate, envy, fear, and doubt, and these things will not only control your life, but will mold your life to conform to their natures.

Thought Projection No. 69: Idle words reveal true character (Matt. 12:36,37).

"I tell you, on the day of judgment men will render account for every careless word they utter; for by your words you will be justified, and by your words you will be condemned." Jesus has been warning His critics about their attacks upon Him and His works. He has pointed out to them, by the use of several metaphors, that what a man does marks the kind of man he really is, and that the outward man is but a public image of the real man he is inside. Now Jesus is saying two important things regarding what comes out of a man. The importance of words cannot be overemphasized. Jesus says that we shall be judged by what we say—words uttered before men. One must keep in mind that this is said only after He had established that what comes out of the mouth of a man is the result of the kind of person he really is inside.

"For by your words you will be judged." This does not mean we shall be judged or saved by "works" in our lives or by what we say or have said. He is not speaking about the use or lack of use of profanity in speech. What Jesus is saying is what he has been talking about all through this chapter: What comes out of man is determined by the nature of that man. The Christian speaks the language of Zion—of Christ, because that is his nature. He has been given the nature that goes with the Kingdom of God. The profane man who is redeemed begins to develop a new vocabulary at once. The old vocabulary cannot express for him the emotions or the thoughts of his mind. He is embarrassed when he lapses into any of the old expressions that are un-Christian in their nature. The mental processes of the Christian are also reconditioned to function within the wholesome atmosphere of the Kingdom of God.

Some years ago, the author led an atheist to accept Christ into his life. His speech was profane before his conversion experience. The day after this religious experience, he returned to his newspaper office and into the old profane atmosphere. The first man to use God's name with an oath in his presence was startled to hear this newly born Christian say, "Please do not profane in my presence the Person I love more dearly than anything on earth."

His profane friend of yesterday did not know what had happened to him and asked, "Joe, are you sick or crazy this morning?" He still could not understand Joe's changed attitude even after Joe explained to him that he was now a Christian and a follower of God, the same God for whom he had no respect yesterday. The words Joe spoke were not the same as the ones he used the day before, because Joe was not the same person; he had been born into the Kingdom of God.

"For every careless word"—this is the "careless" or "unthought-out" word we speak. Anyone can be careful with the words he speaks, and he can mislead people in their evaluation of him by so doing. A "Southern drawl" can be changed into a "Yankee whine" or into a "Missouri brogue" by a speech specialist, or even by a person being careful in the way he is speaking. Let that same individual continue in his speech for a time, and he will drop a careless word (an unthought-out word), and this careless word will reveal his true background. This truth ought to awaken and rebuke the person who justifies his profanity by saying, "I am sorry, but it just slipped out—I was not thinking what I was saying." Jesus says that this is a true index to a man's nature—the things he says spontaneously. The "unguarded" expressions are the "natural" expressions of the real self. Man shall be judged by these for they are the revealer of the inner man, the real self.

Thought Projection No. 70: The sign of Jonah (Matt. 12:38-41).

"Teacher, we wish for a sign from you." But he answered them, "An evil and adulterous generation seeks for a sign; but no sign shall be given to it except the sign of the prophet Jonah." It appears that Jesus is making it too uncomfortable for his accusers over the work (miracles) He has been doing. They shift the subject to another matter by saying to Jesus, "Master, show us a sign." They are asking for a sign, a miracle—something not explained by known natural laws. What has Jesus been doing? If they cannot accept the miracles he performed, nor the maker of miracles as the Son of God, what kind of sign would do? He turns the spotlight back upon them, the thing they are trying to avoid. He does this by referring them back to two historical events. The first of these, says Jesus, "would be the only sign I will give you." The second historical event to which Jesus refers them is to be their own judgment. Let us first examine the "sign of Jonah."

Jesus calls them an evil and adulterous generation. They have been unfaithful to the One and Only True God, to their own laws and traditions. No nation had received more attention nor knowledge from God, the Eternal One, than had Israel; and yet, no nation had caused God more grief by its rejection of Him. He knew that it would be this same nation—the nation of promise—that would reject Him and have Him nailed to a criminal's cross.

They are a "sign-seeking" people. He will give them no "new" sign. They refuse to recognize the many signs all around them. The only sign He will give them is one from their own history, the sign of Jonah. Men through the ages, in their zeal to justify the "whale and Jonah story" or in their eagerness to prove the impossibility for a whale to swallow Jonah, have missed the "sign" of Jonah, have overlooked the real sign. The Bible does not say that Jonah was swallowed by a "whale," but that God prepared a "big fish" to do the job for Him. If God prepared "a fish," and He did, it could have been the one and only of its kind. Does it really matter? The facts of the story are even more incredible—facts which have not been questioned: How men on a ship, caught in a storm, threw a man overboard at his request; and how after three days at sea in a raging storm this man walked into the city of Nineveh, ready to begin a revival meeting that would turn the city away from its sins and back to God. This is the real miracle—this is the "sign of Jonah." The man who came from the grave to repentance! The people of Nineveh must have thought that they were seeing a ghost or a miracle of God. They accepted the miracle and believed his message.

You would have thought that these scribes and Pharisees would have been the first to have accepted Jesus as the promised Messiah after His resurrection from the tomb. They should have remembered the sign of Jonah—his miracle and his message. Jesus said that "the men of Nineveh will arise at the judgment with this generation and condemn it; for they repented at the preaching of Jonah, and behold, something greater than Jonah is here." The men of Nineveh would give testimony against their generation. Jesus was and is greater than the man Jonah; they had accepted the words of a lesser man over those of a greater one, the one they were refusing to believe—Christ, the Son of God. They had eyes to see but refused to see, and they had ears to hear, but refused to hear. This was to be their judgment.

Thought Projection No. 71: The sign of the queen of Sheba (Matt. 12:42).

"The queen of the South will arise at the judgment with this generation and condemn it; for she came from the ends of the earth to hear the wisdom of Solomon, and behold, something greater than Solomon is here." Again, Jesus draws a metaphor from the history of Israel to explain the sin of rejection being committed by Israel. The queen of Sheba had heard of the wisdom of Solomon. She was not of his kingdom, but his fame attracted her attention. She made the journey to see and hear Solomon, and she accepted what she heard and it satisfied her.

Jesus came teaching, preaching, and working miracles in the cities. All the people had to do to see Him and hear Him was to tarry a few minutes on the street corner. He did not disappoint those who came to him—the sick, the lame, the blind, the hungry. Only the spiritually blind refused to have their eyes opened, and the spiritually deaf refused to accept His message of peace and freedom.

If a foreign woman could leave her own country to travel great distances just to see and hear a man like Solomon, how much more ought the people of God to listen to God's Son as He tries to deliver God's message to them? Great as was Solomon, greater still is Christ. "The queen of the South," Jesus says, "will arise at the judgment with the men of His day and charge them with rejecting the greater light." She believed what she saw and what she heard; they were doing neither. What was even more condemning, they were trying to discredit Him in the eyes of the people for whom He came to die and thus to save.

Thought Projection No. 72: The danger of the empty house (Matt. 12:43-45).

"When the unclean spirit is gone out of a man, he walketh through dry places, seeking rest, and findeth none. Then he saith, I will return into my house from whence I came out; and when he is come, he findeth it empty, swept, and garnished. Then goeth he, and taketh with himself seven other spirits more wicked than himself, and they enter in and dwell there: and the last state of that man is worse than the first. Even so shall it be also unto this wicked generation." In these verses, Jesus tells the story of an evil spirit that leaves his home inside of a man. The man decides to clean up his life, to become a clean, moral man. After a period of time, the evil spirit decides to investigate his former home, and he discovers that although the house was cleaned up, no one occupies it, and so he returns with seven other evil spirits, more evil than he was himself. The man's condition is now eight times worse than before.

Jesus was speaking of Israel. She had cleaned herself up, but failed to put into her national life the righteousness of God. "So shall it be also with this evil generation." The scribes and the Pharisees had charged Jesus with working in league with Beelzebub. Jesus turns this around by saying that they are in control of not one, the prince of demons, but eight more demons more wicked than Beelzebub. They had made the mistake of cleaning up their morals, but had failed to put something better in place of the things they had removed. The forces of evil abroad in this world will not let a city, nation, or an individual live in an empty house—no matter how clean it might be.

The danger of an empty life is its very emptiness. God made man with a capacity for moral and spiritual occupancy. If we do not fill this space with Christ's moral standards and the righteousness of Christ, Satan will soon fill these empty spiritual spaces with his own brand of unrighteousness. The mission of Christ is to remove from our lives its sinful nature, and then fill this with His own spirit. The self-righteous man that is filled with nothing is only a spiritual vacuum that will not remain a vacuum very long—Satan will see to it. "Christ lives in me," said Paul. This makes the difference.

Thought Projection No. 73: True brothers of Jesus (Matt. 12:46-50).

During the battle of words Jesus was having with the scribes and Pharisees, the mother and the brothers of Jesus came seeking Him. They, perhaps, mentioned that they wanted to speak to Jesus. Someone conveyed this to Jesus and what He said must have sounded strange to His listeners:

" 'Who is my mother, and who are my brothers?' And stretching out His hand toward His disciples he said, 'Here are my mother and my brothers. For whosoever does the will of my Father in heaven is my brother, and sister, and mother.' "

We do not know the purpose of the members of Jesus' family in trying to speak to Him. They might have been concerned with His safety, as the anger of the scribes and Pharisees was increasing. Perhaps they did not understand the many things He had been saying. We do not believe that He is being rude to them when He replies thus to those seeking Him in behalf of His family. He uses the occasion to ask and answer a very pertinent question. Who are to be the real brothers in the Kingdom of God? Will this be a matter of racial qualification, of religious heritage, or what? He is asking and answering the question, "What is the real brotherhood in the Kingdom of God?"

Jesus points his fingers at his own disciples—the prototype of all the followers of Jesus to come—and says, "Here are my mother and brothers: For whoever does the will of my Father in Heaven is my brother, and sister, and mother." The test of sonship with God, and of brotherhood with Christ, is in doing the will of God, our Heavenly Father. The entrance into this family relationship is Christ Himself: "He came to his own, and his own people received Him not. But to all who received Him, who believed in His name, He gave power to become children of God; who were born, not of blood, nor of the will of the flesh nor of the will of man, but God" (John 1:11-13).

The act of repentance turns man around in his walk away from God and points him back to Jesus. When man comes face to face with Jesus, he recognizes Him as the Saviour, his Saviour, and he commits his life in faith to Jesus. Baptism follows as an act of obedience. This conversion experience places man in God's family. The Holy Spirit gives witness to man's spirit concerning the completion of this act.

20

Matthew 13

Summary: Matthew 13 contains thirteen THOUGHT PRO-
JECTIONS:

74. The sower (Matt. 13:3-9; 18-23) ALLEGORY; NARRA-
TIVE.

75. Why did Jesus use parables? (Matt. 13:10-12) METAPHOR;
HISTORICAL.

76. Hearing and seeing (Matt. 13:13-17) METAPHOR.

77. Tares and wheat (Matt. 13:24-30; 36-42) SIMILE and
ALLEGORY; NARRATIVE.

78. Mustard seed (Matt. 13:31-32) SIMILE; NARRATIVE.

79. Three measures of meal and leaven (Matt. 13:33) SIMILE;
NARRATIVE.

80. Hidden things revealed (Matt. 13:34-36) METAPHOR.

81. Shine like the sun (Matt. 13:43) SIMILE.

82. The hidden treasure (Matt. 13:44) ALLEGORY; NARRA-
TIVE.

83. The pearl merchant (Matt. 13:45-46) ALLEGORY; NAR-
RATIVE.

84. A fisherman's net and a catch of fish (Matt. 13:47-50)
SIMILE; NARRATIVE.

85. The instructed scribe (Matt. 13:51-52) SIMILE.

86. A prophet without honor (Matt. 13:53-58) PROVERB.

Chapter 13 opens with Jesus' leaving someone's house. It is still
the Sabbath. We do not know from our context if Jesus had rested
in this home or not, following His lengthy and tiring discourses with
the scribes and Pharisees. The chapter simply begins with the statement, "That same day Jesus went out of the house and sat beside
the sea. And great crowds gathered about Him, so that he got into
a boat and sat there; . . ." The crowd stood on the beach and listened
to Him as he spoke the thirteen thought projections found in this
chapter. In this series of thought projections, Christ deals with the

Kingdom of Heaven. He describes it, its earthly functions, and what will happen to it in the future.

Without a backward glance into history, it would be very difficult to understand the things Jesus reveals in these discourses. The thought projections have history on their side to support what Jesus said. One must tread very carefully through the maze Jesus is weaving through history, or the modern reader of the New Testament can make the same errors in interpretation that were made by many of the ancient church theologians. Much of the confusion in theology among religions can be traced to these errors.

It is difficult to classify the origin of the figures of speech used by Jesus in some of these thought projections. We find all four forms used in the New Testament among these thirteen thought projections. Three of these fall into the simile-allegory family and one into the metaphor-allegory family. This does not make simpler the interpretation, for they carry a "mixed" heritage. Jesus gives us a great deal of help by making interpretations of two of these (The Sower and The Tares). A study of the symbols or figures of speech used by Jesus will help clarify the others. We believe that Jesus intended thought projections 74, 77, 82, and 83 to be treated as allegories. History seems to confirm this classification.

Most theologians say that only seven parables are to be found in this chapter, though a few claim eight. When the Thought Projection Method is applied to this chapter, we find not seven thought projections, but thirteen. Each has something to say about the Kingdom of God, its Biblical form and those forms it will develop in the ages to come. Writers of theology and religion have had a field day in dividing these parables into groups that mean certain things in history, and some have gone so far as to associate the seven parables (claiming seven parables for this chapter and ignoring the rest) with the seven churches in the book of Revelation. It shall be our approach to these thought projections of Jesus to let each one speak for itself, with the hope that when each of the thirteen has spoken, a complete picture will emerge—a picture Jesus was trying to paint not only for those people before him on the seashore, but for men in all ages to come.

Though Projection No. 74: The sower (Matt. 13:3-9; 18-23).

"And he spake many things unto them in parables, saying, Behold, a sower went forth to sow; . . . some seeds fell by the wayside . . . some fell upon stony places, . . . And some fell among thorns; . . . But other fell into good ground and brought forth fruit, . . . " Thus the parable is given. In verses 18 to 23, the parable is explained. In the third verse of this chapter, Jesus uses the word "parable" for the first time. "He spake many things to them in parables" (thought projections). This was to be His new approach in preaching and teaching. In the thirteenth verse the disciples ask Him why He is using parables (thought projections). He gives them His answer by telling them another parable and then explains its meaning. It seems that He is preparing them to properly evaluate this new technique (an old one brought up to date) of teaching, which he will employ during the rest of His ministry.

It has been suggested by some that Jesus received His idea for His parable of the sower as he sat in His boat that day. He saw a sower in the field broadcasting his seed and observed what was happening to the seed. We should not forget that this was the Sabbath, and no one would be sowing on the Sabbath. It really does not matter whence came the idea, it was a familiar sight to Him and to His hearers.

A sower goes out to sow his field. Some of the seed falls on the hedgerow, hardened by much travel, and rests there until the birds come and eat it up. Other seed is caught and carried by the wind to stony places with little or no topsoil. The seed will spring up quickly, but die just as quickly, for it has no soil to feed its roots nor give anchor. The sun will soon destroy such wheat. Other seeds are carried into the thorny places having good soil, water, and sun, but thorns already have priority on all three and the seed cannot compete with the thorns and will die. The rest of the seed falls on cultivated and prepared soil and will reward the sower with a bumper crop.

Later the disciples ask Jesus to explain this parable to them (verses 18-23), Jesus does explain each part of the allegory upon which this parable is built. This is an example of an allegory expanded into a metaphor-type parable. When Jesus finishes His explanation, we see at once that this is not a parable of the seed but of the soil. The soil has the spotlight. The soil limits what the seed can do or cannot do. The soil determines the abundance or lack of abundance of the crop and the soil holds the key to what the sower will reap or not reap.

Jesus explains each part of this parable. The seed is the word of God concerning His kingdom. This seed is sown in the hearts of men. The heart is the soil upon which the seed falls. If the heart (mind) of man does not understand what it hears, Satan will use this ignorance to steal from it the message of the seed. The rocky soil is the heart with an emotional response, but no spiritual or mental depth for the rooting of the seed. A few "hard knocks" soon destroy this shallow faith, rooted in nothing but the emotions. The seed that falls among the thorns is the seed that falls into the heart of a person with a receptive mind, but the things of the world are more alluring, and the responsibilities of projecting the self in the world soon choke out the spiritual seed that is trying to take root in that life. The fertile soil is that life which has been properly prepared for the message; the seed can take root and grow. This life will produce manifold fruits. This truth is often overlooked in our zeal to get people into the Kingdom. So often improper groundwork or no preparation is made before we attempt to reach for the Kingdom. Soil preparation is extremely important to produce a spiritual crop for God. Productivity in the Kingdom of God shall be in direct ratio to the preparation made of the soil before the seed is sown. Man is to be the instrument used by God for such preparation, but the Holy Spirit must use this tool or instrument.

This is the allegory Jesus is making regarding the attitude of the world to the preaching of the message of the Kingdom. This will be the image (metaphor) of the reactions of men through the ages. This has been, and is still, the reaction of men to the Gospel of Jesus Christ when it is presented. The message is always the same, only the soil is different, but it will be the soil that determines the success of the seed. It matters not who the sower might be, if the seed is sown, the soil must receive it for a crop to be harvested.

Thought Projection No. 75: Why Jesus used parables (Matt. 13:10-12).

"Then the disciples came and said to Him, 'Why do you speak to them in parables?' And He answered them, 'To you it is given to know the secrets of the Kingdom of Heaven, but to them it has not been given. For to him who has will more be given, and he will have abundance; but from him who has not, even what he has will be taken away. This is why I speak to them in parables, . . .'" Jesus answers their question by the use of two thought projections. We shall look at each separately.

A parable, or a thought projection, is given to hide the "mysteries" of the Kingdom of God to some people, and they are used to reveal these mysteries to others. Paul says, "To the unbeliever, the cross is a stumbling block." He says that the cross is a glory to the believer, a way of life, and even an eternity. The real meaning of the cross is but one of many mysteries the unbeliever can never know, but is one of the many mysteries every Christian understands.

Jesus also says in this text that "to him who has will more be added; given to him in abundance, but to those who have not, it shall be taken away from him." This is a paradox the nonbeliever cannot understand—to take nothing from nothing.

The believer's knowledge is increased through Jesus' use of the thought projection method (parables). The unknowns of the Kingdom of Heaven become more knowable when the "knowns" he possesses in Christ are placed alongside "unknowns." To the unbeliever, the "unknowns" of the spiritual kingdom become more unknowable when they are presented in parabolic form. They do not have within their spiritual range or experience anything to cast "alongside" of these unknowns, to identify with them or to make a comparison. The believer's knowledge is increased by such comparisons made in parabolic forms of speech as used by Jesus, whereas the unbeliever's ignorance is only increased by his lack of tools to unravel these mysteries. He has added more ignorance to the ignorance he already possesses in this sphere.

Thought Projection No. 76: Hearing and seeing (Matt. 13-17).

"For this people's heart is waxed gross, and their ears are dull of hearing, and their eyes they have closed; . . ." Jesus continues this discussion by turning to one of the prophets, and He quotes what Isaiah said about his generation (Isaiah 6:9,10), applying it to the people standing before him. They were all aware of the meaning of the words of Isaiah, for history had proven the words he has spoken to be true. Isaiah said that the people had the physical capacity to hear and to see what they wanted to see. They had twenty-twenty vision and perfect hearing, that is, when it came to seeing and hearing what they wanted to see and hear. They lacked spiritual desire to see and hear what Isaiah had to say. They simply turned a "deaf ear" to his voice and said, "Preacher, we cannot understand a word you said in your sermon, and we cannot see in the word of God what you see."

Jesus points out a psychological principle here that is often overlooked when He says, "For the people's heart has grown dull, and their ears are heavy of hearing. . . . You hear what you want to hear and shut out that which disturbs you." Their ears might be stimulated by air vibrations set in motion by the vocal cords of another, but their minds refuse to make an interpretation of the sounds they are receiving. The same reactions are made by the brain as it receives stimulations from the retina of the eye, as the eye picks up stimuli from outside itself. The brain refuses to accept the "call" from outside, because it does not like what it is seeing. Each rejection of a stimulus made to the ear drum or the retina of the eye only adds to the dullness of the ear and the darkness of the eye. It becomes a little harder to hear or see that which you want to see or hear. We have trained our responses to be negative rather than positive.

Nature has built into the human body many defense mechanisms. These are used by the body to reject that which can disturb the peace and comfort of the mind and body. You are aware of a noisy window air-conditioning unit when you first enter into a room, but if you stay in the room long enough, your mind will block out the sound until you are not aware of it. This is why men can work in a noisy boiler room and after a period of time will not hear the noise around them and even carry on a conversation amid all of it. This is what Jesus is saying, "Beware of not hearing, not listening. Your fathers sinned and died, because they hardened their ears and closed their eyes to God's eternal truths."

Thought Projection No. 77: Tares and wheat (Matt. 13:24-30; 36-42).

"Another parable put he forth unto them, saying, the Kingdom of Heaven is likened unto a man which sowed good seed in his field. But while men slept, his enemy came and sowed tares among the wheat, . . . Let both grow together until the harvest: and in the time of harvest I will say to the reapers, Gather ye together first the tares, and bind them in bundles to burn them: but gather the wheat into my barn." Thus the parable is given. In verses 36 to 40, the parable is explained: ". . . and his disciples came unto him, saying, Declare unto us the parable of the tares of the field. . . .

As therefore the tares are gathered and burned in the fire; so shall it be in the end of this world."

Here is a simile Jesus turns into a parable that must be interpreted as an allegory. All this sounds rather confusing, and it would be if Jesus did not also make an explanation of the parable as He did of the Parable of the Sower. Jesus is still talking about the Kingdom. It is a story of a man who has wheat planted in his field, only to have his enemy come at night and plant tares in the same field. His servant asks what to do about it. He is told to wait until the wheat and the tares are ready for harvest; the separation will be made then. This is a simile parable, a comparison by resemblance, and yet, it is allegorical in content, as explained by Jesus, and must thus be interpreted as such, for this is the way Jesus interpreted it.

This story concerns a dastardly act. It is the lowest form of meanness. The wheat planted was to be precious food—life for the starving. Why should anyone deprive the hungry of food just to spite an enemy? This enemy planted bastard wheat among the good wheat. It looked like good wheat at first but as it matured it showed its true nature. It was a bastard wheat because it was not true wheat in its nature. It had not been germinated by a wheat germ, though it looked like a member of the wheat family.

When the servant reports this dastardly act to his master, he asks two questions, "Sir, did you not plant good wheat? How then has it weed?" Then he asks the second question, "Do you want us to go and gather them (the bastard wheat)?"

The master explains the first question by saying he had not sown the bastard wheat seed, only the good seed. The other was sown by an enemy, by someone who wanted to cause him hurt. To the second question, he tells them not to touch the bastard wheat but to wait until both crops are ready for the harvest and then they will be separated. If an attempt is made to pull up the tares, the good wheat crop might be lost in trying to remove the bad plants. The lesser of the two evils is to remove the bad from the good after both have matured. The bad plants will be destroyed then.

Later, the disciples of Jesus ask Him to interpret this parable for them (Matt. 13:33-43). This is the explanation Jesus gives: "The Son of man sows the good seed. The field is the world. The good seeds are the sons of the Kingdom (Christians). The weeds (bastard wheat) are the sons of the evil one, and the enemy who sowed them is the devil; the harvest is the close of the age, and the reapers are angels." Jesus continues and says that the evildoers, like the weeds, are burned: ". . . shall be burned. The righteous (wheat) shall shine like the sun in the Kingdom of their Father."

This method being used by Jesus (parables—thought projections) was new to the disciples. Perhaps they understood this parable and wanted to have Jesus confirm what they had interpreted, or it could be that they still were unable to understand His new method of teaching. We must be grateful for their request for an explanation of this one and the Parable of the Sower, for we have two excellent guidelines we might follow when we come to similar difficult projections of Jesus.

With Jesus' explanation the truths He is emphasizing are easily separated from this story. They are: The Sons of the Kingdom are the results of the "planting" by Jesus. He gives us our birth. Satan will plant his own sons amid the sons of God. We find this is true in the churches. To uproot the sons of the devil from the sons of God in this world is not easy, and Jesus is suggesting that this job be left for the angels to do at the end of the age. It is God's job, not man's. The evil sons will be punished and destroyed, but the Sons of God will "shine like the sun in the Kingdom"—they will shine in the Kingdom.

Thought Projection No. 78: Mustard seed (Matt. 13:31,32).

"Another parable he put before them, saying, 'The Kingdom of Heaven is like a grain of mustard seed which a man took and sowed in his field; it is the smallest of all seeds, but when it has grown it is the greatest of shrubs and becomes a tree, so that birds of the air come and make nests in its branches.'" Here is one of those parables which has suffered much through the ages from the pens of interpreters and theologians, who either do not know or ignore the basic principles used by Jesus when He presents a thought in a narrative parable or a pure thought projection. One such principle is: Jesus never used a subject for a thought projection or a narrative parable whose basic nature was not consistent with the subject being illustrated. If a mustard seed was chosen for a subject, the spiritual truth being illustrated had to conform to the nature of a mustard seed. This knowledge of the mustard seed must be common to those to whom Jesus was speaking. Its nature had to be easily recognizable by anyone in the crowd. The subject should not have to be explained; it must be locally acceptable.

Jesus never violated another fundamental principle in presenting His thought projections: If a subject was used to illustrate a spiritual truth that did not have a "transferable quality," that subject was being used in "contrast." The unjust judge used by Jesus to illustrate prayer is an example. God is not an unjust or dishonest judge. Jesus was saying that if a dishonest judge would hear and grant a request (prayer) of an injured person because she kept worrying him, God would do even more for those of His children who do not give up in prayer.

It is not the nature of a mustard seed to grow into a tree or a large shrub. It was not the nature of mustard seeds in the time of Christ in spite of the attempt of theologians through the ages to find such a seed. Why have they attempted to justify this approach? The answer to this question is to be found in the wrong application of this narrative thought projection. They have read into this illustration a meaning not intended. Jesus was not saying it was the purpose or plan of God to have a very rapidly growing Kingdom. Jesus was not suggesting this here.

We believe that Jesus was warning them of the evil and danger of an abnormal growth of the Kingdom. This would come, but it would be an abnormal growth. It would be as abnormal as for a mustard seed to grow into a tree, a home for nesting birds. This is not the nature of the mustard seed. For such a growth to occur would indicate something abnormal about it. The church did not have such a growth. It cannot compare its growth to that of communism in ratio to time (speed) and numbers.

The growth of the church viewed from this end of history is large, but that growth came at great cost to the spiritual purity of the growing plant; so much so that by the turn of the tenth century, it had little in common with the simple movement started by Jesus. This young religious stream began to have poured into it many ideas from other cultures and religions. It began to change after the third century. The Roman government gradually took over the movement in the fifth and sixth centuries. Then this religious movement took over the Roman Empire and the movement became filled with power, wealth, and worldliness. The birds of prey did come and rest in her limbs. She ruled with an iron hand and tolerated none to oppose her. The lowly Jesus of the hills of Galilee would not have felt at home in the church He started. The mustard seed, the smallest of them all, had become master of all—at a price.

Thought Projection No. 79: Three measures of meal and leaven (Matt. 13:33).

"He told them another parable. 'The Kingdom of Heaven is like leaven which a woman took and hid in three measures of meal, till it was all leavened.'" What a theological time bomb Jesus placed in this one verse of Scripture. It is a parable, for Jesus called it thus, and yet there is no long narrative given—just a statement of fact. This is an example of a parable not being a narrative (story). This theological explosion was not long in making itself felt in history, soon after Christ left this earth to be with His Father. The zenith of this religious leavening force reached a climax before the tenth century, but the church was the one influenced—not the world by the purity of the church. Some of the theological fragments are still falling to earth from this theological time bomb.

One rule always respected by Jesus in His parables—and must be so respected by all who attempt to interpret His thought projections —is: No object used for a thought projection or a parable can be out of character. If Jesus had said, "My Kingdom is like unto a glass of milk," this milk has to be interpreted in the character of milk. It cannot be forced out of character by becoming butter or cheese. Milk, with its milk characteristics, is to be transferred to the spiritual concepts Jesus is trying to express.

The word "leaven" is never used in the Bible as being a good influence, nor is it used to suggest good influence. The transfer of the word "leaven" to a spiritual object always carries the implication of an evil influence; that is, if the true character of the word is upheld. A survey of the meaning of the word "leaven" in the New Testament (as well as the Old Testament) will not reveal one exception to this rule. Jesus was always reminding His disciples and the people to "beware of the leaven of the Pharisees." This is hypocrisy (Luke 12:1). He warns of the "leaven of the Sadducees." This is infidelity (Matt. 16:6). And He warns of the "leaven of Herod." This is worldliness (Mark 8:14-15). Paul uses this term in the same spirit when he warns against "A little leaven leaveneth the whole lump. Purge out the old leaven that ye may be a new lump, as ye are unleavened" (1 Cor. 5:6-7).

One should not take the word "leaven" in verse 33 and ignore the words "three measures of meal," for they all make up the parable; and to ignore parts of a parable is to not have a parable. It would be like describing a house as all windows just because a house has windows.

"Three measures of meal" appears first in the Bible in Genesis 18:6. "And Abraham hastened into the tent to Sarah, and said, 'Make ready quickly three measures of fine meal, knead it, and make cakes.'" The Lord appeared to Abraham as he sat in the heat of the day, in the form of three young men. Abraham recognized the Holy nature of his guests. He ordered a meal of fellowship to be prepared by Sarah, his wife. Later this idea was carried forward with the idea of fellowship (Divine) into the form of worship (Exodus 16:33-36), "Take a jar, and put an omer of manna in it, and place it before the Lord, to be kept throughout your generations." An omer is the tenth part of an ephah (three measures of meal) (Numbers 15:9; 28:12,20; 28:29, and 39:14). The idea it carries is that of a fellowship—man with God and God with man.

The people to whom Jesus was speaking were familiar with these expressions. He was warning them of the danger of any influence of evil, in the present or in the future, that could destroy their personal fellowship with God. The Kingdom of God He brought down to them, restored them to this divine fellowship, which the first man had lost because of his sin of disobedience. Despite His sacrifice, the people faced the real danger of sin—"leavening"— breaking this divine fellowship. History has proven and justified this warning, which was ignored by the church through the ages. The forces of evil leaven have come into the pure church and have made it much like the world today. There is little to distinguish a Christian from the non-Christian; the work of a church from that of a YMCA or a social service agency given to the task of helping their fellowman to get more from this world. The warning has not been heard!

Thought Projection No. 80: Hidden things revealed (Matt. 13:34-36).

"That it might be fulfilled which was spoken by the prophet, saying, 'I will open my mouth in parables: I will utter things which have been kept secret from the foundation of the world.'" Jesus gives us another reason for the use of parables, as He uses a historical parable to explain His purpose.

Jesus is saying several things to His disciples here. Scholarship is not sure as to which prophet Jesus was referring, but an ancient prophet had spoken concerning revelation of hidden truths to be made in thought projections (parables). Jesus is saying that this prophet was referring to Him, and that He was revealing things about God not revealed since the foundations of the world were laid down. What are some of these hidden truths to be found in the thought projections (parables) of Jesus? A study of all the thought projections will give us new information concerning God and His plan for man.

The plan of salvation—the new contract—is to be found, both for the Jew and for the Gentile, in these thought projections of Jesus. The parables about the lost sheep, coin, and Son are three such thought projections (parables). They tell us that man is lost from God, and that God is seeking him. All men are lost regardless of the background they might claim, and if all are lost, all need to be saved.

We discover many new characteristics of God by a study of the thought projections of Jesus. In fact, man's entire concept of God has been greatly altered by these thought projections. What was man's concept of God before these thought projections were spoken? Man had come to think of God as a fierce, demanding, strict and unyielding deity—more to be feared than adored—and worshipped with the slaying of animals as sacrifices. Man obeyed Him because he was afraid not to do so. Love for God was a missing element of worship.

Jesus came, saying in parabolic form, "God is a father, kind, loving, and compassionate of nature, who loves us enough to make sacrifices to prove this love." "God is a shepherd with the heart of a shepherd who will lay down his life for his sheep." Each of the thought projections spoken by Jesus was another view of the face of God the Father to be placed in the theological art galleries of history. Their purpose—". . . reveal things hidden since the foundations of the world"—was formed. How poverty stricken the Bible would be concerning the true nature of God if it were not for these priceless thought projections!

Thought Projection No. 81: Shine like the sun (Matt. 13:43).

"Then the righteous will shine like the sun in the Kingdom of God." We pulled this thought projection out from the parable of the bastard wheat, because it carries a special emphasis beyond the story itself and calls for a closer inspection as to what is being suggested here. It gives meaning to the words of Jesus in Matthew 5:14, "Ye are the light of the world," and to His words in Matthew 5:16, "Let your light so shine before men, that they may see your good works and give glory to your Father who is in Heaven."

We do not agree with the theologians who make a distinction between the meaning of the phrases, "The Kingdom of God and the Kingdom of Heaven." Nor do we believe that one means "all the Christians on earth today, or for any particular age; and the other means those who are dead and have gone to heaven." We believe that both expressions mean the same: All born-again people, the ones who have been brought into salvation through the work of the Holy Spirit upon acceptance of Jesus Christ as their Saviour. The phrase "the Kingdom of God" was addressed to the Gentiles, and the phrase "the Kingdom of Heaven" was addressed to the Hebrew believer, who had been taught never to use the name of God because it was too sacred for human lips to utter.

The "wheat" of our story, said Jesus, are the sons of the Kingdom, His Kingdom. He was looking into the faces of some of these "sons of the Kingdom." He was thinking of the sons of the Kingdom in the ages to come. He saw them as shining lights of truth, His eternal truths. The sons of Satan would try to put out their light, but could not; they would try to dim these lights and might cause some of the lights to be dimmed, but they would never go out. He knew that wherever in the world there was one Christian, there would His light shine forth from that life. You can separate the bastard wheat from the real, for the former had no spiritual glow, but the latter would "shine as the sun." Who can deny that the sun does shine? Even the blind know when the sun is shining and when it is not. Even the sons of darkness know when a Christian is around; the light from the Christian's life will make itself felt upon his environment.

Thought Projection No. 82: The hidden treasure (Matt. 13:44).

"The Kingdom of Heaven is like treasure hidden in a field, which a man found and covered up; then in his joy he goes and sells all that he has and buys that field."

Jesus uses two figures in this short thought projection: "treasure" and "field." A treasure is found by chance by a man who then goes and buys the field so that he might recover the treasure he has found. What does it mean?

Jesus uses the word "field" in relation to the peoples of the world. This is the world of people. "The fields are white unto harvest." This "field" in which the treasure is found is the world. Christ does not buy this world in the sense of a purchase of something that does not belong to Him. The world and all that is in it belong to Him by creation, but the people, by their own choice, have departed from Him under the influence of sin and evil. Jesus sees the "treasure" of these redeemed people, when and if they are brought back into the family of God. We are told by Paul that Jesus endured the sufferings of the cross "for the joys set before Him," and also that we were "bought with a price," not of gold nor silver but by the precious blood of Christ."

Jesus is the man who discovers the treasure-redeemed man, the field is the world (human race); and the joy is the happiness He will have when He (Christ) can return this treasure back to the Heavenly Father. This makes the redeemed the treasure in the field.

We do not believe that Jesus is the treasure of this thought projection. He is a great treasure for anyone to possess, but He cannot be bought, nor do we obtain Him by buying other things. Salvation is not for sale at any price. Christ paid the price for man's salvation and man accepts it as a free gift. Man cannot obtain it in any other way. We do not search for salvation. The Holy Spirit goes in search of the lost man. Christ finds us first, and imparts faith to all who will listen to His voice. Paul says of lost man in Romans 3:11, "No one understands, no one seeks for God."

Thought Projection No. 83: The pearl merchant (Matt. 13:45,46).

"Again, the Kingdom of Heaven is like a merchant in search of fine pearls, who, on finding one pearl of great value, went and sold all that he had and bought it." The parables (thought projection) of the treasure and the pearl are twins but not identical, because there are some marks of difference. In the parable of the treasure, the finder "stumbles" upon the treasure; whereas, in the parable of the pearl, the merchant is out searching for a particular pearl—the pearl of all pearls. He is a buyer of pearls and a world traveler. He searches everywhere for this one pearl, not for himself but for a client who has commissioned him to find such a pearl.

We must reject the idea that Jesus Himself is that pearl. This is not in keeping with His character nor His mission. This idea is a misfit in the pattern of salvation. Man cannot buy Christ, no matter how strong the desire to have Him. It is the shepherd that seeks the lost sheep, not the sheep the shepherd. "For the Son of Man came to seek and save the lost" (Luke 19:10). "The GIFT of God is eternal life" (Romans 6:23). A gift cannot be bought; if it could, it would no longer be a gift. A sinner has nothing acceptable to God, to use to purchase salvation even if salvation were for sale. "When they could not pay, He forgave them both" (Luke 7:42). Isaiah says of the sinner, he is "filthy rags" (Isa. 64:6).

Jesus says that His Kingdom is "like a merchant seeking goodly pearls." Jesus said of himself that He "came seeking the lost" (Luke 19:10). Jesus must be the merchant seeking the one precious pearl, the pearl above every other pearl in beauty and value.

This pearl is the redeemed—the "called-out one" (the church), those who have been born of the Holy Spirit of God. Jesus calls them "His bride." This pearl is born out of suffering. A pearl is the only precious jewel produced by a living organism. Jesus gave it (the church) life by His suffering and dying on the cross of Calvary. The life of a pearl came out of corruptible flesh, an injured tissue. The church, the redeemed, are those who have been born out of sin. The Christian is a "born-out-of-sin" nature made into a precious saint. The GREAT PEARL is the collection of all these individuals into a oneness—the church.

The merchant is seeking the perfect pearl for a particular person. Paul speaks to the Ephesians regarding the church and Christ's desire for it by saying, "Husbands, love your wives as Christ loved the church and gave himself up for her, that He might sanctify her, having cleansed her by the washing of water and the word, that the church might be presented before Him in splendor, without blemish" (Ephesians 6:25-27). Christ will present to God the Heavenly Father the pearl when He returns to earth for it at the end of the ages.

Thought Projection No. 84: A fisherman's net and a catch of fish (Matt. 47-50).

"Again the Kingdom of Heaven is like unto a net, that was cast into the sea, and gathered of every kind: which when it was full, they drew to shore, and sat down, and gathered the good into vessels, but cast the bad away." This parable is similar to the one of the wheat and the tares (13:24-30). In both thought projections we have a mixture of good and bad. The good and bad seed grow together in the same field. They are left together until the harvest comes. In this thought projection, we have a fisherman's net filled with good and bad fish. Again, the good and bad are not separated until a "judgment." The separating of the fish, of the edible from the non-edible, is not done in the boat at the time of the catch, but when all the fish are safely on the shore of the lake. The good fish are sent to market, but the others are cast aside.

The net in this thought projection is the "spreading," the "the broadcasting" of the word of God. It is the message of salvation preached to men. This word will attract all kinds of people. Just as when the net is let down to the bottom of the sea and is brought to the surface with all manner of fish in it, so will the Gospel message, when preached to all types of people, catch or bring into the religious movement the good and the bad. The bad remains so by nature, but many become the good by the work of the Holy Spirit. Separation of these—the spiritually redeemed and the unredeemed in the church—will come at the judgment, not at the time of the "catch."

In this thought projection the fisherman does the separation, but Jesus says that at the judgment, the angels will do this. The fisherman's job is to cast out the net and bring the fish into the boat and onto the shores; the job of separation does not rest with him, but with God.

In both thought projections of the wheat and tares and of the fishermen's net, we see Jesus as a "realist." He wants the church to be a perfect society, but He knows that men will come into the movement and weaken it, because while they may be in the church, He will not be in their hearts. There will always be the "tares" in the church and the "bad fish," but in the end these will be separated from the wheat and the good fish. He will do this and not man.

Thought Projection No. 85: The instructed scribe (Matt. 13:51,52).

"And he said to them, 'Therefore every scribe who has been trained for the Kingdom of Heaven is like a householder who brings out of his treasure what is new and what is old.'" This

simple thought projection is ignored by most scholars in their treatment of the parables of Jesus. And yet, it is the "frosting on the
cake" for all the parables and thought projections found in this
chapter. When Jesus said to His disciples, "Do you understand all
this?" they replied (without much thought) yes. Then Jesus gives
this brief thought projection. He is saying, "If you do understand
these things, you will be like the householder who brings before
his guest things of old and new from his treasure chest. You will
be a scribe who has learned the value of the old as well as the values
of the new. You can profit from each without the loss of the other.
You are a scribe of great wisdom."

Ezra, perhaps, was the forerunner of the scribes. He acted as a
historian for the army, as well as reader and explainer of the law
to the Israelites with whom he lived. Later, other men of letters
performed the function of interpretation of the word of God for
the people. By the age of Christ, these men were jealous of their
interpretations of the law and of their position in the Jewish society
of that day. They had become a separate sect in society.

A scribe had to know the law himself and be able to explain it
to others. As scribe followed scribe, some of the laws were lost under
their interpretations, and these interpretations in some instances replaced the law. Jesus gave these "guardians" of the law a very hard
time; and because of this they grew to hate Him bitterly and were
not satisfied until they saw him hanging on a cross. The very fact
that Jesus would use a "Scribe" as a parable to apply to His own
disciples must have been a shock to His hearers; What was Jesus
teaching in this thought projection?

He is suggesting that these disciples of His, and the other religious teachers of the Gospel of Christ who were to come, are to
replace the scribe, or, at least, to perform as scribes for His Kingdom.
They were to be taught or instructed in the Gospel message and
they were to teach others. "Go ye into all the world and teach all
nations . . ." (Matt. 28:19-20).

This teaching and preaching they were to do would grow out
of the "old" and the "new." The new would grow out of the old
. . . as a new shoot grows out of an old stump. The New Testament, as we now know it, has for its root system the Old Testament.
One cannot be understood without the knowledge of the other.
The message of Christ begins in the book of Genesis. The message
of salvation begins in the same book. We find that the fall of man

and the promise of his redemption begins there. The voices of God's prophets called men into repentance and kept alive the promise which God had made to His people for a Redeemer. From the "new" comes the fulfillment of these promises of God in the form of His own Son, who lives on earth and dies on the cross of Calvary. He is resurrected and now sits at the right hand of God; He will return to earth some day to claim His own. This is the message of the new. Christians are the modern scribes who can and should bring great truths for man to see—both from the "old" and the "new." Christians are trying to interpret HIM for the world, for to know Him is to know eternal life.

Thought Projection No. 86: A prophet without honor (Matt. 13:53-58).

"And they were offended in him. But Jesus said unto them, A prophet is not without honor, save in his own country, and in his own house. And he did not many works there because of their unbelief." Jesus now had finished all His thought projections as recorded in this chapter and had decided to return to His own country, perhaps for a visit with His mother and members of His family. His fame had spread abroad and had even sifted back into His own community. We do not know what He expected from His own friends, but the reception He received disappointed Him. When He arrived, He was not received with any show of enthusiasm or gracious acceptance; just the opposite reaction was thrown into His face. He was met with doubts, sneers, and open contempt.

They shouted something like this at Him, "We know this fellow; he might be somebody in Jerusalem, but we know who he really is in this town." Jesus marveled at their unbelief in the face of the things He had done in other places, and He was unable to help the ones He wanted to help most—His own friends and family. Their lack of faith in Him tied His hands. He could perform no miracles for them because of their lack of faith. Jesus quotes to them one of their own proverbs.

This is an age old story. We tend to underrate the familiar and do not respect that which is nearest us. The family and friends of Jesus should have been among the first to accept Him for what He was and for what He claimed to be, but we have no record of any member of His family—and this includes His mother—accepting Jesus until after His resurrection.

His own community was the greater loser. The blind in the community remained blind, the crippled were still cripples, and the hungry remained hungry after He came and left. Their unbelief locked Him out of their lives. He had lived among them, had, in fact, lived too close to them, and they could not see Him for what he was, because their eyes were blinded by their closeness. The sin of being too close cost them dearly. It always does.

21

Matthew 14

Summary: There are no parables or thought projections in this chapter. It is a chapter of deeds and not words.

Chapter 14 of Matthew contains no parables or thought projections. We find recorded in this chapter the events leading up to the death of John the Baptist. Herod the tetrarch, to please his wife and her daughter, has John beheaded. When the news is brought to Jesus, he retires by boat to a "lonely spot apart." He seems shocked over the news of John's death. The crowds follow Jesus into this desert spot, and when the day is almost gone, the disciples are concerned for the welfare of the people, for they have not eaten all day. Jesus then takes five loaves of bread and two fish and feeds about five thousand men, besides the women and the children. Twelve baskets full of food are left over after the feast.

The disciples take a boat to travel to the other side of the lake. During the night, Jesus appears, walking on the water. Peter sees Him and cries out to Jesus for permission to come to Him. This is granted, but Peter becomes fearful of the water and begins to sink. Jesus rescues him and both return to the boat. A storm arises before they reach the other shore, and Jesus calms the storm by speaking to the winds. Word quickly spreads when he does arrive on shore, and the people bring to Him many of the sick and needy, and He cures them. This chapter is filled with action and not instruction or messages from Jesus. Deeds, not words, mark this chapter.

22

Matthew 15

Summary: Matthew 15 contains six THOUGHT PROJEC-
TIONS:

87. Lip worship (Matt. 15:7-9) METAPHOR.

88. Eating does not defile the body (Matt. 15:11,15-20) META-
PHOR.

89. God must plant if there is to be life (Matt. 15:12-13) META-
PHOR.

90. The blind leading the blind (Matt. 15:14) METAPHOR.

91. Scraps belong to the dogs (Matt. 15:22-28) METAPHOR.

92. The lost sheep of Israel (Matt. 15:24) METAPHOR.

Chapter 15 opens with another attack by the scribes and Pharisees upon Jesus. They could not leave Him alone, for He was a
threat to their own religious security. The weapon they use to
launch their attack is the weapon of "tradition." "Why do your
disciples transgress the traditions of the elders? For they do not
wash their hands when they eat" (Matt. 15:2). This is the opening
barrage in this new attack upon Jesus. They are attacking Jesus
through His disciples.

These religious leaders—these critics—were more concerned with
the continued projection of their rituals, which were based not
upon law, but upon interpretations of their laws, than they were
appreciative of the good Jesus was doing for the people. They had
placed these interpretations of the law above the law itself in importance and value. They were more concerned with keeping these
interpretations than they were in helping the people they were supposed to be serving.

The criticism levied at the disciples for not washing their hands
before eating was not based on the scribes' respect for hygienics or
their concern for lack of hygienics, but rather their anger was aroused
over the failure of these disciples of Jesus to respect and obey the

religious rituals of washing before eating. In their own traditions, superstition had crept in to color some of their rituals. Here is an example of this. They had been taught that the demon "Shibta" would come at night and sit on the hands of the sleeper. The sleeper's hands would become contaminated by this demon and thus had to be washed before they could handle food, or else the food would become contaminated and pass into the body. Only ceremonial washing could remove this danger. It was not the hygienic effect of water that removed the contamination, but the ceremony or the ritual of washing.

Jesus counterattacks the attackers by dropping six little thought projection bombs into their midst. He loads them with the same explosives they had used: their own history (traditions). He says in effect, "If you can use your traditions to attack me and my disciples, our defense will also come from the same arsenal."

Thought Projection No. 87: Lip worship (Matt. 15:7-9).

"You hypocrites, well did Isaiah prophesy of you when he said of you, 'This people draweth nigh unto me with their mouth, and honoreth me with their lips; but their heart is far from me. But in vain they do worship me, teaching for doctrines the commandments of men.' " We find that Jesus is placing two charges in this text against His attackers. He charges them with hypocrisy of worship. "You worship, sing songs of praise to me, make a public expression of worship, but this is all that you are doing—lip service, that is all." Jesus was saying that their hearts were not in what they were doing. They were "performing a religious duty," for duty's sake. There was no spirit of commitment to God in their worship. They were uttering words and making sounds which had no real meaning. Paul speaks of this in 1 Corinthians 13:1-3, "If I speak in the tongues of men and of angels, but have not love, I am a noisy gong or a clanging cymbal. And if I have prophetic powers, and understand all mysteries and all knowledge, and if I have all faith, so as to remove mountains, but have not love, I am nothing, and if I deliver my body to be burned, but have not love, I gain nothing." They key to these verses is also the key to real worship—"Love." This is a response of one personality to another, and it makes worship possible.

Jesus is saying that public expression of worship for worship's sake is not real worship. Rituals practiced for rituals' sake are not real ritualistic expressions. These are mere physical expressions of forms of worship, and worship has to be more than such expressions. Real worship is the heart of man responding to his God, and the reaching out of man to his God. The emotions of the worshipper must be involved, for it is the emotions of man that trigger the decisions of the mind. It is the heart responding to a heart: God does not want, nor does He need the extensions of our personalities (the physical things we offer to Him in the form of a ritual or in a form of worship). He wants our entire personality. When He has this, He is honored by what we offer to him of our substance; without this, what we offer has no meaning nor value. We merely worship Him with our lips, not our hearts.

The second charge Jesus hurls at his attackers in this text is, "You have replaced my doctrines (God's laws) for man-made doctrines." He is saying that they have made a very poor substitution in religion. They exchanged something which had been received from the Eternal God for something from mortal man. Through the ages, they had rewritten God's law and so diluted the meaning of these original precepts given to Moses by God with their own interpretations, that these laws were now lost to the people and their man-made interpretations had become the law itself—had replaced the law of Moses.

Jesus sums this up by saying, "But in vain they do worship me." They are wasting their worship effort, because it is not accepted by God as true worship. It is a worship of interpretations made by man, and these are not acceptable to God. They were guilty of offering to God the wrong thing—rituals and not themselves. They were making "loud noises" with their lips, but their hearts were silent. They were offering Him "things" instead of themselves.

Thought Projection No. 88: Eating does not defile the body (Matt. 15:11,15-20).

Jesus continues His attack upon His critics by exploding one of their pet theories about defilement, when He turns to the crowd and says, "Not that which goeth into the mouth, defileth a man, . . ." Their tradition taught that evil could be brought into the body through the mouth. We already noted the theory behind the ritual of the washing of the hands before eating. This washing was not to give the hands a "physical cleansing" but a spiritual decontam-

ination from the evil resulting from the touch of the evil spirit.
Jesus is saying, "It is impossible to contaminate the soul in this
manner."

Jesus is not justifying complete freedom in our eating habits, nor
is He saying that man can eat anything he wants without harm to
himself. He is not saying man is to have complete freedom to drink
anything he chooses. We have seen men in Africa during World
War II, because of their great thirst, drink contaminated water.
The thirst that prompted them to ignore the orders of our doctors
did not make them immune from having malaria later. We must
keep this statement in its context. Jesus is talking about and dealing
with rituals which had replaced the law originally given to Moses
by God. These commandments had been changed by substituting
man-made interpretations of them. Jesus was attacking these substituted rituals and ceremonies. There are other basic laws that deal
with the diet of man.

Jesus is saying, "Food is taken into your body through the mouth.
It is digested in the stomach and is used by the body to strengthen
the whole body. That which it cannot use for this purpose is discharged as residue from itself."

The body does not care if a thousand demons had used the loaf
of bread, whence came your toast as a dancing platform or for a bed
the night before. The nutritive value of the bread is still retained
in the bread and can be used by the body. A demon is not to be
confused with a virus, however, for no religious ritual will free a
piece of bread of its virus. There are laws dealing with the physical
life of man and there are also laws dealing with man's spiritual
nature. Each operates within its own sphere, even though each can
and does have influence upon the other.

Jesus is asked by Peter in verse fifteen to explain all this; He
does so in verses eighteen to twenty. He says very plainly that eating
with unwashed hands (ceremonially unwashed hands) does not
defile man or make him spiritually unfit to worship God. Man might
carry germs into the body, however, because he has failed to wash
his hands before eating, but this has nothing to do with the spirit-
uality of man.

Jesus then places the spotlight upon the danger spot in the life
of man when he says, "For out of the heart proceed evil thoughts,
murder, adultery, fornication, theft, false witness, blasphemies. These
are the things which defile man: but to eat with unwashed hands

defileth not man." The inner man is the real man, and from inside of man come the evil acts or the good acts.

Thought Projection No. 89: God must plant if there is to be life (Matt. 15:12,13).

"Then came the disciples and said to him, 'Do you know that the Pharisees were offended when they heard this saying?' He answered, 'Every plant which my Heavenly Father has not planted will be rooted up.'" The disciples of Jesus were reacting to the frank and abrupt way Jesus had charged into His critics. "After all, were these men not the religious leaders of their day?" To them, this was not proper protocol. Jesus was hurting their feelings by His frankness.

To this, Jesus makes an even more frank statement when he says, "Every plant which My Heavenly Father has not planted will be rooted up. Let them alone; . . ." The flowers that grow in God's kingdom will be those that God Himself has planted. Any other plant that springs up in his flower garden will be removed—not because it is not beautiful nor fails to resemble the other flowers in a physical way; any such flower will be removed, because God did not plant it.

Jesus makes this quite clear to Nicodemus when He says to him, "Truly, truly, I say unto you, unless one is born of water and the Spirit, he cannot enter the Kingdom of God. That which is born of the flesh is flesh, and that which is born of the Spirit is Spirit . . . You must be born anew . . ." (John 3:3-6). Paul speaks of this when he says, "We are planted together."

Where are the scribes, the Pharisees, and the Sadducees today? What happened to the great burden of their traditions which they had placed upon the shoulders of the people of God? No longer does the smoke arise from their altars of worship. No longer is the air filled with the nauseating odors of animal flesh around every Jewish house of worship. The prophecy spoken here by Jesus has been realized, has been fulfilled:

That which is planted by God grows and continues to live as long as it fulfills the purpose for which it was created. But that which is planted by man in the name of God will run its course and disappear. Its popularity is not its badge of God's approval; time will be the test of its origin—of man or God? It takes more than the usage of God's name by man to authenticate something not planted by God.

Thought Projection No. 90: The blind leading the blind (Matt. 15:14).

Jesus continues His response to the disciples' concern over the "bruised" feelings of the scribes and Pharisees by saying, "Let them alone; they are blind guides. And if a blind man leads a blind man, both will fall into a pit."

What a ridiculous picture Jesus paints here: A blind man attempting to lead a group of blind men through rugged and dangerous country, or through the traffic of a modern "freeway" in an American city. He is saying that the leaders are blind to the spiritual truths they are trying to teach others. They are attempting to guide men through a theological wilderness not traveled by themselves. They are trying to direct men to God without knowing the direction themselves.

It would be the same principle as a man trying to practice medicine without a knowledge of medicine, or trying to perform a delicate operation without any training or experience in methods of surgery. The results would be fatal to the patient. Such a person would keep the mortician busy until he himself was taken out of circulation.

God must call (plant) into His service those who are to serve Him as teachers and ministers. God chooses, and man responds to God's choice. A man does not select spiritual leadership positions; he responds to God's selection of him. The selected one then is trained in the things of God before he attempts to lead others to God. A newly purchased robe does not qualify one for the priesthood of God, no more than a paper of ordination issued by some church qualifies a person to be a spiritual leader of a church. These things come after God makes His selection—not before. Too often, God is forced to take men's decision in this matter, and the Kingdom of Heaven suffers the loss.

A man was standing on a busy street corner in New York City waiting for the traffic light to change. A woman was also waiting near him for the light to change. The man took the woman's arm and escorted her across the street, but near the center of the crossing, he stumbled and almost fell. She, too, almost fell. When they reached the safety of the sidewalk, she turned to him and said, "Sir, you almost caused me to fall in the middle of the street. You were very clumsy, you acted like a blind man." He replied, "I am blind. I took your arm thinking that you knew I was blind and that you wanted to help me across that busy and dangerous street." Jesus is warning of the danger of the blind leading the blind.

Thought Projection No. 91: Scraps belong to dogs (Matt. 15:22-28).

"And, behold, a woman of Canaan came out of the same coasts, and cried unto him, saying, Have mercy on me, O Lord, thou son of David; my daughter is grievously vexed with a devil. . . . But he answered and said, it is not meet to take the children's bread, and to cast it to dogs. And she said, Truth, Lord; yet the dogs eat of the crumbs which fall from their masters' table." Jesus departs from the land of Gennesaret and goes to the coast of Tyre and Sidon. A woman of Canaan comes to Him seeking His mercy and help for her sick daughter. For some reason Jesus ignores her and passes her by. She continues to follow Jesus and to plead in behalf of her daughter. The disciples ask His permission to send her away. They are embarrassed by her attention. He refuses their request and turns to the woman, engaging her in conversation. The play of words between Jesus and this woman is intriguing because of the humor underlying the entire conversation. One can almost see the sparkle in the eyes of Jesus and this woman, see the smiles playing across their faces; and yet, Jesus projects a great truth for all men and gives notice of God's change of plans concerning the promise made to Abraham.

The key to the story is found in verses twenty-six and twenty-seven. " 'It is not fair to take the children's bread and throw it to the dogs.' She said, 'Yes, Lord, yet even the dogs eat the crumbs that fall from their master's table.' "

This woman was not one of the promise; she was a Canaanite. He is saying to her that he came to administer to His own, to fulfill the promise made to Abraham. He came to give bread to the house of Israel. He is to be that bread. He is the promised Messiah. He is not dealing here with their refusal to accept Him as their Messiah. He is merely identifying Himself with His mission.

She replies, "Perhaps this is all true, but even so, I might be a dog in status to those for whom you came, but even a dog has privileges. They can expect scraps to be tossed to them from the table of the privileged. I am willing to just eat the scraps you toss to me. These 'scraps' will satisfy the need of my sick daughter." This, in substance, is what she is saying to Jesus.

The comparison Jesus is making between Israel and her own background was not done to embarass or humiliate her, but to test and strengthen her faith. Jesus must have been satisfied by what he saw in her, for he quickly terminates this play of words filled with humor, and says to her in dead seriousness, " 'O woman, great is thy faith! Be it done for you as you desire.' And her daughter was healed instantly." He does not touch the body of the sick child, nor does He go to the home of the sick girl. The mother's faith is great enough to span space and time, the cure is one by remote control. She does not say what Mary and Martha said to Jesus when He returned to find His friend Lazarus dead: "If you had been here, our brother would not have died." Her faith was greater.

We should not leave this story without a glance at the word that Jesus uses for "dog." This is the only place in the New Testament that this particular word is used. Dogs were scavangers, and because they had to fight other dogs, they were fierce, ugly, and dangerous when hungry. Jesus did not use the word describing this kind of dog, but one that was used for a pet of children. "You do not expect me to take the food of the children and give it to their pets" is what Christ m

The woman responds to the twinkle in the eyes of Jesus, for she replies in the same vein, "No, Lord, but even the children will share their food with their pets; I expect you to do as much for me." She was not wrong in her understanding of the heart of the Saviour, nor was she disappointed by the response of Jesus to her faith in Him!

Thought Projection No. 92: The lost sheep of Israel (Matt. 15:24).

"But He answered and said, I am not sent but unto the lost sheep of the house of Israel." In His conversation with this woman of Canaan, Jesus uses a metaphor that ought not to go unnoticed. It is worth recovering from the oblivion of its background. When the woman asks Him for help for her daughter, Jesus says unto her, "I was sent only to the lost sheep of the house of Israel." This raises some provocative questions.

Jesus says He came "only" to the "lost sheep" of the "house of Israel." Did He not come also to the lost Gentiles, non-Jewish people? Did He come only to save a part of the Jewish people? Or did He come to save the whole house of Israel? Answers to all these questions can be found by examining the entire New Testament. One must remember the purpose Jesus had in mind as He talks with this woman of Canaan, as he searches for these answers.

We do not believe that Jesus meant that He came only to save Israel. He came first to His own, but His own rejected Him and He turned to the Gentiles. Jesus said that He came to seek and to save the lost, and that all men were lost. He presented himself first to His own, and even if they had received Him, He still would have presented Himself to all men. The cross was the goal of His life, for it took Calvary's cross to save both the Jew and the Gentile—the one under the promise and the ones living outside of the promise.

"The lost sheep" of the house of Israel: "He came to save the lost." Jesus said that He could not save the righteous man, for such a person felt no need for Christ or for what Christ had to offer him. He was resting in his own self-righteousness. He seemed to satisfy all his own spiritual needs. No one will seek to be found until he realizes that he needs to be found. A man is not lost until he realizes he is lost, and since Jesus came only to seek, to find, and to save the lost, only the lost of the house of Israel can be saved by Jesus. The lack of man's awareness of his lostness does not mean that he is not lost. He simply refuses to recognize that he is lost. Christ had nothing for such a person in that age, nor does he have anything for such people in our age.

23

Matthew 16

Summary: Matthew 16 contains six THOUGHT PROJECTIONS:

93. Bad weather prophets (Matt. 16:1-4) METAPHOR; HISTORICAL.

94. The leaven of the Pharisees and Sadducees (Matt. 16:5-12) METAPHOR.

95. Peter the rock (Matt. 16:13-18) ALLEGORY.

96. The keys to the Kingdom (Matt. 16:19) ALLEGORY.

97. Peter is called Satan (Matt. 16:22-24) METAPHOR.

98. You must lose life to gain it (Matt. 16:24-28) METAPHOR.

The Pharisees and the Sadducees, natural enemies within Jewish theology, were united in their effort to trap and destroy Jesus. They had little else in common in their separate theologies, but both parties knew that Jesus was a threat to them and must be hushed, silenced, or destroyed. They did not stop their united effort until they saw Him hanging on the cross of Calvary. In this chapter, Jesus deals first with these men. In chapter 16, our first two thought projections of Jesus come in answer to a request made by the Pharisees and Sadducees, "And the Pharisees and Sadducees came and to test Him they asked him to show them a sign from heaven."

Thought Projection No. 93: Bad weather prophet (Matt. 16:1-4).

"He answered them, 'When it is evening, you say, "It will be fair weather; for the sky is red." And in the morning, "It will be stormy today, for the sky is red and threatening." You know how to interpret the appearance of the sky, but you cannot interpret the signs of the times. An evil and adulterous generation seeks for a sign, but no sign shall be given to it except the sign of Jonah.' " Television has made the average American keenly aware of weather conditions across the country. Almost every television set in America is tuned in at least once every day to some weather report. Many predicate what they will do the next day by what they learn from these reports the night before. No longer do we take our chances on the weather to play golf, fish, or visit in certain areas of the country. We make our decision after we have seen the weather report. We are becoming experts in prognosticating the weather. This has been a game man has played since he first noticed the changes in the weather. Man has learned to use the latest scientific instruments to protect himself from the weather. He can now guard against storms, tornados, and hurricanes because of the forewarnings of such weather disturbances. Man needs this knowledge for survival.

The answer that Jesus gives to His testers is based in this knowledge. He says to them, "You students of the weather, how can you be so blind as to other things around you? Use the same power of observation regarding Me as you have used in the study of the weather each day. You ask Me for a sign; you already have the only sign I shall give you. It is the sign of Jonah; go and study it."

These men were not seeking a confirmation of the authority of Jesus nor His Messiahship; they were only attempting to discredit Him in the eyes of the people. They wanted to cause him public embarrassment. They would not have accepted any "new" sign He might have given them, for they had been blind to the many signs of His Messiahship to be seen in the people He touched and healed.

These same men already accused Him of working miracles, curing the sick, raising the dead, making well the crippled, giving sight to the sightless, and feeding, on at least two occasions, many thousands of people, in and through the power of Satan. They refused to apply their own theology to Jesus which taught that only good comes from God and evil must come from Satan.

Jesus knew also that if He failed to furnish them with a public display of His power of miracles—and for their entertainment— they would say that He lacked such power to produce the proof they demanded. "We refuse to believe in Him for He failed to show us proof of His divine powers by working a miracle that we could accept." This could be their defense to the people.

"You ask for a sign?" Jesus asks. "You have them all around you, but you refuse to see them. Then go into your own history, for you will find one there. This sign of Jonah will be my only sign to you." This sign is still the only sign man needs for proof that Jesus is the promised one. This was the sign upon which Paul staked his own acceptance of Christ. This sign of Jonah was to certify the validity of Christ's mission to earth and to authenticate His divine character. Jesus continues by saying, "You seek a sign? a wicked and adulterous generation seeketh after a sign; and there shall no sign be given unto it; except the sign of the prophet Jonah." Jesus has reminded them of this sign of Jonah before, but it seems that they still have not been able to translate the message.

They were familiar with the story of Jonah, the rebellious messenger of God who refused to accept God's orders to preach to the wicked city of Nineveh. He had been caught at sea, going somewhere else in a storm that threatened his life and the lives of all on board. He knew that the crew and passengers on his ship were right in their conclusion that God's wrath was kindled against someone on the ship; it was then, and only then, that Jonah came forward and confessed his guilt, requesting that he be thrown into the sea. He did not want others to suffer for his disobedience. This was done. A God-prepared fish swallowed Jonah, and after three days, it cast Jonah alive onto the shore. Jonah, having learned his lesson, proceeded to Nineveh to preach God's message of repentance. The results were astounding to Jonah, for the people repented of their sins, and God spared their city.

The sign of Jonah was not the great fish. This was only God's background for the real miracle. The people knew that Jonah had been cast into the sea during a great storm. They knew nothing about the great fish that saved Jonah's life. The miracle to them was that a man, who had been dead or at least should have been dead, could come walking into his town preaching a message of repentance: He was a resurrected man; let the record show he had died at sea; here he was alive after three days and three nights in a storm at sea with no lifeboat or raft; it had to be a God-made miracle, and it was to the people of Nineveh.

Jesus was looking toward His own death, burial, and resurrection. He would be placed among the dead. His tomb would be sealed and He would be counted by the Romans and others as a citizen of the dead. As the sign of Jonah was his restoration to life from the dead, so would the sign of Jesus' own resurrection validate and authenticate His divine Sonship with God. He was saying to them, "You have observed My miracles, heard Me speak, and heard of My supernatural birth; but the proof of My divinity, proof of My true relationship with God the Father is not found in any of these things. It will be found only in the sign of Jonah, the resurrection." We do not doubt His divine birth, His miracles, and we accept His teachings and try to follow His examples. We accept what the Scriptures have to say about Him and believe that He is the promised Messiah, but all these things come to rest and find their support and proof in this sign of Jonah. It is the sign of the empty tomb: Christianity will stand or fall on this (1 Cor. 15).

Thought Projection No. 94: The leaven of the Pharisees and the Sadducees (Matt. 16:5-12).

"Then they understood that he did not tell them to be aware of the leaven of the bread, but of the teaching of the Pharisees, and Sadducees." These words leave no doubt in the minds of any reader of the New Testament as to what Jesus was saying by this thought projection. The disciples did not misunderstand, nor did the Pharisees and the Sadducees miss His point! He was speaking of the "DOCTRINES" of these two sects. Their doctrines were leaven. What is meant here by the leavening of the doctrines of the Pharisees and Sadducees?

We have already noted in Matthew 13:35 the nature of leaven in the Bible. There are not two kinds of leaven in the Bible, only one. It is never used in the sense of goodness, nor of good influence. It is always used as the chemical action of fermentation, the breaking up of an organic compound. It works quietly but persistently to do its job of fermentation. It does not stop working until its job of "leavening" is finished.

It was in this sense that Paul used the word "leaven" in his Corinthian letter, warning the Christians of the danger of the Judaizing teachers. He said, "A little leaven leaveneth the whole lump." These teachers were trying to superimpose Pharisaism, which Paul calls leaven. This meaning of leaven has been lost through the ages; today its meaning has become the "good influence" of a Christian person or church in a community. This change has been the result of a misinterpretation. Jesus used this word in its original meaning: an influence of evil that would weaken good by its evil influence.

What, then, is the meaning of the leaven of the Pharisees and Sadducees? Were these not two respected schools of Jewish theology? Were not these men spiritual leaders within the religious

Jewish community? To what was Jesus making this odorous comparison?

What Jesus meant by the leaven of the Sadducees was the materialistic approach they made toward religion and toward life. All their religious practices and beliefs were based upon a materialistic concept of life. It provided for and encouraged indulgences in every form of materialistic living.

The Pharisees were just the opposite in their approach to religion and life. They professed to believe in angels, spirits, and the resurrection of the dead. But they so completely covered over these doctrines with their traditions that the people could not get beneath to the vital doctrines they were covering. Traditions had replaced spiritual assets.

Two words can cover the word leaven as it is applied to the Pharisees and the Sadducees: "materialism" and "traditions." Jesus could have said, "Beware of the materialism preached by the Sadducees and the traditions preached by the Pharisees, for they will keep you from finding and knowing God."

Leaven works slowly, insidiously, and it does not stop working until the whole lump of dough has been affected. If some of this contaminated dough is placed into unleavened dough, its leavening influence will continue. This writer has eaten sourdough pancakes which contained elements of yeast that had been put into dough more than fifty years before. Each time the batter was used, a small amount was retained and placed in more unleavened dough to continue its work.

History is a mirror that reflects the truth of this unheeded warning by the Christian church. Traditions and materialism are still the two greatest dangers to the Christian church. These two have wrought chaos in the Christian movement in all ages. Their danger is that they work from within the Church, leavening pure doctrines to become doctrines not consistent with the word of God as found in the New Testament.

The Sadducees and the Pharisees both taught the religion of the one and only true God. But what they taught stood in opposition to the other, and both could not be right without the other being wrong. The test of either school was not to be found in the "cloth" of the church, not its "traditions," but in Christ Himself. He is still the test for any doctrine. "What think ye of Me, where do I fit into your religious life?" asks Jesus.

Thought Projection No. 95: Peter the rock (Matt. 16:13-18).

When Jesus arrived on the coast of Caesarea Philippi, it seems that He decided to give His disciples a little theological examination to check up on their progress. This consisted of only one question, "Whom do men say that I the Son of man am?" Jesus first addressed this question to the crowd before facing the disciples with it. He gave them an opportunity to listen and reflect upon the answers from the crowd. Various answers were given; none satisfied Jesus, and He turned to His disciples and addressed them with the same question, "But whom say ye that I am?"

He was saying to them something like this, "You have heard the answers from the crowd. The people have divided opinions about Me, and none seem too sure of the answers they have given. This is to be expected under the circumstances, but the really important thing to Me at this moment is not what they think of Me, but what do you think of Me? What have these many months meant to you in regards to your understanding of Me and of My mission?" This was a point of crisis. If the disciples had no more knowledge of Him than the voices that came to him from the crowd, much had been lost, and there was not much time left to recover this loss. Calvary was not far away and time was running out. Much was hanging on their answer to His question.

There must have been a long pause, each man's eyes searching the face of the other, each asking with his glance, "Who will speak up for the rest of us?" Peter, being less timid than the others, became their spokesman, and says, "Thou art the Christ, the son of the living God." Peter, more correct than He might have supposed, must have swelled with pride (this shows later) at what Jesus said to him and to the rest of the disciples.

Jesus responds to this answer from Peter, first by issuing a warning that what Peter has said did not come by logical reasoning of man's mind, nor as a result of theological instructions from others, but as a direct revelation of the Holy Spirit. Man was not to glory in this discovery.

The Holy Spirit revealed to John the Baptist on the banks of the Jordan that Jesus was the "lamb of God which taketh away the sin of the world." (John 1:21.) It was the revelation of this same Holy Spirit which revealed Jesus to them as the Son of the living God. They had nothing to boast of themselves; the Holy Spirit had been their teacher concerning who Christ was. This is still God's method of teaching men concerning Jesus and Himself. All other sources of knowledge are mere instruments used by God in the hands of man that work under the authority and power of the Holy Spirit. It is through the work of this same Holy Spirit that the sinner finds God and becomes acquainted with the saving work and grace of Christ Jesus. After this warning to Peter and the others, Jesus continues with His explanation.

There are three general views as to the meaning of this thought projection of Jesus. "Thou art Peter, and upon this rock I will build my church and the gates of hell shall not prevail against it" (Matt. 16:18). The largest single body of Christians in the world, the Roman Catholic church, teaches that Peter is the "rock," the supreme authority of the church, and that this authority has passed down from Peter to the popes of the church. This, they claim, makes them the one and only true church of God.

Another view of this text suggests that it is not Peter the man, but what Peter said concerning Jesus which is the foundation of the Christian church. Men must believe that Jesus Christ is the Son of the living God. The Greek grammar and structure is offered in proof. "Peter the man" is masculine, but the "rock," the foundation, is neuter and does not agree in gender with Peter.

A third view is based upon the usage of the word "rock" referring to God in each case. Jesus was addressing Hebrews and was using a figure of speech that could only mean one thing, the rock was God. Moses said in his closing message to Israel, "Their rock is not our rock; their God is not our God."

We can put the last two ideas together and come to an acceptable solution to this text. God is the Eternal Rock. Salvation rests only in Him. He is and must be the one foundation of the Christian church. Jesus is saying, "Upon this (God) I will build my church." Peter had just said that Christ was the Son of this Eternal Rock (God). The grammar is correct and the figure of speech is correct and violence is done to neither theory.

If Peter the man was to be the rock, he was made of soft sandstone, for he crumbles a few minutes later, and Jesus calls him "Satan" (16:23). He had taken Jesus aside and rebuked Him over something that Jesus had said. Peter was already suffering from a "big head," but Jesus quickly brings him down to earth by saying to him, "Get thee behind me Satan."

Peter's statement did advance man's concept of God—the Eternal Rock—one step nearer. Jesus had declared that to see Him was to know God. Peter is saying that he knows that this is so, for in answering the question, "But who do men say that the Son of man is?" and "Who do you say I am?" Peter declares that he has seen God in Him. "Thou are the Christ, the Son of the living God." To know Jesus is to know God, and to accept Jesus is to accept God: This is the meaning of what Peter is saying.

It has been suggested by some theologians that the Hebrew nation was God's first church—the "ecclesia." It had failed God, and now it was rejecting God's only Son, who was sent by the Father as the promised Messiah. God had furnished the Hebrew nation the Messiah in the form of His only Son.

Some theologians have thought that God attempted to establish His church—the "ecclesia"—on several occasions, and that the Hebrew attempt was only one such attempt, the first being the creation of Adam and Eve, who had failed God.

God followed this with an attempt to establish His church—the "eccelesia"—with Noah and his family. But Noah and his sons soon turned away from God after the flood. Jesus now is saying, "All past attempts to establish the church—the "ecclesia"—by family, by nations, or by marriage have failed. This is the final plan, and it will not fail. My church, My ecclesia, is to be made up of individuals of all nations, tribes, and families. These members of the church are to be those who will accept the fact that I am the only Son of the Heavenly Father, who, in accepting Me accept Him, and those who will commit themselves into His care and love." God had not failed to establish and maintain the "true ecclesia"; men have failed the church and in doing so, failed God, but the church cannot fail, for it rests upon the Eternal Rock—God. The church fails only when it leaves the security of THE ROCK. But when it does this, it cannot be the ecclesia.

Thought Projection No. 96: The Keys to the Kingdom (Matt. 16:19).

"And I will give unto thee the keys of the Kingdom of Heaven: and whatsoever thou shalt bind on earth shall be bound in heaven: and whatsoever thou shalt loose on earth shall be loosed in heaven. Then charged He his disciples that they should tell no man that he was Jesus the Christ." If God is the Eternal Rock, and if the true church—the ecclesia—is made up of only those who have heard the voice of God and responded to this voice in surrendering their lives to Him, and, thereby, have been the recipients of the regenerating work of the Holy Spirit, we should not have much trouble finding the answer to the question that is raised in verses 19 and 20. We only have to apply the laws governing thought projections and narrative parables.

"Key" is a symbol of authority in the Bible. It is still used today as such. We still speak of giving the "keys of the city" to certain famous visitors. We say that "such and such person is the 'key' to our solution." We often say of an invididual, "He is the key man." The key was a symbol of the order of scribes. It was used as an insignia of their office. The scribes were the interpreters of the moral law; they were the "Keys" to unlock these moral laws for the people. Jesus was speaking to people who understood the usage of this word.

The church, not Peter, was to be the key until Christ returned for His "ecclesia," His "bride," the church. This church would replace the scribes as the voice of interpretation of His life to the world. The church would present the eternal plan of salvation that Jesus brought down to earth. This plan would go out from the church to all men through the salvation offered by God. To those who would receive this message and respond to it, God would affirm the contract in Heaven. Jesus was saying in our language of today, "You are the church; present the contract of salvation to man; ask men to sign this contract, and when they do, it will be signed by Me in Heaven. It is binding upon Me. I will see that it is fulfilled and the gates of hell shall not prevail against it." This is a tremendous statement of victory for the Christian. If the Christian and the church attack Satan and the evil in this world, Satan and evil cannot withstand such an attack.

Too often, we wait for the attack upon the church by the world. We say we cannot be defeated. The attack never comes and the church dies of dry rot. The church is not to be a defensive institution but, rather, an offensive force! The church is an aggressive force against evil and sin at all times. The church cannot lose if it attacks the evil forces of this world, but the church cannot win unless it attacks. Victory comes for the church when it is in pursuit of the enemy, and not in being pursued by the evil forces in the world. The church is at war with evil and the war shall not end until Christ returns for His victorious bride!

Thought Projection No. 97: Peter is called Satan (Matt. 16:22-24).

"Then Peter took him and began to rebuke him, saying, Be it far from thee, Lord: this shall not be unto thee. But He turned and said unto Peter, Get thee behind me, Satan: thou art an offence unto me: for thou savourest not the things that be of God, but those that be of men." From verses sixteen to twenty-three, we see a man dropped from the gates of heaven down to the doors of hell. Peter had enjoyed the supreme spiritual revelation of the Holy Spirit in recognizing the true nature of Christ as being the True Son of the Eternal God. From this pinnacle of theological greatness, he is plunged into the depth of shame. The same Master who had praised Him a few moments before, now calls him the evil one—Satan. The same One who had raised him so high, now drops him flat on his theological face.

If Peter became the first pope of the early Christian church by the statement made by Jesus a few moments before, he was quickly dethroned from his high office and defrocked when Jesus said to him, "Get thee behind me Satan." And Jesus tells him why: "You are a hindrance to me; for you are not on the side of God, but of men."

Peter seemed to still be basking in the afterglow of his early experience of being singled out by Jesus for praise, and had, perhaps, let some of this "glow" flow into his mind, making him believe he had an extra portion of divine wisdom which overshadowed the wisdom of Jesus, for he began to correct a statement made by Jesus. Jesus had said that He must return to Jerusalem, suffer many things from the hands of the elders, scribes, and chief priests, and in the end, be put to death, but He would arise after the third day.

Upon hearing this, Peter took it upon himself to take Jesus aside and rebuke Him for saying these things. "Do not talk like that; stop acting so foolishly, and stop this nonsense about being killed and being resurrected after the third day." This was in substance what Peter said to Jesus. He had now reached a point in his relationship with Jesus that he felt that he could change and even improve on the plans of Christ.

Jesus turns and says to Peter, "Get thee behind me, Satan." Return to the place where you belong, in the rear. Peter was acting as Satan wanted him to act. Peter was now tuned to Satan's channel and was receiving him loud and clear. If this can happen to someone as close to Jesus as Peter was, it ought to serve as a warning to all Christians. It is only three verses from PETER THE ROCK to PETER THE SATAN, and it took Peter only a few minutes to make the descent.

Thought Projection No. 98: You must lose life to gain it (Matt. 16:24-28).

"Then Jesus said unto his disciples, If any man will come after me, let him deny himself, and take up his cross, and follow me. For whosoever will save his life shall lose it: and whosoever will lose his life for my sake shall find it." Jesus concludes this chapter with a paradox on life when He says the way for a person to gain a life is to lose a life. What is Jesus suggesting by this thought projection? Can a person have a life if he does not have life, or does one have to die in order that he might live?

Jesus had just said that if anyone wanted to be a disciple of His, he should demonstrate this fact by denying himself, and take up his cross and follow Him. If one would submit his own personality—lose himself in the personality of Jesus—he will discover the meaning of real life, the real person he is.

Millions live and die on this earth without really living at all. They are born, eat, breathe, reproduce themselves, and then die, but without learning the secret of what living really is. Jesus once asked what a person would give in exchange for his soul, and if one should gain the wealth of the world but still lose his soul, what has such a person gained? He has not really lived. The soul is the one thing that distinguishes a man from a beast of the field. This has to be developed if life is to have meaning.

Jesus is asking and answering His own question, "Is there something more to man than the physical side that lives only to satisfy the basic human drives and needs of the human body? Of course there is," says Jesus, "for the spiritual man is housed within the physical framework of the body." This is the real you that must be discovered and liberated from its physical prison. Man must regain his freedom from the slavery of the physical body. When the spiritual man is liberated, the physical body becomes the slave to the spirit; he is no longer the slave of the physical body. The unliberated man is subject to all the laws of life and death and imprisoned by them; whereas, the Christian is freed to live life at its best. Only Christ can free the spiritual man from his physical prison.

24

Matthew 17

Summary: Matthew 17 contains three THOUGHT PROJEC-
TIONS:
99. The Coming of Elias (Matt. 17:10:13) ALLEGORY.
100. Mustard seed faith (quality versus quantity) (Matt. 17:14-
20) SIMILE.
101. Who should pay taxes? (Matt. 17:24-27) METAPHOR.

This chapter opens with Jesus and three of His disciples retiring
to the top of a mountain for prayer and meditation. Jesus takes
with Him Peter, James, and John. Soon after they arrive at the
summit of the mountain, Jesus is transfigured before them, "And
He was transfigured before them, and His face shone like the sun
and His garments became white as light. And behold, there appeared
unto them, Moses and Elijah." A heavenly conversation is held
between Jesus and these two heavenly hosts.

Impulsive Peter breaks into this heavenly conversation and
makes a suggestion: "This experience justifies a memorial. Three tab-
ernacles (booths) should be built, one for each of the two heavenly
guests and one for Jesus." But before Peter can finalize his plans, a
cloud overshadows them and a voice speaks out of the cloud and
says, "This is my beloved Son, in whom I am well pleased; listen
to Him." This puts an end to Peter's construction plans for three
booths. He falls to the ground with the other two disciples and
remains silent until Jesus suggests they return to the other disciples
at the foot of the mountain. He warns them to tell no man of this
experience until after His own resurrection.

As they walk down the mountain, with the vivid experience of
seeing Moses and Elijah in person and hearing the voice of God
still fresh in their minds, they seem to be confronted with a disturbing question. They had seen Elijah (Elias) and they remembered
the words of Malachi 3:1 and 4:5. Malachi prophesied that Elijah

228

was to come and prepare the way for the Messiah. If this sudden appearance of Elijah on the Mount of Transfiguration is the fulfillment of this prophecy, Elijah is a little tardy in his appearance and derelict in his duties in preparing the world for the appearance of Jesus, for Jesus has been on earth now for thirty years.

They do not question that Jesus is this promised Messiah. This is not the point in question; the transfiguration experience has erased all doubt of this for the moment: They had seen Moses and Elijah (all three witnessed this), and all three had heard the voice of God speak saying that Jesus is His divine Son. But everything else is now completely out of focus as they look at these events through their theological glasses. This is the problem that prompts their question. This gives us our first thought projection in this chapter.

Thought Projection No. 99: The coming of Elias (Matt. 17:10-13).

"And the disciples asked him, 'Then why do the scribes say that first Elijah must come?' He replied, 'Elijah does come, and he is to restore all things; but I tell you that Elijah has already come, and they did not know him, but did to him whatever they pleased. So also the Son of man will suffer at their hands.' Then the disciples understood that he was speaking to them of John the Baptist." By this statement Jesus quickly restores their theological equilibrium and equanimity of mind. Jesus identifies the prophecy of Malachi with the person of John the Baptist, who was beheaded after preparing the way for Christ. John was but a figure of Elijah (Elias). He had come and prepared the way for Jesus by baptizing Jesus and by declaring that Jesus was the "Lamb of God which taketh away the sin of the world" (John 1:29). Having finished his mission, he left the stage of life to Jesus.

The OFFICE OF ELIJAH and not the PERSON OF ELIJAH is the point of this prophecy of Malachi. John did what Elijah was commissioned to do. He prepared the way among the people for the will of God to be carried out. The people, to whom Elijah was sent, rejected his message, but the message was given. The people did not heed the message of John the Baptist, but it was given just the same. The people to whom John was sent killed John, and Jesus said that He, neither, would be spared the fate of John.

Thought Projection No. 100: Mustard seed faith (quality versus quantity) (Matt. 17:14-26).

"Then Jesus answered and said, O faithless and perverse generation, how long shall I be with you? how long shall I suffer you? bring him hither to me . . . And Jesus said unto them, Because of your unbelief: for verily I say unto you, if ye have faith as a grain of mustard seed, ye shall say unto this mountain, Remove hence to yonder place; and it shall remove; and nothing shall be impossible unto you." As Jesus and his three disciples approach the crowd gathered at the foot of the mountain, a man detaches himself from the crowd and comes to Jesus. He is in great distress. He has brought his son who is an epileptic, who when seized, would often fall into the fire and water. The man kneels before Jesus, saying he has brought his son to the disciples, but they failed to do him any good. "Could and would He, Jesus, cure his son?"

Jesus cries out, looking not at the father of the afflicted boy, but toward his helpless disciples who failed in this ministry, "O faithless and perverse generation, how long am I to be with you? How long am I to bear with you? Bring him to me." Then Jesus cures him of his affliction.

The disciples of Jesus come to Him privately and ask why they failed to cure this young man. "Wherein have we failed? What did we lack?" They were honest in their effort to cure the man, but something was wrong. Jesus never did discredit or ignore an honest question, nor did He ever let one pass without an answer. No one has anything to fear from a doubt, if he will face up to it and carry it to God and seek an answer from Him.

Jesus replies to their question by saying, "Because of your little faith. For truly, I say to you, if you have faith as a mustard seed you will say to this mountain, 'Move hence to yonder place,' and it will move; and nothing will be impossible to you." Much is lost in the translation of this Scripture. Most of the translators give emphasis to the quantity of faith. This is not the point of emphasis. Each of these disciples had much faith. This was, perhaps, their basic problem. They approached this sick young man with the attitude, "Stand back, crowd, so you can get a better look at the miracle we are about to perform." No doubt, they had left their room with faith running out of the pores of their skin and were alert to the first opportunity to demonstrate it to the world. Here was an opportunity to demonstrate their faith.

Jesus finds at the foot of the mountain an embarrassed and subdued group of disciples. They had failed miserably and completely in their mission. They knew this; the crowd and the father of the sick boy knew it. Their failure would not go unnoticed by the enemies of Jesus, and it would be held against Him, not them. But why this failure? This is the question Jesus is attempting to answer for them. It cannot be found in translating the adjective "little" as one of quantity. They had faith—lots of it; but the wrong kind. It took quality.

The mustard seed used by Jesus as a simile here was not chosen because of its size (smallness), but because of its nature. Even the smallest of seeds have the power of life and growth, for within their smallness is the nature of life. When the mustard seed allows its nature to respond to the warmth of its creator's sun rays, it finds life that conforms to the purpose for which God has created it. Its secret is found in living within the sphere of the creator's purpose for its life. It is a matter of quality and not quantity.

The difference between a pound of coal and a pound of diamonds is not quantity but quality. Both are made of carbon, but the nature and state of the carbon determines the value of each. One is used as cheap fuel and the other is treasured because of its beauty and great value.

The power of faith in the life of a Christian is not found in "how much" he has, but in the nature of that faith. The Christian's faith must be of the same nature as the faith found in the life of Christ. Jesus lived within the will of the Father and sought to honor the Father in everything He did. Satan tried to get Jesus to misuse his faith in God when he tempted Him to turn stones into bread and feed himself after His forty-day fast. Jesus refused to do this for it would not have honored God but Satan.

A faith lived within the will of Christ will keep the Christian from using this faith for the glory of self or for the fulfillment of selfish desires. This kind of faith is a sacred trust, and we will safeguard it from misuse by ourselves. We will not use it foolishly. We will be like the owner of a well-trained dog that loves his master dearly. The owner of the dog says, "I must be careful of the command I give my dog, for he will obey all of my commands." We should strive not to increase the amount (quantity) of our daily faith, but the nature (quality) of our faith. It is the quality of faith that gives us the power and not the quantity. "Lord increase the quality of our faith." This ought to be our daily prayer.

Thought Projection No. 101: Who should pay taxes? (Matt. 17:24-27).

"And when they were come to Capernaum, they that received tribute money came to Peter, and said, Doth not your master pay tribute? He saith, Yes. And when he was come into the house, Jesus prevented him, saying, What thinkest thou, Simon? of whom do the kings of the earth take custom or tribute? of their own children, or of strangers? Peter saith unto him, Of strangers. Jesus saith unto him, Then are the children free. Notwithstanding, lest we should offend them, go thou to the sea, and cast an hook, and take up the fish that first cometh up; and when thou hast opened his mouth, thou shalt find a piece of money: that take, and give unto them for me and thee." When the disciples and Jesus enter Capernaum, Peter is approached by a tax collector and asked if Jesus, his Master, pays taxes. When this question is relayed to Jesus by Peter, Jesus instructs Peter to go fishing. Peter takes Jesus at His word and goes fishing to catch only one fish, the one with the required tax money lodged within its mouth. This money is used to pay the tax.

What was the nature of this tax? Some scholars suggest that it was a temple tax—a religious tax—placed upon the Jewish people beyond the tithe. Others say that it was a civil tax of the Romans. Its nature is of little importance to the thought projection Jesus is presenting. This is found in verses twenty-five and twenty-six. "What do you think, Simon? From whom do kings of the earth take toll or tribute? From their sons or from others?" And when he said, "From others," Jesus said to him, "Then the sons are free. However, not to give offense" go fishing for the money and pay this tax.

Should the Christian pay taxes to support a government that might be non-Christian in nature, or should he pay civil taxes at all? Jesus uses this thought projection to give us an answer to both questions. The Christian is both a citizen of the world and of heaven. He has obligations to both kingdoms. He is to fulfill responsibilities to his civil government and to God. Taxes must be paid but the tithe also must be returned to God. Paying one does not excuse a Christian from the obligation he has regarding the other.

Jesus said that He could claim for himself and for His disciples an exemption from the tax, but not to give offense (create problems for Himself and for His disciples), it would be better to pay the tax. The king of this thought projection is the king of a country. His subjects are his children, and the strangers are those who trade with his country, or men he has conquered. The king levies a tax, not upon his own children (subjects) but upon others.

25

Matthew 18

Summary: Matthew 18 contains nine THOUGHT PROJEC-
TIONS:
102. Entrance into the Kingdom (Matt. 18:2,3) SIMILE.
103. Greatest in the Kingdom (Matt. 18:4) SIMILE.
104. Stumbling blocks to children (Matt. 18:5,6) METAPHOR.
105. Cut off hand, foot (Matt. 18:7,8) METAPHOR.
106. Angels and children (Matt. 18:10,11) METAPHOR.
107. The lost sheep and the 99 (Matt. 18:12-14) METAPHOR;
NARRATIVE.
108. Loosing and binding (Matt. 18:18) METAPHOR.
109. Seventy times seven is not 490 (Matt. 18:21,22) META-
PHOR.
110. The king and the unjust servant (Matt. 18:23-35) SIMILE,
NARRATIVE.

Chapter 18 opens with a question by the disciples addressed to
Jesus. They ask, "Who is the greatest in the Kingdom of God?" It
concludes with the story of the servant who sought and received forgiveness of a debt he could not pay his master, but who would not
forgive a small debt owed to him by a fellow servant. This question
triggers nine thought projections by Jesus dealing with the entrance
requirements into the Kingdom, marks of greatness, stumbling
blocks to children, removing hindrance into the Kingdom, angels, a
shepherd's heart, loosing and binding, the liberal heart of the Christian, and why we should forgive others.

We do not know what prompted this question by the disciples
that set off this chain reaction of thought projections. Perhaps, Jesus
had been observing certain attitudes building up in the minds of His
disciples, and this question opened the door for Him to say some
things the disciples needed to know.

Thought Projection No. 102: Entrance into the Kingdom (Matt. 18:2,3).

"Truly, I say to you, unless you turn and become like children, you will not enter the Kingdom of Heaven." Their question was not, "How to enter into the Kingdom, but who was to be the greatest, to hold the highest position in the Kingdom?" Jesus is saying, "You are concerned about rank in the Kingdom; whereas, you ought to be concerned about how people get into the Kingdom." "Being in God's Kingdom is more important than the rank one might hold in it." Jesus is placing the emphasis where it belongs.

Jesus sent His disciples out one day, two by two, to preach the message of salvation to the lost. They came back later, rejoicing that they had been able to command evil spirits and to work miracles. Jesus stops them in their tracks by saying, "You are quite happy with the power you have had over the forces of evil, and in your power to work miracles, but you should be rejoicing not in these things, but in the fact that your names are written in the book of life." Again, Jesus is placing the Christian emphasis where it belongs. Conversion is the most important thing that can happen to any man, for without conversion, man is nothing, but after conversion he takes the position in God's Kingdom as a son of God.

Jesus then gives them an example on how they will come into the Kingdom, and how they are to lead men into the Kingdom of God. He calls a little child to him and gathers him in His arms, saying, in substance, "Did you notice how this child responded to My invitation to come to Me? Perhaps, this child had never seen Me before I called him to Me. He had heard his parents talk about Me and was eager to see Me, but we were strangers until today."

"What marked the action of this child?" continues Jesus. "Learn this and you will know how one is supposed to enter My Kingdom." Jesus could have said, "A child is teachable, humble (natural), possesses simplicity of action, is trusting and unspoiled by the world. The attitude of a child is, 'I will trust you until you teach me not to do so, and I will commit myself to you until you make me fear you.'" This is what Jesus is trying to say to His disciples. This is the way anyone must approach Christ for salvation—in the simplicity of faith.

Thought Projection No. 103: Greatest in the kingdom (Matt. 18:4).

Jesus now turns to the question asked, "Who is the greatest in the Kingdom of Heaven?" His reply is, "Whoever humbles himself like this child, he is the greatest in the Kingdom of Heaven." The word "humble" carries with it more than the idea of a meek person, or the submission of one's will to another (servant and master relationship). The word suggests more the spirit of knowledge-ableness of a child. The normal and unspoiled child is "all eyes and ears," searching for knowledge of the things around it. It does not put a question mark around something new and say, "I must certify it before believing it," but accepts it for what it appears to be to him.

When one becomes satisfied with his knowledge of Christ, God, and the things of the Kingdom, he begins to die spiritually and intellectually. The healthy child will grow in all areas of his life. This is normal for a child; if this all-around growth is absent, we have an abnormal child. Jesus is saying that to become great in His Kingdom, grow as the child grows, and the secret of that growth is in its spirit of humbleness. Humbleness produces greatness in God's Kingdom, for it allows God's grace to develop the Christlike spirit in those who are humble, and who are submissive to the will of God. The mark of greatness is found in Christian likeness to the Master Himself.

Thought Projection No. 104: Stumbling blocks to children (Matt. 18:5,6).

"Whoever receives one such child in my name receives Me; but whoever causes one of these little ones, who believe in Me to sin; it would be better for him to have a great millstone fastened around his neck and to be drowned in the depth of the sea." Jesus is saying that it is a serious matter to stand in the way of a child trying to come to Him, and it is a serious matter also to cause him to sin after the child has come to Jesus. Both of these ideas are found within the context of this Scripture.

Jesus deals with the way to enter into His Kingdom by using a child's simple faith and trust in coming to Him as an example of how men must come to Him. He turns His attention now to those persons who would block children from coming to Him. It is a serious matter to keep a child away from Chirst. The figure of speech Jesus uses here suggests that death to a parent is preferable—if a choice must be made—to that parent's blocking a child's salvation. The parent is charged with the responsibility of bringing the child to Christ. It would be better for the parent to err on the side of right than on the side of wrong; to encourage the child to make an early decision for Christ than to delay this.

This warning includes the danger of adults' causing young Christians (children) to sin. This is often done by example more than by direct leadership into sin. The warning is not limited just to children, however, for every newly born Christian is called by Paul a "Babe in Christ," and he says all are in need of proper food and shelter. This must come from adult Christians.

Years ago, this writer heard a man, who had been a member of his church for many years, stand up and discourage a young Christian who had offered his skills as a carpenter to his church in his off time. The older church member said to this new Christian, "When I was a new Christian, I did the same thing, but I have learned better, and I do not do this any more." He then turned to the group of men in the room and said, "He will also learn the same thing." The man who had tried to put a stumbling block in the way of this young Christian's growth was found dead a few days later in his yard in a hole he had been digging. When this writer gazed at his dead body lying in that hole, he thought of this text.

Thought Projection No. 105: Cut off hand, foot (Matt. 18:7,8).

"Wherefore if thy hand or thy foot offend thee, cut them off, and cast them from thee: it is better for thee to enter into life halt or maimed, rather than having two hands or two feet to be cast into everlasting fire." These are harsh and unacceptable statements of Jesus to people in the world who do not know what is offered in Jesus. Jesus is not trying to create the impression that these things are the conditions one must meet to become a Christian. He is saying that if such a choice faced man, it would be better for man to enter life maimed or lame, better to enter life with one eye than face the alternative—eternal hell!

The non-Christian cannot within his own strength gain victory over the flesh in many areas. When the Holy Spirit comes into the life at conversion, this is the strength he needs to gain mastery over the weakness of the body. It would not help the non-Christian to cut off his hand, if by so doing, he thought this would bring him salvation. Jesus is saying that the one who sincerely wants to be saved would be willing to do this or anything to have the gift of eternal life.

If heaven is a place of perfection, and we believe that it is, there are no blind saints, no armless or feetless children of God. In the light of these facts, the choice is not an impossible one, for even if it took such sacrifice to become a Christian, our limitations would be confined only to this earthly life. The burden of these Scriptures is not this, however, but on the comparison of spiritual values with the values of the world. Any kind of life here on earth is worthwhile if man is assured of the abundant life of eternity, but nothing the world might offer is worth the loss of heaven!

Thought Projection No. 106: Angels and children (Matt. 18:10,11).

"Take heed that ye despise not one of these little ones; for I say unto you, That in heaven their angels do always behold the face of my Father which is in heaven. For the Son of man is come to save that which was lost." The attention of Jesus is again focused on the children in His audience. We wonder what caught His attention again? Perhaps another child came to him, or others began to cling to him, as children will do to those they love. He speaks to the crowd and His disciples, saying, "See that you do not despise one of these little ones; for I tell you that in heaven their angels always behold the face of My Father who is in heaven." Angels of children beholding the face of God the Heavenly Father!

Much is said about the function of angels in the Bible, and yet so little is said about the work of angels in our Christian world today. We have neglected our angels. The writer of the Hebrew letter says, "Are they [angels] not all ministering spirits sent forth to serve, for the sake of those who are to obtain salvation?" (Hebrews 1:14). "Even so, I tell you, there is joy before the angels of God over one sinner who repents." "The angel of the Lord encamps around those who fear Him, and delivers them" [the angels deliver them] (Psalm 34:7). "For He will give His angels charge of you, to guard you in all your ways" (Psalm 91:11). "On their hands they will bear you up lest you dash your foot against a stone."

Jesus says that an angel is assigned to each child, and this angel sits gazing on the face of God. "Beholding the king's face" in the parlance of the Far East means to be admitted into the king's immediate presence, to enjoy his special favor and confidence. Thus the angel knows the Father's wishes for each of these children, and it matters not if they are "little children," or later, "new babes in Christ." Could this also mean that God's angels guard the children before they reach the ages of personal accountability? We believe it does.

"See that ye despise not one of these little ones." If God thinks enough of them to assign an angel to guard them, you ought to likewise place great value upon them. This reminds us of the attitude of the English during the bombing of their cities during World War II. They sent the children to rural areas, and some even to America. They said, "The children must be saved; the British Empire rests in their hands." Adults might smile when a child chooses to accept Christ, and we might rejoice when an adult makes the same decision. We believe that in heaven there is greater joy over the conversion of a child, for a child has a life he can give to God; whereas, the adult can only give God half a life, or a part of life.

Thought Projection No. 107: The lost sheep and the 99 (Matt. 18:12-14).

"How think ye? if a man have an hundred sheep, and one of them be gone astray, doth he not leave the ninety and nine, and goeth into the mountains, and seeketh that which is gone astray? And if so be that he find it, verily I say unto you, he rejoiceth more of that sheep, than of the ninety and nine which went not astray. Even so . . ." Jesus shocked His hearers with the demands He made for entrance into the Kingdom of God when he said that they might have to cut off hand or foot, or pluck out an eye. He warned them against being stumbling blocks to little children seeking Him, saying it would be better for anyone doing this to perish by drowning in the sea with a great stone tied around his neck. What kind of God was this to make such demands? He suddenly shifts the focus from a person seeking God, to God himself. He seems to want to erase any false idea of God from their minds which they might have misconstrued from the emphasis He had made in bringing into focus the importance of their decision to follow Him. Christ was not trying to frighten them into the Kingdom of Heaven, but He wanted them to be realistic when they examined the alternatives.

Jesus paints a word picture of a shepherd who has brought his sheep into the sheepfold at the close of the day: He counts each sheep as it passes into the safety of the pen. When he finishes counting, he discovers that one of the sheep is missing. He closes the door to the pen and goes out into the night, searching until He finds the one lost sheep. The love of the shepherd's heart has sent the shepherd out to seek and to find the one sheep.

Jesus could have pointed out to the people that the shepherd, when he finds the sheep, does not scold it, beat it, nor punish it in any form. He picks it up tenderly, puts it on his shoulders, and walks over the rugged hillside, protecting it from the dangers of the night, not stopping until he replaces it in the flock. He is happy because the one lost sheep was safely back with the other sheep. This was the thing that really counted!

Jesus could have pointed out to the crowd that just as the shepherd does not play percentage with his sheep, neither does God. The shepherd could have said, "I have ninety and nine sheep safely tucked away for the night—only one percent lost; why worry about that small percentage point!" The one percent sent the shepherd back into the night to find the one lost sheep, and he did not sleep until He had found it and returned it to the flock. God the Father is the Good Shepherd with a shepherd's heart. He loves His sheep—all the sheep—and He has sent Jesus to seek and to save those lost sheep. This is the message of this parable. The sheep have nothing to fear from this kind of a shepherd.

Thought Projection No. 108: Loosing and binding (Matt. 18:18).

"Verily I say unto you, Whatsoever ye shall bind on earth shall be bound in heaven: and whatsoever ye shall loose on earth shall be loosed in heaven." Once again, we have pointed out to us the importance of the church, "the called-out-ones-of-God." In this thought projection, Jesus discusses the question of right relationship between the brethren. He says that if a brother sins against another brother, let the brother against whom the sin is committed go at once and tell his brother of the wrong. If the wrongdoer refuses to listen, the sinned-against is to take two witnesses with him and return to the brother, trying again to make the matter right. If the wrongdoer still refuses to listen, then the other brother is to take the matter to the church. If he refuses to listen to the church, that brother is to be treated by all "as a Gentile [nonbrother] and a tax collector [to be avoided]." Jesus then gives us this thought projection, "Truly, I say to you, whatever you bind on earth shall be bound in heaven, and whatever you loose on earth will be loosed in heaven."

God will abide by the church in such matters, said Jesus. The church does have the power of excommunication. Christ gives the order for such action. He gives the church its authority. He gives the church a plan of action. It starts with a man-to-man contact. If this fails, a committee waits on the offending brother, and if this fails, it is carried directly to the church. If the man refuses to listen to the action and to the decision of the church, he is to be excommunicated by the church and to be treated by all as an outcast.

If a person is a Christian, such treatment would break his heart, and he would seek to become reconciled with his offended brother and the church. If that brother has never been born again but had got into the church without a changed nature, he will be quite happy to remain outside of its fellowship. God will base His own actions toward that brother by the decision made by the church. The comfort and security offered by the Holy Spirit will be lost to him as well as the stimulation he had received from the friendships in the church. These things will help bring the offending brother to repentance, to the fellowship of the church.

Thought Projection No. 109: Seventy times seven is not 490 (Matt. 18:21,22).

"Then Peter came up to him, and said to him, 'Lord, how oft shall my brother sin against me, and I forgive him? As many as seven times?' Jesus said to him, 'I do not say to you seven times, but seventy times seven.'" Peter was being very generous by suggesting that the Christian ought to forgive another seven times seven (49); the law only required four times. We feel that Peter was expecting a word of commendation from Jesus for his generous attitude. He was willing to go the seventh mile instead of the legally required four miles of forgiveness: Instead of words of commendation, Jesus removes some wind out of his theological balloon by saying, "Forgive not seven times seven, but seventy times seven. Take the bottom out of your basket of forgiveness, so that it can never be full." There is no limit to the Christian's spirit of forgiveness. Jesus demonstrated the greatness of his own spirit of forgiveness when He was dying on the cross of Calvary, as He cried out to God the Father, "Forgive them, for they know not what they do." The Christian is to live a life of forgiveness, because his life is one that came to him from God's heart of forgiveness.

Thought Projection No. 110: The king and the unjust servant (Matt. 18:23-35).

"So also My Heavenly Father will do to everyone of you, if you do not forgive your brother from your heart." To give emphasis to what He was saying, Jesus tells a story about a man who was in great debt to his king. He owed an enormous debt, one that he could never pay. When the king decided to call in this debt and demand payment, the servant pleaded for mercy, saying he could not pay it then, but if the king would be patient he would pay it in the future. He pleaded with the king not to sell his wife and children to satisfy this debt. Out of compassion for the servant, the king agreed.

Later, this same servant faced a fellow servant who owed him a small debt. He demanded payment of this small debt from the fellow servant; he took him by the throat and tried to force payment. When this failed, he had the servant thrown into prison for his small debt. Other fellow servants reported this matter to the king, who in turn called this unmerciful servant before him again and had him punished for his failure to pay his own debt, saying, "You wicked servant! I forgave you all that debt because you besought me; and should not you have had mercy on your fellow servant, as I had mercy on you?"

Jesus then gives us the key to God's treatment of those who come to Him for forgiveness: "So also My Heavenly Father will do to every one of you, if you do not forgive your brother from your heart." You must remember, Peter's question was, "How often should I forgive my brother who sins against me?" and that this question followed the method Jesus suggested in treating a church brother who had sinned against a fellow member. Broken fellowship is a serious matter with God. Jesus said that the world would judge our Christianity by how we love the brethren. God would treat us in the same manner we treat our brethren. If we live with each other in the spirit of forgiveness, we will also live in the spirit of forgiveness with God.

26

Matthew 19

Summary: Matthew 19 contains five THOUGHT PROJEC-TIONS:

111. Two become one (Matt. 19:5,6) METAPHOR.

112. To marry or not to marry; to divorce or not to divorce (Matt. 19:10-12) METAPHOR.

113. The Kingdom belongs to children (Matt. 19:13-15) METAPHOR.

114. A Camel and the eye of a needle (Matt. 19:23-27) META-PHOR.

115. The last shall be first (Matt. 19:30) METAPHOR.

Jesus crosses over the Jordan into the region of Judea, where he heals many people. The Pharisees will not let Him alone and follow Him, hoping to find something in what He said or did that might be used against Him to discredit Him in the eyes of the people. They agreed that He must go at any cost. It is the Pharisees who now take the ball to carry in this game against Him—a deadly game that can have only one end, His death. Thus begins chapter 19 of Matthew.

Thought Projection No. 111: Two become one (Matt. 19:5,6).

". . . For this cause shall a man leave father and mother, and shall cleave to his wife: and they twain shall be one flesh. Wherefore they are no more twain, but one flesh. What therefore God hath joined together, let not man put asunder." We find hidden in this discourse of Jesus on marriage and divorce a small thought projection that can be easily overlooked in the glaring light of the larger subject the Pharisees had thrust upon Jesus. It is found in these words, "For this reason, a man shall leave his father and mother and be joined to his wife, and the two shall become one. SO THEY ARE NO LONGER TWO BUT ONE."

244

When and how does this unity take place? How can two people become one? On another occasion Jesus said of Himself and God, "If you have seen Me you have seen the Father . . . I am in the Father and the Father is in Me [We are One]" (John 14:9-10). We know that husband and wife will not merge into a physical "one" while they stand at the marriage altar. We know that Jesus and God have two separate personalities. There must be another answer to the problem of the "physical oneness" suggested by this text.

"For this cause," goes back to the words preceeding the statement, "from the beginning, God made them male and female." The sex difference between male and female is the cause of unity in marriage. There would be no marriage in the human race if it were not for the God-implanted sex drives in the male and female. This is the "marriage drive" that leads into unity of marriage. This is not to suggest "raw sex" as the "marriage drive." "Raw sex" should be labeled "physical passion." There is nothing evil about the marriage drive. The emotion called "Love" must have this drive as an active ingredient mixed with common interests and other factors to produce real love. You can have raw passion without love, but you cannot have pure love without passion.

God protected the male and female sex instincts in the human race by a set of moral laws which include marriage. It is this protection that brings two persons together in marriage, and unity is completed in the marriage act of sex. It is more than a unity of ideals, ideas, and common interests. Jesus is dealing here with the sex problem of the human race. The problem would not be a problem if proper marriage relationships were always healthy and normal. It is God's way to give supreme joy of unity and also to protect the reproduction of the human race. There is nothing evil in this sex relationship, and it only becomes evil when it is misused out of marriage or abused in marriage.

Thought Projection No. 112: To marry or not to marry; to divorce or not to divorce (Matt. 19:10-12).

"Is it lawful to divorce one's wife for any cause?" The Pharisees ask Jesus this question. Twenty years before the birth of Christ, Hillel, a great teacher of Israel, died. He left an interpretation of Deuteronomy 24:1 which reads like this: "A man may lawfully divorce his wife for any reason that might render her distasteful to him." He based this interpretation on the possibility that at the time of marriage, the wife had some blemish that made her unsuited for marriage; thus, the husband could give her a bill of divorcement and return her to her father. Jesus is being asked his opinion of this interpretation of Hillel.

The School of Shammai held the opposite view on the question. Divorce was to be granted only on the grounds of unchastity by the wife. If Jesus agreed with the interpretation of Hillel, He would offend those who did not support Hillel's liberal view on divorce; if he agreed with Shammai's interpretation on marriage and divorce, He would create disfavor among the liberal faction. The Pharisees knew they had Jesus boxed in on all theological sides. No answer he could give would satisfy the crowd before Him.

Both teachers, Hillel and Shammai, had appealed to Moses as the source of their authority; however, each had drawn an opposite opinion from the law of Moses regarding this subject. Jesus went to a higher authority than the law of Moses for His reply. Jesus went beyond their interpretations of the law of Moses to God Himself— the One Who gave Moses the original law. "Have you not read that He Who made them from the beginning made them male and female?" Jesus questions. "For this reason son of man shall leave his father and his mother and be joined to his wife, and the two shall become one. So they are no longer two but one. What therefore God has joined together, let no man put asunder."

Jesus approved of Shammai's interpretation of the law of Moses regarding divorce; i.e., unchastity being the only ground for a divorce. Elsewhere, Jesus deals with the sin problem involved in divorce, and with who has the authority to remarry, and who should not remarry lest he live in sin.

Later, the disciples of Jesus say to Him, "This is a hard saying." They are admitting they held to Hillel's interpretation of the divorce law of Moses. Jesus agreed with them that it was a hard saying, and that all men could not nor would not live up to it; yet this was not to justify man's breaking the original law of God on this subject. Marriage is to be broken only by death.

Jesus then projects a thought for them to consider to further illustrate the seriousness of this question of divorce. He says that some men are eunuchs from birth. They are born impotent and lack the capacity for the sex act of marriage. Other men are made into eunuchs by the acts of men, and others make a choice to become eunuchs to serve God.

Eunuchs were used by the Romans as guards for their wives. The word "eunuch" means "a guardian of the chambers." Men who were born as eunuchs were chosen for this duty by their masters, or slaves were made into eunuchs for the same purpose. Some men felt that a wife and family would be a hindrance in serving God, so rather than live under constant sex temptation, they allowed themselves to become eunuchs.

Jesus concluded that this was a difficult choice for any man to make, but that no one was required to make the choice to become a eunuch to serve God. If one could not serve God without yielding to his sex drives out of marriage, then it would be the choice to make. Jesus was not suggesting that if one became a eunuch for the Kingdom's sake, that he would have "special favors with God." No special honor would be given to either class. The choice to be or not to be a eunuch was to be made in the light of each man's limitations and his desire to serve in the Kingdom of God.

All men do not have to marry, but if one chooses to marry, he must face the limitations the choice of a wife places on himself. The woman should also face carefully the responsibility of her choice of marriage, for God only recognizes one cause for divorce—unchastity.

Thought Projection No. 113: The Kingdom belongs to children (Matt. 19:13-15).

"Then there were brought unto him little children, that he should put his hands on them, and pray: and the disciples rebuked them. But Jesus said, Suffer little children, and forbid them not, to come unto me: for of such is the Kingdom of Heaven. And he laid His hands on them, and departed thence." We already noted in chapter eighteen Christ's attitude toward little children. Parents brought their children to Jesus, and asked Him to lay His hands upon them and to bless them. The disciples, thinking that these children and their parents were disturbing the Master and, wanting to protect Him, suggest to Jesus that He give them permission to send them away. Jesus says, "Let them come to Me." Then He gives us another thought projection concerning children: "Do not stop them (do not hinder them in their attempts to come to Me); for to such belongs the Kingdom of God."

Jesus is not here projecting a theological thesis on the plan of salvation for children or for adults. He is making a general observation and statement. Children loved him and were not afraid of Him. Children have this same attitude of trust and confidence toward all people until someone destroys this attitude in them. Jesus is simply saying, "My kingdom shall be made of people possessing this kind of attitude, confidence, and trust in Me and toward My Heavenly Father. This pure, unrestrained confidence and faith you see in the hearts of these children is the mark of the members (children) of my Kingdom."

In our present age, where theology attempts to dethrone God and bring Him down to the level of sinful man, we need to recapture this childlike characteristic of the children of the Kingdom as suggested here by Jesus. "What do we think of Jesus?" should find its answering echo in the attitude of the child of God: "For to such belongs the Kingdom of God."

Thought Projection No. 114: A camel and the eye of a needle (Matt. 19:23-27).

"Truly, I say to you, it will be hard for a rich man to enter the Kingdom of Heaven. Again I tell you, it is easier for a camel to go through the eye of a needle than for a rich man to enter the Kingdom of God." This thought projection cannot be taken out of its context. A rich young man approached Jesus (16-23) and asked Him the secret of eternal life. He wanted to gain possession of this kind of life. Hidden beneath this request was an even greater desire. This is seen in the answer given to him by Jesus. He wanted to understand this "eternal life," its fullness and completeness, for he felt that something was missing from his own life. His wealth had failed to bring him what was being offered to men by Jesus. "What lack I yet?" is the young man's question. Jesus replies, "If you would be perfect . . ."—this is what the young man wanted—the perfect life— the life that satisfied.

Jesus states the terms for the complete life: "Go, sell what you possess and give to the poor, and you will have treasure in heaven; and come, follow Me." Upon hearing these terms, the young man leaves in an attitude of great sorrow. He knew what he wanted, but he was not willing to pay the price to get it.

Jesus turns to His disciples and gives us this thought projection: "Truly, I say to you, it will be hard for a rich man to enter the Kingdom of Heaven. Again I tell you, it is easier for a camel to go through the eye of a needle than for a rich man to enter the Kingdom of God." This stuns the disciples.

The old theology of the disciples taught them that wealth was a sign of God's approval and blessing. They had been fed on a theological diet that taught that men became rich because God's favor was upon them, and others became poor because God's favor had been withdrawn from them. "If the wealthy are not in God's grace, and if God does not favor the rich, then who is favored? If the rich cannot be saved, who can be saved?" This idea was a shocker for them.

Many attempts have been made by theologians and scholars of the Bible to explain this simple thought projection. Some have suggested that the "needle's eye" was the gate in the wall of Jerusalem through which passed only the people. It was made large enough for only a man to pass through. Animals and carts had to use the larger gates. Now if a camel would get on his knees it might be able to pass through the gate (needle's eye), suggesting that a spirit of humbleness on the part of man would get him into the Kingdom of God. The rich would not do this; or it was harder for them to do this than the poor. Thus, it was hard for a rich man to be saved. This seems an acceptable theory. However, there are too many improbables for this theory to be accepted as the thought Jesus is trying to present.

It has been suggested that a camel could be passed through the eye of a needle by reducing the camel to a liquid and then pouring this liquid through the eye of a needle. Such a theory does violence to all the principles respected by Jesus in the use of parables and thought projections. The people to whom He was speaking would not have understood such an application.

The key to this thought projection is found in the words, "With men this is impossible, but with God all things are possible." This statement by Jesus follows the question, "Who then can be saved?" The question is not how to put a camel through the eye of a needle, but how to be saved. Jesus is saying that salvation *by* man is as impossible as trying to put a full-grown healthy camel through the eye of a sewing needle.

Only God saves. Man cannot save himself. The rich young ruler was not willing to give up that which stood between himself and God. To this young man, the barrier was his money and all that it could buy for him. He would be willing to spend a part of his money for salvation, but not give it all away and stand before God with nothing. To another person, it might not be money, but pride, ambition, an unwillingness to give up certain sins, and so on. Jesus says the young man is not willing to "come and follow Me."

"What must I do to have eternal life?" Turn loose that which is holding you back, says Jesus to all men. Repentance is the turning away from that which is standing between you and Christ, and then walking toward Him. Jesus can save only those who come to Him.

Thought Projection No. 115: The last shall be first (Matt. 19:30).

"But many that are first will be last, and the last first." This is the conclusion Jesus makes after the disciples had asked Him about their reward for following Him. He says to them that they will be rulers in His Kingdom and will sit on thrones with Him in the latter day to judge Israel. He then gives this reverse order of things, "But many that are first will be last and the last first." This statement is used by Jesus several times. It suggests that God's evaluation of values is not man's, nor man's God's. Jesus came to His own first, and when they rejected Him, the Gentiles replaced Israel in God's plan. The Gentile world will be moved from last place in God's program to first place.

27

Matthew 20

Summary: Matthew 20 contains three THOUGHT PROJEC-
TIONS:
116. Laborers and the vineyard (Matt. 20:1-16) SIMILE; NAR-
RATIVE.
117. Drinking from the cup of Jesus (Matt. 20:20-23) ALLE-
GORY.
118. To be great, one must be small (Matt. 20:24-28) META-
PHOR.

Chapters 19 and 20 should have no break between them. Jesus
has been speaking to His disciples about the cost of following Him,
the reward of doing this, and concludes this by saying, "But many
that are first will be last and the last first." The first word in chapter
twenty is "for": "For the Kingdom of Heaven is like unto . . ." The
thought is continued from the nineteenth chapter. The subject is
the same: the cost and reward of following Jesus. Three thought
projections are found in this twentieth chapter, and each has to do
with the relationship of the Christian to Christ, and to the Kingdom of God.

Thought Projection No. 116: Laborers and the vineyard (Matt.
20:1-16).

Jesus tells the story of an owner of a vineyard. The crop of grapes
is ready to harvest, and unless they are picked at once they will be
lost. The owner of this vineyard goes out into the labor market to
secure men to pick the grapes. He finds a few men and hires them
to work twelve hours for a penny. Later he returns to the market place
to find more men; he hires all he finds and sends them into the
same vineyard to work for nine hours. He hires more workers three
hours later and sends them into his vineyard, and even one hour
before the day is over, he hires still other men. At the end of the

day, the owner calls all the men in to receive their wage for the day. He gives each man a penny, the amount he promised for a day's labor. The men who worked twelve hours grumbled because they received the same pay as the men who workd only one hour.

The question Jesus is raising in this story is, "Did the owner do right or wrong by his men? Did he underpay or overpay the men?" It seemed that the men who worked twelve hours were underpaid, while the men who worked only one hour were overpaid (they were quite happy about this). What was Jesus trying to teach by this story? The answer can be found when we relate this story to the question of Peter in chapter nineteen, "Then Peter said in reply: 'Lo, we have left everything and followed you, what then shall we have.'" Peter is saying, "Since we have served You longer than others, ought we not receive more for our service to You?"

The owner in this thought projection defends himself with this explanation: "I have kept my contract with you (the men who had worked twelve hours), and I have paid you the wages we agreed upon before you entered my vineyard. What have you against me if I have kept my word; you have received what was promised you, have you not? Can I not be a generous man if I choose? This is my land, my grapes, and my money. If I choose to pay the same wage to all the men who worked today, regardless of the number of hours each worked, this is my business. You have no complaint if you receive that which was promised you."

Jesus concludes this story with the words, "So the last shall be first, and the first shall be last: for many be called, but few chosen" (Matt. 20:16). These words are almost the exact ones of verse thirty of chapter nineteen, "But many that are first will be last; and the last first." To get the full meaning of this narrative, we need to look carefully at the entire story. Several salient points should not be overlooked:

1. The men hired to work in the vineyard were not working at the time the owner approached them to go into his vineyard. They were idle and waiting for someone to hire them.

2. They agreed on the wage and hours they would work before entering the field. A contract was made between the owner and workmen. This contract was kept by the owner and the workers.

3. The owner of the vineyard returned to the labor market for more workers later. He found idle men each time wanting work to do. He made a contract with each group and kept the contract. He

agreed to pay each new group what he considered right. The penny offered those who worked twelve hours was agreeable to those men; the others supposed their wage would be in ratio to this figure and the hours worked.

4. The owner asked each group before hiring them, "Why are you idle? Are you free to work for me, and do you want to work?" Each replied, "We want to work, but no one will hire us."

5. At the end of the day, each group received the pay agreed upon by both parties; the first group received one penny as per agreement, and the others received the pay that the owner thought to be right (this was their contract). Now if the owner thought the men who worked only one hour were worth the same money as the one who worked twelve hours, he owed them the penny wage. They had agreed to accept the owner's evaluation of their time.

6. The only complaint made against the landowner came from the group who was hired to work twelve hours for a penny. The others were satisfied, for their silence said their wage was acceptable to them.

The last words of Jesus in concluding this narrative are significant. He says, "Many are called but few are chosen." These men were called into work because they had chosen to labor in this particular field. They could have offered themselves to be shepherds, craftsmen, and so on, but they made themselves available for the kind of work needed by the owner of this field. This was why he selected them. When Jesus asks them why they are not working in their chosen field, they reply, "No one will hire us." The owner replies, "I will; come with me. I choose you because you are available to be chosen."

All the men who are chosen to labor in the vineyard are paid the same wage. This wage is not determined by the length of service (hours worked), but by the fidelity of opportunity. Each used the offered time of service to the best of his ability and was faithful to the opportunity offered to him to work.

This thought projection teaches that it is not "how long one has been a Christian" that determines the reward he shall receive for his service to God, but how well he served during the period of life lived in Christ. Reward is to be based on the fidelity to the opportunities we have to serve. "Well done, thy good and faithful servant . . ." Jesus did not say, "Well done, successful servant," nor, "Well done, servant of long length of service." "Faithful" is the key to reward. To be faithful is all God asks of us all.

We are not to misconstrue this narrative to mean that a wasted life can be erased by a few moments of service in God's kingdom. Christ is not suggesting that such a person will be rewarded in the same degree as a saint who has given a life in faithful and fruitful service. He is saying, however, that one can enter into the Kingdom of God late in life, and although many years have been wasted, God can use that life even for "one hour." He can do nothing to redeem wasted years, because such a person has not been faithful to his opportunities. If one has had many opportunities to enter into the "vineyard of God" to work and refused such opportunities, he lacks "fidelity" to opportunities, and he will not receive the same reward as those who have been faithful to their opportunities. In our story, each laborer goes into the vineyard at his first opportunity, and each receives the same reward for his faithful service. If a person has no opportunity to enter the Kingdom of God in early life because of circumstances beyond his control, and upon his first opportunity accepts Christ and enters into the program of the Kingdom, his reward will be based not on the length of that service but upon his fidelity to his opportunities.

Thought Projection No. 117: Drinking from the cup of Jesus (Matt. 20:20-23).

A woman makes a selfish request of Jesus for her two sons and creates discord among the disciples of Jesus, but how patient Jesus is with her: Jesus often takes what seems to be a foolish question, and turns it into a lesson with eternal values. He does this in answer to the mother of the two sons of Zebedee. She asks that her two sons be seated on either side of Jesus when He sets up His eternal Kingdom. In other words, she wants her two sons to be second in command in the Kingdom of God and to be above the rest of the disciples.

Jesus asks her a question in turn, "You do not know what you are asking. Are you able to drink the cup that I am to drink, and to be baptized with the baptism that I am baptized with?"

These two sons of Zebedee are present with their mother when she makes her request to Jesus. Jesus knows that they are asking the question through their mother, and so He gives the two sons the answer directly. This is why Jesus asks, "Are you able to drink from my cup?" They reply, "We are able."

The fact that these two men approached Jesus with this request through their mother, combined with the nature of their request—to be second in command of the Kingdom—and their thoughtlessness in answering the question of Jesus with, "We are able," is indicative of their lack of qualification for the position they are seeking. Their answer suggests that they did not know nor understand what Jesus means when He asks, "Are you able to drink the cup that I am to drink?"

To what is Jesus referring when He says, "Drink of the cup," and "Baptized with the baptism that I am baptized with?" or "Can you do these two things?" Perhaps, the sons are thinking about the baptism of John the Baptist, and the supper in the upper room later. We believe that Jesus was referring to neither of these two events.

We must go to the garden of Gethsemane to find this cup. As He looks into the cup of death—the cup of sin—we hear Him cry, "Let this cup pass from Me, Father." The agony Jesus suffered in this garden can never be known to man. Man shares in this cup, when man becomes a Christian, but man can never know the greatness of the agony suffered by Jesus when he took on sin to make it possible for us to overcome sin. He drank of the cup so that the human race might not be destroyed by the contents of the cup.

Jesus said, "You will drink of this cup." They and every Christian drinks from this cup. Every Christian shares in the death of Christ on the cross, and many have shared in the sufferings of Christ. All of the disciples died for the cause of Christ, and history tells us that in dying they honored the name of Christ. "We are able" might have been spoken out of ignorance of what lay ahead, but the Spirit of Christ shares their future with them and He makes them "able."

Thought Projection No. 118: To be great, one must be small (Matt. 20:24-28).

The request of the mother of James and John upsets the other disciples. They resent the request and the method used in presenting it to Jesus. Jesus turns to the other disciples and teaches them a lesson, a lesson still needed by all Christian workers of all ages. It is a lesson in humbleness and the need for brotherly love among all of God's children on earth.

Jesus says to His disciples, "You know that the rulers of the Gentiles lord it over them, and their great men exercise authority over them. It shall not be so among you; but whoever would be great among you must be your servant and whoever would be first among you must be your slave; even as the Son of man came not to be served but to serve, and to give his life as a ransom for many."

In the world, the relationship of ruler and man, prince and servant is one of exercised authority, one over the other. This is not the order of the relationship in the Kingdom of God. It is not a king-servant relationship, nor the pulpit-pew relationship. The pew is not to serve the pulpit, nor the people the pope or pulpit. The pulpit serves the pew, and the pope or pulpit is the servant of the people. Power of leadership comes from service rendered the people. Leadership of the Kingdom of God comes out of service to the Kingdom. All men in the Kingdom are brothers in Christ, serving not one another, but all serving Christ together. Some might rise to positions of leadership, but it will not be leadership or authority with a certain rank or position, but leadership born in love for the people being served. This kind of leadership comes from within the church—not placed in the church from without. This is leadership not by authority but of fellowship of love and respect from those being led. The road of leadership—the school for leadership in the church—is the road of service to the church.

28

Matthew 21

Summary: Matthew 21 contains seven THOUGHT PROJEC-
TIONS:
119. A den of thieves (Matt. 21:13) METAPHOR.
120. Out of the mouths of babes (Matt. 21:16) PROVERB.
121. The cursed fig tree (Matt. 21:18-21) ALLEGORY.
122. The two sons (Matt. 21:28-32) METAPHOR; NARRA-
TIVE.
123. The dishonest husbandman (Matt. 21:33-41) ALLEGORY;
NARRATIVE.
124. The rejected cornerstone (Matt. 21:42) ALLEGORY.
125. Kingdom taken away from Israel (Matt. 21:43) META-
PHOR.

Chapter 21 shows Jesus coming to the close of His ministry. It
opens with His entrance into Jerusalem, riding on a colt, with people
throwing their garments and flowers before Him. The people shout,
"Hosanna to the Son of David! Blessed is He Who comes in the
name of the Lord! Hosanna in the highest!" This is the earthly high
point in the life of Christ on earth. He is for the first time, receiving
the public acclaim due Him. Only He knows that these same voices
would change their words of praise and acceptance of Him into
words of rejection: "Crucify Him, Crucify Him . . ." He knows how
fickle a crowd is.

Jesus goes to the temple for the last time. He must have loved the
house of worship, for what He saw taking place in the temple area
of God's house of worship, causes Him to resist such goings-on with
physical force. He turns over the tables of the money changers,
and of those who sold objects of sacrifice to the people for a greedy
profit. Here we have the first of seven thought projections uttered
by Jesus in this chapter.

Thought Projection No. 119: A den of thieves (Matt. 21:13).

"And said unto them, It is written, My house shall be called the house of prayer; but ye have made it a den of thieves." Jesus is referring to two Scriptures found in the Old Testament. Isaiah records these words, "I will bring to my Holy Mountain and make them joyful in my house of prayer; their burnt offerings and their sacrifices will be accepted on my altar; for my house shall become a house of prayer for all people" (Isaiah 56:7). Jeremiah 7:11 says, "Has this house, which is called by my name, because a den of robbers in your eyes? Behold I myself have seen it, says the Lord." The house of the Lord, a den of robbers; this is the metaphor Jesus hurls at them. "See, it is not a place for prayer, but a place being used to rob those who come to make their sin-offerings—a den of robbers."

It takes more than a name over the doors of a building to make that building a church or a house of God, or a temple of God. In the seventh chapter of Jeremiah, verse four, he says, "Do not trust in these deceptive words, 'this is the temple of the Lord, the temple of the Lord, the temple of the Lord.'" The name of God placed on a building does not mean that God can be found within its walls, nor does it mean it has His approval or sanction.

Jesus could have said, "What is the first thing a worshipper sees and hears as he approaches the house of prayer? He hears the cry of the salesmen and the money changers trying to attract customers. When the would-be worshippers get through the den of thieves, they are in no condition to really have fellowship with the Heavenly Father. This building, which was erected to the glory of God, has become known abroad and in the city as a house where the worshipper is robbed: You have changed the meaning of the House of Prayer into the Den of Thieves."

Jesus, in reminding these people of the words of Jeremiah, is also warning them of the wrath of God, which is promised to those who abuse God's house of worship. In verse 12, chapter 7 of Jeremiah, God instructs the people who have thus abused the house of God to go back and study what happened to Shiloh. Shiloh was the first house of worship to which God allowed His name to be associated. He promised to wipe it out—to do the same to any house of God not used to honor God in worship. It takes more than a name to make a building. It takes more than the name of God over the doors of a church to assure the worshipper of God's presence there.

Thought Projection No. 120: Out of the mouths of babes (Matt. 21:16).

". . . And Jesus saith unto them, Yea; have ye never read, Out of the mouth of babes and sucklings thou hast perfected praise?" The blind and lame are brought to Jesus in the temple area, and Jesus cures many. Children, seeing these things, cry out, "Hosanna to the Son of David." This disturbs the chief priests and the scribes, and they grow indignant at the reaction of the people. They ask Jesus, "Do you hear what these are saying?"

Jesus' reply to this question gives us our second thought projection in this chapter. He says, "Yes; have you never read, 'Out of the mouth of babes and sucklings thou hast brought perfect praise?' " This is a quotation from the eighth Psalm, verse 2, "Thou whose glory above the heavens is chanted by the mouths of babes and infants." In flinging this quotation at His critics—a quotation which had become a proverb—Jesus is giving emphasis to a modern psychological principle. He is saying in effect, "You have learned from your experiences with children that a young child will give expression to truth as he sees it." The frankness of children is still an embarrassment to many parents. Children have to be taught to lie, and they learn this from adults. If you want to know the truth, ask a child.

It seems that these religious leaders were more concerned about the children crying out, "Hosanna, to the Son of David," than they were over the miracles Jesus was performing. Where had these children learned this about Jesus? Who had taught them to associate what they were seeing in Jesus with the promise made concerning the son of David? These professional theologians had a right to be puzzled; were they not the theologians, the ones who had all such answers? And yet, these children knew something about Jesus they did not know.

We do not believe that God gave these children a "special revelation" concerning Jesus. They were looking at Jesus with uncluttered vision, and they saw Him as He really was. The theologians were unable to do this, for they were looking at Jesus to discover his weaknesses and faults. The glasses they were wearing needed changing, for they were reading into Jesus what they wanted to see, and could not see the truth of His life. They had "eyes to see, ears to hear; but they could neither see nor hear."

Thought Projection No. 121: The cursed fig tree (Matt. 21:18-21).

"Now in the morning as he returned into the city, he hungered. And when he saw a fig tree in the way, he came to it, and found nothing thereon, but leaves only, and said unto it, Let no fruit grow on thee henceforward forever. And presently the fig tree withered away." We find here the only thought projection of "action" in Matthew's Gospel. Jesus demonstrates rather than speaks his thought. He leaves the city of Jerusalem and passes a fig tree on the side of the road. He is hungry and turns aside to pluck some fruit from the tree. He finds no sign of fruit and places the curse of death on the tree. The next day, his disciples notice the tree as they pass this spot. To their amazement, the tree is already showing signs of death. The leaves on it have begun to wither. The thing that prompts their surprise is not in the signs of death they see in the tree, but that death should come so quickly, "How did the fig tree wither at once, so quickly?"

Modern critics of Jesus would say that Jesus performed this miracle out of anger. It angered Him to find no fruit on this tree. They would say, this ought to be classified as a miracle, not as a thought projection or parable. They would also add that this act of Jesus was not consistent with His divine nature, for He used His power not in a constructive way, but in a destructive way. Some would challenge the fairness of his action. It was not the tree's fault for having no figs; it was not the season for figs. He was expecting the unusual from this tree. He had no right to expect this tree to bear figs for him out of season, and in anger, He killed it.

Fig trees in that area of the world bear a preseason crop. This tree should have had some preseason figs, for it was in full leaf. It had no figs on it, preseason ripe or green. He saw no figs on it. Jesus was not seeking an abnormal thing of this tree, but the normal.

This tree suggests that to all persons passing, it has fruit for the weary and hungry traveler. It is a deceiver. Its life is a living lie. "And when He saw a fig tree in the way, He came to it and found nothing on it but leaves only. And he said to it, 'May no fruit ever come from you again.'" Jesus is saying by His action, that this tree deceived Him, but it would deceive no one in the future. Death would be its mark henceforth.

This tree is marked by its green and beautiful leaves. Leaves are the producer of the fruit, and these leaves are saying to the traveler, "Look at my leaves, come and eat," but when the traveler stops, he finds no fruit.

The disciples are confused by what they have seen and ask Jesus a question—not about the reason of the tree's death, but about the quickness of its death. Jesus gives them a strange answer. He says that if they have faith and doubt not, they could have said the same thing to the same tree and got the same results; or they could have told the mountain in back of the tree to move and it would have moved itself to another location.

They had asked how the tree was made to die so quickly. He told them the key to spiritual power in His kingdom was the faith of the believer. This faith is not a blind acceptance, but it rests within the believer's acceptance of the will of God for his life. If man's will is subject to the will of God, he will not be led by the Holy Spirit to request foolish and selfish things of God, but will seek only those things that will honor the name of God. This kind of faith places nothing out of the range of the Christian's prayer power.

This Scripture should not be isolated from the events dealing with the entrance of Jesus into Jerusalem and the cleansing of the temple. He was at the peak of His earthly popularity, but was saddened by the rejection of Himself by the ones He had come to redeem. All His opposition had come not from the enemies of the Jewish people, nor from unbelievers beyond the promise of Abraham, but from Israel itself. Their lack of faith was their reason for rejecting Him.

As Jesus walked in the temple on Solomon's porch one day, a group of the Jewish leaders stopped Him and asked Him this question: "How long dost thou make us to doubt? If Thou be the Christ, tell us plainly," and He said unto them, "I told you and ye believe not; the works that I do in my Father's name, they bear witness of me. But ye believe not because ye are not of my sheep, as I said unto you. My sheep hear My voice and I know them and they follow Me" (John 10:23-27).

Jesus, by destroying this fig tree, is saying in a miracle-parable way that since His own had not lived up to the opportunity that God had given them—to be the mainstream of God's blessing to mankind—that He was now declaring henceforth that God's plan was changed. Israel would no longer be the "fruit-bearing tree" for God to the world, but the honor would be given to peoples of the world who would bear His fruit through and because of their faith in Christ. To such would be given the secret of eternal life, and they would be God's proclaimer—not the men of Israel. No longer would those seeking knowledge concerning God turn to them for this fruit, but men would turn to the Gentile believers.

Someone has said that since the time of Christ, history is but a graveyard of nations which were given the opportunity to be God's heralds of truths, but which did not carry out this assigned mission. As each nation failed in this mission, it declined in power and influence, and another nation took its place. This same thought can be carried over into the life of religious denominations and to local churches. It can be brought down to the individual Christian.

The world is not interested in the "leaves," but the fruit it sees coming from our lives. Leaves are beautiful, but one does not eat the leaf of a fruit tree; men seek for food the fruit produced by the leaf. The fruit of the Christian's life is not its leaves—the social aspect of Christianity—but the life of another Christian. A pecan tree does not come from a planted leaf, but from a planted pecan—the fruit of a pecan tree. Too often we confuse the fruit and the leaf of the Christian life. You can have a fruitless tree with leaves, but you cannot have fruit without leaves. The test of the tree is to be found in its fruit-bearing ability—not in its leaves. Faith is the raw ingredient needed to produce the fruit in a Christian life. This was lacking in Israel, as we demonstrated by Jesus in His thought projection.

Thought Projection No. 122: The two sons (Matt. 21:28-32).

"A certain man had two sons; and he came to the first, and said, Son, go work today in my vineyard . . . Whether of them twain did the will of his father? . . . Verily I say unto you, that the publicans and the harlots go into the Kingdom of God before you. For John came unto you in the way of righteousness, and ye believed him not: but the publicans and the harlots believed him: and ye, when ye had seen it, repented not afterward, that ye might believe him." Jesus returns to the temple the next day and is met again by the scribes and elders who had prepared a question that they thought would put Him in a theological mousetrap. They ask Him, "By what authority are you doing these things, and who gave you this authority?" But Jesus did not answer their question, but asks them one instead. He says, "If you will answer my question, I will answer your question."

He then asks, "The baptism of John, whence was it? From heaven or from men?" This sprang the trap on them, for if they said it was of men, the answer would stir up the multitude, but if they said it was from heaven, the multitude would ask them, "Why have you not accepted it?" Silence was the only answer they could safely give, and they answered him not. Jesus then said, "Neither will I tell you by what authority I do these things."

Jesus turns to the crowd and tells a narrative about two sons. Their father requested each to go into his field to work. The oldest son first said he would not go into the vineyard. The second son did agree to work, but then did not go; whereas, the first son changed his mind and went, after all, into the vineyard to work. Then Jesus asks, "Which of these two sons did the will of the Father?" The crowd shouts, "The first son."

Jesus told them they were right, it was the first son. Then He says, "Truly, I say to you, the tax collectors and the harlots go into the Kingdom of God before you. For John came to you in the way of righteousness, and you did not believe him, but the tax collectors and the harlots believed him; and even when you saw it, you did not afterward repent and believe him."

Jesus went straight to the point of their rejection of Him. John had prepared the way for Him. The people had accepted the preaching of John and many had repented and followed John. John had declared Jesus to be the promised Saviour, but the theologians, instead of shouting with joy over this revelation, tried to discredit John and rejected his message. It was the hated tax collectors, the harlots, and the common sinners who believed and followed Jesus. True sonship is not to be found in the kinship of two persons, but in the fellowship. The two sons of the thought projection were of the same parents, but only one followed the will of his father, although both had expressed views they did not carry through. The theologians could claim the bloodstream of Abraham, but they were not acting as the sons of the promise should act. Sonship is revealed not by words, but by deeds.

Thought Projection No. 123: The dishonest husbandman (Matt. 21:33-41).

"But when the husbandmen saw the son, they said among themselves, This is the heir; come, let us kill him, and let us seize on his inheritance." It seems that Jesus was not satisfied with his exchange of theological blows with his critics, for He continues with another narrative. He tells of a landowner who had leased out his land. This man had spent much money in improving his land holdings and expected a handsome profit at the end of the season. He moved to another country, feeling that he had made a good investment. In due season, he sent servants to collect the rent from the husband-men. To one servant the husbandmen gave a beating; they stoned a second and killed a third. The landowner then said to himself, "They will respect my son, so I will send him." But when the son arrived, the tenants said to themselves, "Come let us kill the son, the heir of this land, and we shall keep all this for ourselves." They carried the son outside of the vineyard and killed him. When Jesus finishes his story, He asks the crowd, "What will this landowner do to these men?" They reply at once, "He will kill them and cast them out of his vineyards and get other tenants who will pay him rent for the usage of the land."

The meaning of this story was not lost upon the chief priests and the scribes, nor did they fail to get its application, for Jesus said to them, "The Kingdom of God will be taken away from you and given to a nation producing the fruit of it." Matthew has said that these men knew that Jesus was speaking concerning them, and that they would have taken Him and killed Him then, but they were afraid of the crowd's reaction to this act; for the people knew and accepted Jesus as a great prophet. First they had to destroy this belief before they could safely kill Him. This became their new pro-gram.

There can be no question as to whom each character in this nar-rative represents. The owner of the vineyard is God; the vineyard, the program of God in reaching men in the world; the servants sent to collect the rent are the prophets who have spoken to the people of God through the ages. The Son that the evil renters killed is Jesus. This story is but a mirror of the nation of Israel. The punish-ment of the evil ones by the landowner is a picture of the wrath of God to come upon those who rejected and killed Jesus. This message was too plain and clear for them to misunderstand. It is understand-able why they hated Him so much. He made them see their real selves and what they saw was not pleasant to the eye. They knew of only one way to remove this reflection of themselves: break the mirror. This they did at Calvary.

Thought Projection No. 124: The rejected cornerstone (Matt. 21:42).

"Jesus saith unto them, Did ye never read in the Scriptures, The stone which the builders rejected, the same is become the head of the corner: this is the Lord's doing, and it is marvellous in our eyes?" Jesus is quoting Psalm 118:22-23. David talks about the need of salvation. He asks God to open the gates of righteousness for him that he might enter and give thanks to God. Then he says, "You have answered me and become my salvation (Psalm 118:21). He follows this with the Scripture quoted by Jesus, "The stone which the builders refused is become the head stone of the corner." The saviour is the rejected rock. He is to be the door of righteousness, and salvation will come from Him.

Jesus is saying here that He is that rock of salvation. God has given this stone to be the cornerstone of His Kingdom, but the men (nation) chosen by Him to build upon this stone, reject it and refuse to use it. Henceforth, this stone will be given to other peoples of the world and they will build God's Kingdom upon it.

This is in keeping with the words spoken by Jesus to Peter, "Upon this rock, I will build my church and the gates of hell shall not prevail against it." Jesus is God in the flesh. He is the eternal rock of salvation for man. The Christian life can have no other foundation upon which to build. No other foundation can nor will stand the test of life and the test of death. Through this rock, men will obtain righteousness, and because of this righteousness, they can share in the Kingdom, its wonders, and its glories. They can share in the blessings of this Kingdom as heirs and joints heirs with Christ, the very Son of God who made this eternal relationship possible by His death.

Thought Projection No. 125: Kingdom taken away from Israel (Matt. 21:43).

"Therefore I tell you, the Kingdom of God will be taken away from you and given to a nation producing the fruits of it." This is really a summary of all the things Jesus has been saying in this chapter. Jesus pointed out the failure of the religious leaders to accept Him as the promised One of God, and most of the people of Israel had also rejected Him. Their sin was one of unbelief. They were blind to the truths revealed by God the Father and to the signs of the Holy Spirit, as Jesus used the power of the Holy Spirit in many forms of miracles.

Israel had failed God in the harvest season. All the cultivating, the seeds planted by the prophets through the ages, and the compassion which the Eternal God had lavished upon them were for one purpose—to prepare Israel to properly accept Jesus, the promised Messiah, when He arrived on earth. This they failed to do, and this was unforgiveable. Jesus said, "You forced God to turn the foundation stone of the Kingdom of God over to someone who did not have your training, nor your preparation, but they had something greater, a simple childlike faith in Me." This faith would be fruit borne in the ages to come. History has justified this choice.

With this choice comes a warning, a warning history has verified: A people or nation chosen by God to scatter His precious seed of salvation will be removed from its favored position whenever they, too, fail to bear fruits of the Kingdom of God. This same truth holds for individual Christians. It is a truth a denomination cannot ignore, nor can a local church. The seeds of the Kingdom must be scattered for God, and the crops must be gathered. God will not let this work be neglected. To neglect our responsibility in this area is to be rejected and replaced by someone who will do the will of God for Him.

29

Matthew 22

Summary: Matthew 22 contains three THOUGHT PROJEC-
TIONS:

126. The king's wedding banquet (Matt. 22:1-14) ALLEGORY,
NARRATIVE.

127. Dual citizenship and dual responsibility (Matt. 22:21,22)
METAPHOR.

128. The dead shall be like the angels (Matt. 22:29-33) SIMILE.

The thought projections in the last chapter dealt with responsibility. Jesus had placed his hand on a very sore spot with these
religious critics, for they could not avoid the application Jesus was
making to Israel. The last of these thoughts so disturbed them that
they wanted to kill Jesus at once, but were held in check by the
fear of what the multitude might do to them if Jesus was harmed.

Chapter 22 opens with these words, "And Jesus answered and
spake unto them again by parables, . . ." Matthew does not record
any question asked of Jesus that prompts this statement. The answer
Jesus gives grew out of what he saw and felt in the eyes and minds of
the chief priests and Pharisees. He knew that they hated Him, and
that they wanted to kill Him. He gives them another story that
illustrates their failure as God's chosen people to measure up to
what God expected of them. The emphasis of the story is not on
responsibility as is found in the thought projections in chapter 21,
but it deals with the neglected privileges offered by God.

Thought Projection No. 126: The king's wedding banquet
(Matt. 22:1-14).

"Then saith he to his servants, The wedding is ready, but they
which were bidden were not worthy. Go ye therefore into the
highways, and as many as ye shall find, bid to the marriage. The
parable tells the story of a king who holds a wedding banquet for

267

his son. He sends his servants across the country to call the ones whom he has selected. It is a banquet by invitation only. It seems that these persons have been informed of the forthcoming wedding feast and that this call is merely to confirm the exact time and get a confirmation from those who are coming. The king is shocked at the refusal of these people to come.

He sends his servants out a second time to these people and has them announce the menu: "This will get them here," he thinks. He says, "Tell them I have prepared my dinner. It has already been cooked, ready to be eaten; my oxen and my fatlings are killed, and all things are ready; come unto the marriage."

Not only do the people refuse to come, but they make light of his invitation, and each turns back to his daily work. Others take the servants with wedding invitations, abusing some and killing others.

The king reacts at once upon hearing of these outrageous actions. He calls out his army, slays the murderers, burns their homes and destroys their cities.

Other servants are sent out to gather people to the wedding feast. They are found on the highways, and in the hedges of the towns. "It matters not who they are; tell them to come and enjoy my feast." The servants carry out the king's orders, and the banquet hall is soon filled. The king looks over the crowd and remarks that those who had been invited and had not come showed how unworthy they were by their refusal of his gracious invitation.

As the king reviews his guests, he is shocked to see one guest who does not have on the special wedding garment he has provided for all his guests. He calls this unrobed guest into his presence and asks him why he has failed to properly robe himself for the occasion. " 'Friend, how comest thou in here not having a wedding garment?' And he was speechless." The original language suggests a deeper and broader meaning than this. It suggests that not only did the guest not have on a wedding garment, but he refused to take one when it was offered. He was an "individualist"; he would wear what he wanted, where he wanted. He possessed superior knowledge over his host as to what was the proper clothing for a wedding feast! He had placed his own personal opinion above that of the king.

The king's treatment of this man is just as severe as that dealt out to the invited guest who refused to come, and who killed his servants bearing his invitation. "Then said the king to the servant,

'Bind him hand and foot, and take him away, and cast him into outer darkness; there shall be weeping and gnashing of teeth.'" The first group made light of the king's invitation by refusing to come; whereas, this man made light of the wedding by coming out of uniform. The actions of each are an insult to the king, their host. Each created an embarassing situation for the king. All who refused to come and the one that came but refused the king's wedding garment sinned against divine privilege.

The religious leaders standing before Jesus with hatred in their hearts represented God's chosen people, Israel. The promise of Abraham had been theirs. They had feasted at the table of God since the day of Abraham. God had honored them with great leadership and with great prophets to instruct them. Now God was inviting them to the wedding feast of His Son. God was welcoming them to meet the bride, the church; but these favored people would have no part in this marriage feast. They were too busy being religious to come to the feast. They were more anxious to kill God's messenger, Jesus, than they were to eat of the bread from the Son's hands.

Again, Jesus is saying through a thought projection that God now was forced by their own decision to turn to other peoples to carry out His promises to man on earth. These chosen ones made themselves unworthy of the promise made to Abraham, their spiritual father, and God was turning to people considered by them to be outside of God's divine favor. Just as their failure to respond to His invitation made them unworthy of the wedding banquet, the acceptance by the unworthy made them acceptable.

The postscript in the form of a sidelight story of the improperly clothed guest adds a "one-two punch"—a punch line and a warning to all people in the future. This addition to the original story says for man to beware! For even if you are a replacement for someone who has refused to attend the wedding, this does not give you divine privileges. You still must be robed in the right garment. It will be the king's garment that justifies your presence at the wedding feast.

Jesus once warned that "except your righteousness exceeds the righteousness of the Pharisees and Sadducees, you cannot (will not) see the Kingdom of God." The righteous and the unrighteous need to enter God's Kingdom in the inherited righteousness of Christ Jesus. This is the wedding robe we must wear at the wedding banquet. This is given to us at conversion by and through the work of the Holy Spirit. Each person that stands before God at the judgment, if he enters into eternal life with Christ, must have on the garment of Christ, a garment woven out of Christ's righteousness.

Thought Projection No. 127: Dual citizenship and dual responsibility (Matt. 22:21,22).

"Then saith he unto them, Render therefore unto Caesar the things which are Caesar's; and unto God the things that are God's." This verse is akin to the verses in chapter 17:24-27. Both deal with the same subject, What is the relationship of the Christian to his government? Should the Christian pay taxes?" In chapter 17, Jesus is confronted with a question of paying a certain kind of tax, but in this text it is a question of paying homage to Rome in the form of a tax. This is a "loaded" question: "Tell us, then, what you think. Is it lawful to pay taxes to Caesar, or not?"

If Jesus said yes, He would have been charged with siding with the hated Romans, but if he said no, He would have brought the wrath of the Romans upon himself in suggesting that the people not obey the law of Rome.

Jesus responds by asking them for one of their coins. "Whose picture do you see on the coin you are holding in your hand?" They reply, "Caesar's picture." "Then the coin belongs to Caesar, and you owe respect to him for he is your ruler. Render unto Caesar that honor that belongs to him in keeping with his position, and render unto God that which belongs to God."

The principle enunciated by Jesus here is one for all Christians in all ages, in whatever country they live. We have civic obligations and these must be kept by every Christian. The Christian also has obligations toward God, Christ, and the Church. These, too, must be discharged. We are dual citizens living in two worlds with obligations in both.

Thought Projection No. 128: The dead shall be like the angels (Matt. 22:29-33).

"For in the resurrection they neither marry nor are given in marriage, but are like the angels in heaven." The Sadducees, who did not believe in the resurrection of the physical body, come to Jesus with a question concerning a woman who had married seven brothers, after the death of each. The question posed is, "In heaven whose wife of the seven brothers would she be?" This is a loaded question. The Sadducees did not believe in the resurrection. They had quoted the law of Moses to justify this question, but they thought they could trap Jesus into an impossible situation with it.

Jesus points out two errors that their question reveals about themselves. Jesus says, "You err in not knowing the Scriptures whence comes your quotation," and, "You are not the scholars of the Holy Scriptures that you would lead others to think you are. You are twisting the Scriptures in your attempt to trap me into giving a false answer."

The second error which their question points up is, "You neither know the Scriptures nor the POWER OF GOD. You are underrating the power of God." Jesus could have said, "You reject the physical resurrection of body. You imply that God cannot do this." He also meant that by their question they were implying that God could not work out the tangled situation. They were passing an earthly observation of man to God, which would be binding upon God Himself. "This is what Moses says a woman must do, if her husband dies without giving him an heir; she must marry his brother. This happens seven times to a woman; now what can God do about untangling this marriage problem? Whose wife is she to be in heaven?"

Man shall be "like the angels" in heaven. This is the answer Jesus gives them. Marriage is God's pattern for man on earth. The human race has come about as a result of marriage. Death ends this pattern. Those who have made "sex" their God here on earth would not be happy, even if they could get to heaven by by-passing God's plan of salvation. Angels are not given to sex reproduction of themselves. Each angel is a separate creation of God; not so with earthly man, but man will become a "sexless" race upon death. The power of God will bring this to pass—both the resurrection of the Christian and what he will be after death. We do know that whatever form we might possess, it will be a "living one." "Have you not read what was said to you by God, 'I am the God of Abraham, and the God of Isaac, and the God of Jacob?' He is not God of the dead, but of the living." Death is going to be a great adventure for the Christian!

30

Matthew 23

Summary: Matthew 23 contains seven THOUGHT PROJEC-
TIONS:

129. The seat of Moses (Matt. 23:1-15) METAPHOR.

130. Which is greater, God or the altar? (Matt. 23:16-22)
METAPHOR.

131. Straining at a gnat and swallowing a camel (Matt. 23:23-
24) METAPHOR.

132. Clean outside; dirty inside (Matt. 23:27-32) SIMILE.

133. White sepulchres full of dead men's bones (Matt. 23:27-
32) SIMILE.

134 The snakes of hell (Matt. 23:33-36) METAPHOR.

135. Jesus weeps over Jerusalem (Matt. 23:37-39) SIMILE.

Chapter 23 of Matthew records Jesus' last visit to the temple.
He would leave it, never to return again. His earthly ministry is
now growing to an end. He knows that the hatred of his critics will
soon lead to his death. We find Him at the temple area with His
disciples, and as always, like dogs barking at the moon, the Pharisees,
the scribes, and the Sadducees are there ready to discredit or em-
barrass Jesus if they can.

These seven thought projections Jesus casts before His disciples
and the crowd are broadcast in the midst of eight woes. He began
his public ministry with the eight beatitudes and is now closing
his public ministry with eight woes. They stand over against the
other, and each gives an answer to the other. You will find no place
in religious literature where more brutal frankness is expressed than
what Jesus enunciates here. Jesus strips the masks off of these religious leaders and exposes them to the full glare of the truth of
God. It is not a pretty picture at best. He uses words like "hypocrites," "fools," "blind fools," "blind guides," "white sepulchres,"
"serpents and murderers." This is not the language of the drawing
room: It is the preaching of the frontier and the old-fashioned tent

revival. It was not well received by these critics and brought the expected reaction. Their desire was intensified to rid themselves of this man called "Jesus."

This entire chapter is a continuous discourse and contains seven thought projections Jesus uses to drive home his message. It is a message of excommunication of the Hebrew people not from salvation, but from their privileged position of being God's instrument through which God would speak to the world. This is more like a funeral service than any to be found in the Bible. "The Kingdom of God shall be taken away from you and shall be given to a nation bringing forth fruit."

Thought Projection No. 129: The seat of Moses (Matt. 23:1-15).

"For they bind heavy burdens and grievous to be borne, and lay them on men's shoulders; but they themselves will not move them with one of their fingers." Here lies the danger of a priest-ridden society. History is filled with such examples. Jesus is touching a very sensitive nerve here. He makes this striking statement, "The scribes and Pharisees sit in Moses' seat." They assume the authority of Moses. They speak "Ex-Cathedral"—out of the seat of authority. They make Moses say things that he did not say with their interpretation of the laws of Moses for the people. They eagerly take the position of Moses, but are less concerned with the purity of his theology. Jesus makes eight charges against these religious leaders:

1. They place religious duties and demands upon the people which are too heavy and too impossible for the people to carry themselves. Religion is no longer of the "spirit" but become "labor-laws" to be performed.

2. The leaders are always "up-staging," wanting to be seen and recognized; to be honored and to have special privileges. They want to be called "Rabbi." They are not acquainted with the spirit of meekness or the humbleness of Jesus.

3. They "shut up the door" of the kingdom of God but would not go in themselves nor let others go in. They are the doorkeepers of the Kingdom, but keep the key well hidden, even from themselves.

4. They want to be the "Fathers" of the people. Jesus warns the people to call no man "Father" except God himself (spiritual father).

5. They are charged by Jesus as being guilty of taking advantage of widows.

6. They make prayer a mockery, praying long prayers to be heard and seen of men.

7. They are most zealous to make a proselyte to their religion; but when they do get one, he is twofold worse off spiritually than before.

8. They do not raise even a finger to help their people in their spiritual struggle with the many burdens they themselves have placed upon the people.

Jesus is saying to these people, and to us today, that man does have his limitations and his spiritual capacities. To demand more than man has the capacity to do is wrong, and to overload a man with laws he cannot carry himself is an act of sin. We ought not to forget that though Jesus was speaking to the leadership of the Hebrew people, in this crowd were His own disciples also. No religious leader has a moral right to ask his people to do anything he is not first willing to do himself.

The Christian ought to recognize his own limitations and strive to live within them with the joy of doing his best for the Master. He ought to trust God to supply all his needs, not all his "wants." Even an animal is not expected to carry beyond his own weight. Christ does not expect us to have to carry a load of any kind beyond the spiritual capacity we have developed. Paul says that man will not be tempted beyond his capacity to resist.

Thought Projection No. 130: Which is greater, God or the altar? (Matt. 23:16-22).

"Woe unto you, ye blind guides which say, Whosoever shall swear by the temple, it is nothing; but whosoever shall swear by the gold of the temple, he is a debtor! Ye fools and blind: for whether is greater, the gold, or the temple that sanctifieth the gold?" Jesus drops another spiritual bomb among them. He tells them to stop trying to do the "twist." Of course, Jesus was not thinking about the dance craze of a few years ago. He was talking about these religious leaders twisting God's truths around to mean something God did not intend for them to mean. Again, He charges the religious leaders with the words, "Blind guides, ye fools and blind guides."

Jesus then tells them why they are blind. He says they are taking God's truths, and because they are ignorant or just do not care, are twisting them to mean something other than what God intended. Nor do they care what harm they are doing to the very people they are supposed to be serving, by making these twisted applications.

"Ye fools and blind: for whether is greater, the gold, or the temple that sanctifieth the gold?" They were teaching that it was not wrong to swear by the temple, but they could not swear by the gold in the temple. Jesus asks, "Does the gold make the temple sacred to God, or does the temple make the gold sacred?" The answer to Jesus and to them was quite obvious. The gold only became sacred (set apart for God's usage) when it was brought into the temple and offered to God. The temple was greater in God's sight than the gold offered to him in the temple. They had twisted the truth around to meet their own wishes.

The second charge of doing the twist is found in verses 18 and 19: "And, whosoever shall swear by the altar, it is nothing; but whosoever sweareth by the gift that is upon it, he is guilty. Ye fools and blind: for whether is greater, the gift, or the altar that sanctifieth the gift?" Jesus has charged the religious leaders with twisting the meaning of the altar and the gift being made on the altar. They could swear by the altar, but they could not swear on the gift resting on the altar. Again, Jesus points out the obvious error of their theology. It is the altar that makes the offering holy unto God, not the offering that makes the altar holy. The beef burning on the altar is an acceptable sin offering to God, but the same beef cooking on a stove at home becomes a juicy steak. The only difference between the two is the location of the fire applied to the meat.

Jesus sums all this up in these words: "Whosoever therefore shall swear by the altar, sweareth by it, and by all things thereon, and whoso shall swear by the temple, sweareth by it, and by him that dwelleth therein. And he that shall swear by heaven, sweareth by the throne of God, and by him that sitteth thereon."

Those religious leaders had assumed the authority to change unholy things into holy things, and holy things into unholy things. They had replaced God's authority for man's authority. There are three special warnings offered in these Scriptures for the people.

There is the danger of the wrong kind of spiritual leadership. "The blind leading the blind"; fools attempting to lead the ignorant.

What a combination; a blind person, who is also devoid of sound reason, that is, a fool, trying to lead blind people and ignorant people from earth to heaven.

Jesus warns of the danger of setting aside holy things for unholy things. What God has declared holy, remains holy until He declares them unholy. God has said that the tithe was holy unto Him. Today, men say the Christian does not have to tithe; that this is not binding upon him. God has said that we are stewards in regard to our time and talents, but we say that these things belong to us.

Jesus also warns that man is not to use holy things to justify unholy things. What crimes have been committed in the name of religion: How often we blame our mistakes on the Holy Spirit, and how often we claim the credit for what God has done for us!

Jesus says that we are not to separate in our minds God and his throne, the temple and its gold, and the altar and the sacrifice upon the altar. The relationship that one has with the other gives spiritual value to both. Those who handle holy things of God oftimes, because of the very nearness of these things, forget that all these things have been set aside by God to be His own and that man has no right to consider them his own to change as he might choose, to meet a particular situation in life. God's Holy Word, the Bible, is still God's last word to man: It contains God's plan and program for man, and His Kingdom here on earth.

The Pharisees and Sadducees, and scribes had taken upon themselves the right to change the Law God had presented to man by Moses. This is why Jesus charges them with "twisting" the truth.

Thought Projection No. 131: Straining at a gnat and swallowing a camel (Matt. 23:23,24).

"Woe unto you, scribes and Pharisees, hypocrites! For ye pay tithe of mint and anise and cumin, and have omitted the weightier matters of the law, judgment, mercy, and faith: these ought ye to have done, and not to leave the other undone. Ye blind guides, which strain at a gnat, and swallow a camel." Jesus is still speaking to the same crowd to whom He had delivered the first two thought projections. This thought projection must have brought smiles to some of the people in the crowd, perhaps, even laughter; but to others, the story was a knife that cut into their thick theological skins and it brought forth blood.

What a scene—a wedding, no doubt, with the guests standing around talking and drinking wine. Suddenly, one guest calls a servant and says to him, "Fetch me a strainer, I see a gnat in my drink." The other guests watch him with a great deal of interest—after they have examined their own drinks. He carefully strains out the gnat and gives the strainer back to the servant, the small gnat safely caught within its mesh.

Then Jesus throws His punch line, which must have brought a roar of laughter from the crowd. "Then," says Jesus, "the fastidious man, ignoring the dirty camel now in his wine glass, drank both the wine and camel without batting an eye, finishing off his drink with a look of self-satisfaction on his face."

What is Jesus saying here? He had just charged the scribes and Pharisees with spiritual blindness and with twisting God's Holy truths around to meet their personal needs. They had magnified some of the law, but neglected other laws of God. They had become willing instruments of a twisted theology. The law had become more important to them than the people. As a result of this, they had become blind to many of God's truths and were leading the people astray.

They had misunderstood God's values. The gnat (a pure insect or animal in their theology) was to be "strained out," but the camel (an unclean animal) could not harm them. The tithe (money)— even the tithe of their vegetables, all the material things of man— was more important to them than the spiritual things of God. "You have omitted the weightier things of the law: judgment (which means to act equitably toward others, to avoid hurting others by deed or by word); mercy (sharing God's mercy with others); and faith (being true to your word given to God and man)—these (judgment, mercy, faith) ye ought to have done and not leave undone." One word covers all this: "hypocrisy." They were teaching one thing, but living something quite different. The smell of spiritual death was hanging around these men of life and light, but their light had gone out, and their spiritual lives were on the wane.

Thought Projection No. 132: Clean outside; dirty inside (Matt. 23:25,26).

"Thou blind Pharisee, cleanse first that which is within the cup and platter, that the outside of them may be clean also." Cleanliness was important to the Jewish people. They brought the concept into their religious life, and it became such a passion with them that their religious leaders spent most of their time making things "pure." This idea was in the background of the thought projection of the gnat and the camel, and it is the center of this thought projection of Jesus.

"Picture being invited to a meal," says Jesus. "Look at the table-cloth, spotless; the tableware, spotless too. One cannot but admire the beauty of the dishware; hours must have been spent on it to get it so beautifully clean. One can eat without fear of committing the sin of contamination."

Jesus must have paused to give emphasis now to the real point of His story. "With spoon in hand and poised over the dish of food, you behold that this beautiful serving dish is filled not with cere-moniously clean food, but filled with extortions and excess." Jesus leaves them with their mouths open, with their taste buds crying for food—food they cannot eat.

Jesus hit these religious leaders where it hurt. It was their job to see that everything was clean, undefiled. They cleaned only one side of the spiritual dishes for the people, and the wrong side at that! He was saying to the people that it took more than clothes to make a man, or a robe to make one an authority for God in spiritual mat-ters. It was the life inside of the man that marked him for what he really was, not what he wore over that body. They were the known "professionals" of religion, but in becoming such, they had lost per-sonal touch with God and with people for whom Christ came to save. They had lost the law in searching the "letters" of the law. They had shifted their emphasis from the compassion of God to a rigid keeping of the law of God.

Jesus was not condemning cleanliness, nor was He undervaluing its importance. He is saying that cleanliness is not an end in itself but a means to an end. Man ought to keep clean, but he should not spend all his energies and time just keeping clean. "This," says Jesus, "you should do: Keep clean dishes on the table, but be sure that the food inside of that clean dish is just as clean."

Thought Projection No. 133: Whited sepulchres full of dead men's bones (Matt. 23:27-32).

"Woe unto you, scribes and Pharisees, hypocrites! For ye are like unto whited sepulchres, which indeed appear beautiful out-

ward, but are within full of dead men's bones, and of all un-
cleanness. Even so ye also outwardly appear righteous unto men,
but within ye are full of hypocrisy and iniquity." It is understandable
why the scribes, the Pharisees and the Sadducees hated Jesus. He tore
off the false mask of religious piety from their faces and exposed
their true natures to the people. Jesus saw through their religious
piety and called it by the name it was—"a sham." What Jesus taught
in this one chapter was enough to arouse their hate to the point of
murder, and murder Him they did.

What was it in these words that infuriated these religious leaders?
What did Jesus have in mind when he spoke them? This thought
projection is a two-pronged attack on their hypocrisy. They are
compared to "whitewashed sepulchres," which were so whitewashed
that no one could become contaminated or "unclean" should he
touch them by accident. These sepulchres contained the bones and
remains of dead bodies. They were clean and beautiful on the outside, but like the dishes, were filled with "extortions and excess,"
their impurity inside covered up by their outer coating.

The second prong of the attack dealt with the practice of building tombs or monuments for the prophets. By so doing, the leaders
were trying to create the impression that they were better than their
fathers, who were guilty of killing these prophets. They were trying
to justify themselves by blaming their fathers and others for the
death of the ancient prophets. Jesus explodes their balloon of hypocrisy filled with the gas of false piety.

Jesus could not have made a more repulsive comparison. Here
are the "purifiers" being called the "contaminators." Their own lives
were not "fountains of pure cleansing water"; instead, from their lives
came that which was destroying the good in others. They needed to
be avoided—as white tombs were avoided.

Herein lies a warning to each new generation. Each generation
ought to examine carefully that which it believes. It should not
justify mistakes of the present by blaming them on the past. Each
generation is to be judged by its own age and not by another.

Again, Jesus is giving great emphasis to the fact that external
religion must be consistent with the inner man. What man is inside
cannot be lost in the external things he surrounds himself with in
this world. The inner man is the true outer man. A new suit each
week will not cure the cancer of a sick body.

Thought Projection No. 134: The snakes of hell (Matt. 23:33-36).

"Ye serpents, ye generation of vipers, how can ye escape the damnation of hell?" At each utterance of a new thought projection, the crescendo of Christ's wrath against religious hypocrisy reaches a higher level. The people were enjoying the whiplashes of Jesus as He applied them to the scribes and Pharisees, for was it not these men who had burdened them down with duties they could not do? In Jesus, they found a new champion for their cause! But they are rudely awakened from their daydreaming by these words of Jesus. He now turns to the people around him, for He knows their thoughts, and they, too, are without excuse for what they have done, and are to do to Him. "Ye serpents, ye generation of vipers, how can you escape the damnation of hell? You cannot rely upon the abuse and mistakes of your religious leaders; no, you have to face the blame, too."

Their fathers had been guilty of murdering God's prophets, and they would also be guilty of the same offense. They could not shrug off their father's sin, for they were to share in the same sin in their own generation. "Verily, I say unto you, all these things shall come upon this generation." History has recorded the accuracy of this statement by Jesus. Who drove the nails into the hands of Jesus and thrust a sword in His side? "The guilt," says Jesus, "will not be upon a Roman soldier, but upon them." All who reject Him share in the guilt of His death. Men are the product of their generation and must share the guilt of that generation.

Upon whom was Jesus pouring out this righteous anger? He was not speaking to the Romans, nor the pagans of the world. No, he was speaking to His own. The religious leaders were the leaders of his own Jewish people, and this crowd was made up largely of the Jewish population. They fell down the religious scale, from the high position of being God's chosen people with a precious promise, to that of snakes or vipers. From the highest form of life to the lowest form—a snake. From the throne of David, to the dust of the streets of the world: this is the comparison Jesus is making. Sin never stops until it drags man down to the lowest level of life, and there was no lower level for this race than that of a snake. What a warning there is in this thought projection for all men!

Thought Projection No. 135: Jesus weeps over Jerusalem (Matt. 23:37-39).

". . . How often would I have gathered thy children together, even as a hen gathereth her chickens under her wings, and ye would not! Behold, your house is left unto you desolate." It seems that the fire from the religious wrath of Christ had burned itself out with this last outburst of passion, for the last thought projection Jesus makes in this series is one of compassion that speaks of a broken heart. He has come to the terminal point of his ministry, the end is a few hours away. It is a sad picture He paints of a mother hen trying to protect her chicks from the danger of the hawk, only to see her chicks, one by one, die because they refuse to use her body as their shelter. He says, "Because you have done this to yourself, your house is left unto you desolate."

Jerusalem was a symbol for the Jews. Its very name meant the presence of God. It was to them a Holy City, not unlike Paris to the French. When the German army overran Paris in World War II, France gave up her fight; her heart was taken and she lost the will to resist. This is the symbol here. Jesus is not thinking about the city of brick and wood, but for what the name "Jerusalem" stood. His Jewish background and training are speaking for Him here.

Jesus is saying to them, "I loved you and tried to save you: I would have done so if you would have allowed me, but you refused. Now you are left alone to face the world, and later to face the Father of wrath." He sees their plight, and what he sees makes him weep for a people who will not weep for themselves.

31

Matthew 24

Summary: Matthew 24 contains eight THOUGHT PROJEC-
TIONS:

136. When the lightning begins to gather (Matt. 24:27)
SIMILE.

137. When the vultures begin to gather (Matt. 24:28) ALLE-
GORY.

138. The four winds of earth (Matt. 24:31a) METAPHOR.

139. The ends of heaven (Matt. 24:31b) METAPHOR.

140. When the trees begin to bud (Matt. 24:32-35) SIMILE.

141. When the floods begin to come (Matt. 24:36-42) NAR-
RATIVE; SIMILE (Historical).

142. When the thief breaks in to Steal (Matt. 24:42-44) META-
PHOR.

143. When the steward is left on his own (Matt. 24:45-51)
METAPHOR.

Chapter 24 shows Jesus, after finishing His lectures of the "woes,"
leaving the city of Jerusalem for the last time. His trial and crucifixion will follow His next visit to the city. He crosses over Kedron to
Mount Olivet. As he is walking with His disciples, they point out
the various buildings of the temple. He breaks into their conversation
about these buildings to make a prophecy. He says, "See ye not all
these things? There shall not be left here one stone upon another
that shall not be thrown down."

His disciples must have remained speechless the rest of the
journey to Mount Olivet, for they wait until they reach it before
asking Him for an explanation of His statement. "Tell us when these
things shall be?" they ask Jesus. "What shall be the sign of thy
coming and of the end of the world?"

They ask three questions of Him: When will the temple be
destroyed (he said it would be sometime in the future)? When
will He come back? When will the world come to an end? We have

what is called "The Olivet Address" of Jesus, given in explanation to these three questions.

Jesus first cites some preliminary historical events that must occur before the end of the age occurs. They are five in number. False Christs shall come and mislead many. Wars and rumors of wars will come. Famine and pestilence and earthquakes will increase. Many Christian witnesses shall be killed and hated. The Gospel will be preached to all the world and there will be the fulfillment of Daniel's prophecy. Jesus then given them six little "When" thought projections that have to do with His return to earth.

Thought Projection No. 136: When the lightning begins to gather (Matt. 24:27).

"For as the lightning cometh out of the east and shineth even unto the west; so shall also the coming of the Son of man be." This thought projection has to do with the "nature" of His return. We need at once to face two questions as we try to grasp the full meaning of this thought projection of Jesus.

What is the meaning of "like lightning"? Learn the nature of lightning and we have the answer to this. Lightning has been defined as a "spark discharge, sometimes oscillatory in character, which takes place between two charged clouds or between a cloud and the earth." This is caused by rain drops charged with positive electrons and grounded with negative electrons—energy flows between the two charges. When such conditions occur, there is lightning.

Lightning is universal and is to be found everywhere in the world. All men have some experience with lightning. Its function is to provide "food" for the air and earth. It causes "ozones" to be released, and it produces nitrogen for the soil of the earth, without which we would have no plant life on earth.

The source of lightning is from above; it generates itself in the heavens. Only a small part of lightning set in motion reaches the earth. Most of its energy is released in the atmosphere above the earth. And in releasing its energy in the heavens, or in sending great flashings of power to the earth, it creates one of the most beautiful displays of nature's power. Man's fear of lightning has robbed lightning of its rare beauty.

The second question is What application is Jesus making here? He is picturing the brilliance of His return. He has just warned of

"False Christs" coming to deceive the people. He is saying, "Do not worry about such things, My return will be as brilliant as a flash of lightning." You do not confuse a flash of lightning with the sudden flash of a match touched to a cigar in the blackness of a night. Nor should men confuse these false Christs with the coming of Christ. His coming will be like lightning.

His coming will be marked by swiftness like unto the suddenness of a flash of lightning. A flash of lightning on a stormy night, even to the most alert eyes, will always surprise the watcher by its suddenness. So will the return of Christ be like lightning. Christians in every generation have been on the alert for His return, and so will be the generation living when He returns, yet His coming will be swift and sudden, even to those who are watching for Him.

Lightning is unpredictable. It can strike at any moment during a rainstorm and strike almost any object. You may see the signs of lightning in the heavens, but where it will strike, no one can be certain. Because of this particular characteristic, it has become a proverb that "lightning does not strike in the same place twice" (this is not true however).

Jesus is reminding His disciples that in comparing His return to lightning, two aspects of lightning ought not to be forgotten: lightning is a blessing to those who are prepared for it, because it purifies the air and blesses the earth with needed food; but it is also a killer and a destroyer. So will His return have a twofold meaning and function to man. To the children of God, it will be a "purifier"—the Christian will be raised from a corrupt grave to become an immortal being. The unprepared man, however, will be cast into an eternal hell for unending punishment. "For as the lightning cometh out of the east and shineth even unto the west; so shall also the coming of the Son of Man be."

Thought Projection No. 137: When the vultures begin to gather (Matt. 24:28).

"For wheresoever the carcass is, there will the eagles be gathered together." This is a strange saying to contemplate after having thought of the glory of Jesus return in the first thought projection of this chapter. After dealing with the NATURE of his return, Jesus turns now to the JUDGMENT aspect of His return. He uses the figure of a carcass attracting the scavengers of the air, the undertakers of nature. The word "eagle" here is not the eagle known to us as king of birds. It is the word for "scavenger." Few people realize how useful to man these scavengers of the air are, for they keep much pollution out of the air and land.

Again we need to ask and find answers to two questions to fully understand the meaning of this thought projection of Jesus. What usage is Jesus making of the word "Scavenger"? The second question is, What application is Jesus making in this comparison?

These "eagles"—scavengers—have an unusually keen sense of smell. They seem to "sense" death, even before it occurs. At least they arrive on the scene soon after death does occur. They live off the dead and offer no man to the living.

They are disliked by man, and yet, most nations of the world protect these "soarers" of the air. They fill a need in the life of man, and this need outweighs his dislike for the flying scavenger.

They have great range. The sky holds not a single sign of life as far as the eye can see. Then, suddenly, out of nowhere, a speck appears, another and another, until you have many scavengers of the heavens overhead; then you, too, catch an unpleasant odor. After they have done their job, they disappear just as quickly. You ask yourself, Whence cometh they, and whither goeth they?

They are birds of judgment. They take over after death. They do not question how or why an animal died, nor do they concern themselves with the kind of animal it is. They have one job to do— remove every ounce of flesh from the carcass of the animal as quickly as possible. Not a pretty comparison here to the return of Christ. Nor will the judgment of the sinner at His coming be a pretty sight. "What a man sows; that will he also reap." Christ's return is that payday.

What application is Jesus making here for his disciples? Jesus is deliberately painting the most repulsive picture he can of His return. The first of these pictures is a thing of beauty; this is a contrast to that one. This is a view of the other side of the coin of His return.

It pictures the terrible annihilation and complete destruction that will be the result of His return. The Christian dead and the living Christians will be caught up with Him at His return; the rest will be left in a sinner's jungle without aid of God nor help of the Holy Spirit. The world will be a madhouse.

Nothing is more worthless than the flesh of a dead animal left to rot in the heat of a desert—its only value is for the scavenger's food. The only value man has after death is the spiritual value he receives from God when God makes him a child of God. The millionaire who dies without Christ in his life, his real value after death?—scavenger food, nothing more.

There is a meaning hidden in this comparison for the Christian, too. At death, our old sinful natures will be shed, and at the coming of Christ we shall shake off the dust of our earthly bodies, leave them in the grave, and arise with the glorified body promised the Sons of God. The "old man" of sin is annihilated for us forever.

Death teaches one thing to all men who will look and listen. The real values of this life are to be found not in the external possessions of a man, but in the eternal values he has built—or allowed to be built—into his life. The scavenger of death will strip us of every external possession we have acquired in this life, but it cannot remove a single spiritual eternal value we possess in Christ.

Thought Projection No. 138: The four winds of earth (Matt. 24:31a).

"And he shall send his angels with a great sound of a trumpet, and they shall gather together his elect from the four winds, . . ." There are two thought projections in this thirty-first verse of Matthew. They both deal with the same subject. Often the casual reader of the Bible condemns the scientific inaccuracies he assumes to be in the Bible. His error in his appraisal of the Bible is to be found in his failure to recognize the figure of speech used by Jesus to illustrate a truth He places before the people.

"The four winds" is not a mathematical analysis of air currents nor is it a meteorological report. Even today, we say, "the north wind," "the south wind," "the east wind," or "the west wind" blows. These are merely points of reference—basic points of reference. They are used by the general public, even today, to describe wind direction. Our wind gauges carry these four reference points.

Jesus is saying here that at His return to earth, He will send the angels to gather His elect—the Christians—from all parts of the earth. These are the Christians alive on earth at the time of His coming. These Christians will come before Him not for salvation, but to have their works judged and rewarded. Their presence before Him is the assurance of their salvation—they are His elect.

Thought Projection No. 139: The ends of heaven (Matt. 24:31b).

"And he shall send his angels with a great sound of a trumpet, and they shall gather together his elect, from one end of heaven to the other." From "one end of heaven to the other" is not a description of the geographical position of the dead elect—the deceased Christians. It suffices us to say that it matters not where the dead in Christ are—to be with Christ, or near Him, or to be under His attention would in itself be sufficient.

Jesus is not giving us a physical description of heaven, suggesting that it has an "end," "corners," and so on. We say today—without doing an injustice to the vast store of knowledge in the physical sciences we have at our disposal—"He is going to the ends of the earth!" We know what is meant by such a statement, but will the reader of that statement a thousand years from now know? Or will he say, "What ignorance! Did not the people in 1975 know that the world is round and has no ends or corners?"

Jesus is saying, "At my return to earth, I will send out my angels into all the earth to gather my elect who are alive on earth. I will also gather all the elect who have died and are no longer citizens of the earth." Jesus is speaking of the general resurrection of the Christian dead and of the gathering of the living Christians to stand judgment for their stewardship of their Christian lives lived or being lived.

Paul speaks of the order of these events: "The living shall not precede the dead," "The dead shall be raised first," etc. The reference here is to the bodies of the dead; the living shall follow their resurrection to meet Christ at His return.

Thought Projection No. 140: When the trees begin to bud (Matt. 24:32-35).

"Now learn a parable of the fig tree; When his branch is yet tender, and putteth for leaves, ye know that summer is nigh." We all have seen on television, news cameras shift from one scene to another; so it is here in this chapter: Jesus is shifting His spiritual camera from one idea to another. He is projecting different thought projections concerning His return. He has already given two ideas relating to His return: the glory of that return, and the destruction that will come with it. They dealt with the "how" of it, and now he turns to the "when" of it in this thought projection.

The physical aspect of this figure of speech must be considered. Jesus said, "Learn from the fig tree." What can a tree teach us about His return? The tree teaches us that God has an order of events for everything. The seed is planted; a tender shoot appears from out of the seed and becomes a fruit-bearing tree. Blossoms are brought forth by the tree in spring, then green fruit appears, and this, in turn, ripens into edible food. God's invisible power is slowly at work from the seed to the plucked fruit that gladdens the heart of man. This power at work is following God's plan for that tree.

Man learns when to plant the seed, how to nurture the seed into life and stimulate this growth with water and fertilizer. He knows, by study of the pattern of the fig tree, when to expect fruit from the tree. This is the way God operates in all of His creation— by a controlled plan. Learn the plan and use it. This is God's desire for man in all areas of life.

The application Jesus is making in this thought projection is found in the five statements He makes in this figure of speech. "Learn (parable) of a fig tree." He tells men to study the designs of God left in the world by God. "When the branches are yet tender, it putteth forth leaves and ye know that the summer is nigh." This is a figure of speech used in reference to the nation of Israel. "Heaven and earth shall pass away, but my word shall not pass away." It is a warning that His Holy Word is eternal and can be trusted. Safety is found in the Word of God for all men in all ages.

Jesus has shifted from general terms to the people before him in these last two statements. "This generation shall not pass away until all these things are fulfilled." This is spoken in answer to the question concerning the destruction of the temple. Jesus is not speaking of the temple, for the word used by Him for "generation" means also "tribe, race, or class of people." He is saying that the Jewish people will continue until the prophecy he is now making concerning the end of the world is fulfilled. The temple was destroyed in A.D. 70, and men in every age since Abraham have tried to stamp out the Jewish people, but without success.

"So likewise, when ye shall see all these things, know that it is near, even at the door." Jesus is speaking to all men who want to learn. To the seeker of truth in any field, will come knowledge. To the man who lives with a closed mind, will come nothing but darkness.

Thought Projection No. 141: When the floods begin to come (Matt. 24:36-42).

"But as the days of Noe were, so shall also the coming of the Son of man be." Here we find Jesus drawing from the pages of religious history for his next figure of speech. His reference is to Genesis 6:5-13. He tells his hearers to review their own history; go back and examine the days preceding the great flood, the days of Noah. "Discover for yourself," says Jesus, "the conditions leading up to the Great Flood, and you will know what the condition of the world will be just before my personal return to earth."

That age of Noah was marked by great sin, evident in the national life of the people of that day. Greed, corruption, selfishness, war are the visible signs of a sinful people. They produce—give birth to—moral decay in the life of the people and set free the sex passions of man. The next and final step downward is spiritual decay. The spirit of God cannot live within the lives of such people. In Noah's day, the cycle continued, becoming more repulsive to the Holy nature of God each generation, until God wiped all out with a flood. To read Genesis 6 is like reading a daily newspaper from any city in America today.

This age was marked by emphasis upon personal pleasure. There is nothing wrong with personal pleasure until it becomes the master of a life, and man becomes a slave to it. Men lived in Noah's day for the pure physical pleasure they got out of life. Life was measured by what physical pleasure it gave. "And in that day . . . they were eating, drinking, marrying, and giving in marriage, until the day Noah entered into the ark." This was their life. They had no time for God—all of their time was spent draining the last ounce from the world of pleasure for themselves. There is nothing wrong with the four things mentioned, if each is kept in its right order and proper place. Life is meant to be more than physical pleasure for man.

Indifference and ignorance of God's plan marked the age of Noah. "And knew not until the flood came, and took them away; so shall it be the coming of Man." God's timetable spares no man, for all must live by it and will die by it. Man might prolong his earthly life by a few years by exercise, diet, and medical knowledge, but an accident can erase all these advances in a second.

This timetable of God for man is not a mysterious thing which man cannot discover for himself, nor is it left hidden and in the custody of only a few theologians of the ages. When man seeks to know and follow the will of God; God reveals himself and His will to the sincere seeker. God wants every man to know Him and to know God's plan for this world.

Jesus concludes this thought projection by pointing that what was true in the day of Noah will also be true at His return: There was (and shall be) a horrible awakening. This awakening will come too late to be of value to anyone not prepared for His return.

"There shall be two in the field; one taken and the other left; two women grinding corn at the mill, the one shall be taken and the other left." Words seem to jump out at the people like shots from an enemy's gun. What a horrible word this will be to the unprepared: "Separation." "One taken and the other left." We see broken homes and broken friendships. Too late—the door of the ark is closed to the wail and cry of the ones shut out. So will it be at the return of Christ. Final, absolute—no turning back the clock for a second chance, nor for another decision in favor of Christ. This is it for mankind—prepared or not prepared. Man has already made his decision and God will accept and abide by this decision.

Thought Projection No. 142: When the thief breaks in to steal (Matt. 24:42-44).

"But know this, that if the goodman of the house had known in what watch the thief would come, he would have watched, and would not have suffered his house to be broken up." In this thought projection, Jesus gives emphasis to the responsibility of the individual Christian in every age regarding the return of Christ. If we, who profess to be Christians, lose sight of Christ's return, the world will never know of that return to earth of Christ to claim His own from out of the world.

Jesus paints a familiar picture for His hearers. They all knew that the houseowner had to protect his family and himself from the thief who would attempt to dig into his house and rob him. The owner could not depend upon a modern police force to protect him at night. So he would construct his house to give him the maximum protection, and he would so arrange himself each night to be alert to any danger that might arise from an attempt of a thief to force an entrance into his home. This picture Jesus paints is one of an alert houseowner who surprises the thief as he breaks into the house. The thief thought he would be successful in his attempt to enter and rob, only to find himself captured by the houseowner. Jesus is saying, "Be alert at all times for my return."

Jesus was a realist. He knew that his disciples and his followers in other generations would face persecutions, and that His delay in returning would cause many to become careless and even discouraged. Some would face misunderstanding from the world, even from their own families and friends. This would weaken their faith in His delayed return. Others would be caught up soon in "business as usual." Peter and the other disciples were quick to return to their fishing boats after the death of Jesus on Calvary.

The new Christian's enthusiasm of his conversion experience is often like the "honeymoon period" of newlyweds; it is soon forgotten by many when the daily routine of married life takes over. The old Christian, too, often becomes so involved with the housekeeping duties of the Kingdom, that he may lose sight of the return of Christ. You must, says Jesus, keep alert to all these dangers that would rob you of the enthusiasm and the vision you have in this new relationship with the Heavenly Father. "Let nothing destroy this in you."

Thought Projection No. 143: When the steward is left on his own (Matt. 24:45-51).

"Who then is a faithful and wise servant, whom his lord hath made ruler over his household, to give them meat in due season? Blessed is that servant, whom his lord when he cometh shall find so doing." This series of thought projections begins in answer to three questions raised by the disciples of Jesus. They want to know when the destruction of the temple and Jerusalem will take place, and when He will return to earth to claim His own. Jesus has spoken of His return being like lightning, the gathering of vultures over a dead body of an animal, trees budding, a thief breaking in; and now He concludes by a twofold thought projection dealing with two stewards—one is good and the other bad.

The society of Jesus' time was built on absentee-ownership. Land came to some as a gift for service to their government, by conquest, by war, or by purchase. The owner of property would place a steward over his holdings and charge him with the responsibility of making a profit for him. Workers would be secured by this steward to work the land. These might be men who worked by the day, or slaves brought in to work the land. The steward stood between the landowner and these servants. The owner did not concern himself with the men who worked his land; he dealt only with the steward. The steward was charged with a twofold responsibility: one toward the owner, and the other toward the men who worked the land. Jesus pictures two stewards; one takes care of his servants, and the other mistreats them. The first is rewarded by the owner (well-treated servants produce more), but the steward who mistreats his men is banished by the owner.

What application is Jesus making here? It is interesting that Jesus never pictures God's children as "servants" but as stewards. Stewards of what? We are stewards of our time, our talents, and our money. All these things belong to God. We use them for profit for God, and, in turn, receive profit from God.

We are stewards of the Gospel of Christ. So were the Jewish people the stewards of the promise of God. They failed in this stewardship and rejected the Son Himself, and Christ turned to new stewards—the Gentiles—and turned over to them His earthly holdings. The Christian's position is like unto that of the two stewards in this story of Jesus. We stand between the servant and the owner. We stand between God and the sinner. We are to bring the two together. We are and were selected by the Owner to do this— "called" says Paul; and with this "call" comes the responsibility to be good stewards of the message of God.

32

Matthew 25

Summary: Matthew 25 contains three THOUGHT PROJEC-
TIONS:
144. The ten virgins (Matt. 25:1-13) SIMILE; NARRATIVE.
145. The talents (Matt. 25:14-30) SIMILE; NARRATIVE.
146. Separation of the sheep and goats (Matt. 25:31-46)
SIMILE; NARRATIVE.

Chapter 25 contains three narrative-type thought projections.
There is no break in the discourse of Jesus between the previous
chapter and this chapter. The word "Then," with which this chapter
begins, ties all of the previously given thought projections in chapter
24 with the three in this chapter. They, too, are given in answer to
the questions asked of Jesus by His disciples concerning His return.

Most theologians agree that in the first of these three narratives
by Jesus, He is dealing with the individual's responsibility (Christian)
for his own preparation for the return of Christ. The key word is
"WATCH." The second narrative deals with the imperial responsibility of the church. God owns all, and all that a Christian has belongs to God. We are stewards of all things in life. The last of
these narratives deals with the finality of the choice we make concerning Christ.

Thought Projection No. 144: The ten virgins (Matt. 25:1-13).
"Then shall the Kingdom of Heaven be likened unto ten virgins,
which took their lamps, and went forth to meet the bridegroom. . . .
And while they went to buy, the bridegroom came; and they that
were ready went in with him to the marriage: and the door was
shut." Look first at the story itself. It is a story of a wedding feast.
Life was drab for the average person of that day. Only the rich got
much joy from life. Two great events made up all the social life of
the average citizen of the land—a wedding and a funeral. For brief

moments in their lives, they had the spotlights of glory focused upon them.

Jesus tells the story of such a wedding. Ten maidens wait for the groom to arrive with his bride. When he arrives, all will go in with him and his bride for a feast. For some it might be the first time that they will get all the food and wine they can consume.

Jesus gives an unusual twist to the story. He pictures five of the ten maidens suddenly awakening to the fact that they are without oil for their lamps. They try to beg or buy some from the others without success. By the time they return from the market place with oil, the door is shut and they have missed all the food and fun.

The listeners to this story would feel no sympathy for the five locked out. The thought of the warm food and cool drinks should have kept them awake. Food was too precious to be wasted, and too many people gladly would have taken the places of these five careless maidens. It was unthinkable for anyone to pass up such an occasion as this. If the crowd's reaction could have been recorded, it would have registered approval of the groom's action of the "lockout" of the five foolish maidens and a strong disapproval of the foolish maidens.

What is the application being made by Jesus? He was coming to the end of His earthly ministry. He was rejected by those to whom He came, and He knew that they would soon ring down the curtain on Him as the promised Messiah. They had not been ready for his first visit, and he did not want them to make the same mistake when He returned for His Bride, the church.

God had prepared a "feast" for the Jewish people. He had offered all to come to the feast and share in the fulfilled promises He made to Abraham and His children. God now turns and offers to the Gentiles the same wedding feast. You cannot buy your way into a wedding; you come only as an invited guest.

Guests are invited to a wedding for one purpose. This is to honor the groom and his bride. Guests are not there to receive honor and praise, but they are there to offer these to the hosts—the groom and the bride. Too many people today have not learned this fact concerning God's invitation of worship. We attend church with the attitude, "Here I am, God, You ought to feel real good because I am here—You know I am doing you a special favor by being here, for I came at great personal sacrifice."

The use of a wedding feast by Jesus for this thought projection is not without intent. This is a joyful occasion. It is time for everyone to be happy and to forget the worries of life. The only unhappiness present is in the hearts of five maidens who did not have the foresight to be prepared for the coming of the groom and his bride.

The return of Christ for His bride—the Church—is to be a joyful occasion, but only for those who are prepared, because they have made previous preparation for His coming. This is the main point of emphasis in this narrative—five had prepared and five had not. All came to the same spot together, all had fallen asleep, all had their lamps burning, and all awakened at the same time—time enough for all to have trimmed their wicks and replenished the oil in their lamps. This is their one point of difference, and it makes a difference to five of the virgins: Five did not bring enough oil. They were unprepared for the delay of the bridegroom.

God does have laws of segregation, but these laws are not based upon the color of one's skin, or a difference of language, or education, or even the greatness of one's sins. When all men face God and Christ at the final judgment, there will be two classes of people; there will be a segregated crowd before the judgment seat of God. One group will be made up of those who failed to prepare for this occasion. They did not take Christ into their lives. The other group will be those who are standing under the shadow of the cross of Calvary. They have been to Calvary and share in Christ's atoning death.

It would be easy to say that the five were not prepared because the "oil" of the spirit was missing from their lives (Holy Spirit). This would be true of every lost person, but Jesus is not illustrating the plan of salvation here, only the tragedy of anyone not being prepared for His return to earth, and the joy that comes to those who are prepared for His return.

These five unprepared maidens tried desperately to correct their mistake. They tried to beg oil for their lamps and tried to buy it in order to get in. The time for borrowing and buying was over. Nothing they could do could change the results for them—they were shut out forever. How shocking were the words of the bridegroom to these five women, "But he answered and said, Verily I say unto you, I know you not." I claim no knowledge of you.

Jesus then turns to the crowd and says, "Watch therefore, for ye know neither the day nor the hour wherein the Son of Man cometh." This is eternal segregation. But it is segregation by man's own choice for God never forces His will upon any man.

Thought Projection No. 145: The talents (Matt. 25:14-30).

"For the Kingdom of Heaven is as a man travelling into a far country, who called his own servants, and delivered unto them his goods. And unto one he gave five talents, to another two, and to another one; to every man according to his several ability; and straightway took his journey." This parable is often confused with the one similar to it found in the Gospel of Luke. It is not the same, for the time and place for each is different. This deals with the talents and the one in Luke deals with the pounds. The word "talents" comes from the Greek word "*talantos*." It is not a noun of quality but a noun of quantity. It does not mean that three men were given three sets of qualities to use (abilities), but that each was given a certain amount of something. Talents are aspects of God's Kingdom given to us; responsibilities in the Kingdom God expects us to discharge for him.

It is often said that the talents of this parable mean that we have a talent to sing, make money, and so on. These are native abilities that we ought to develop and use for the glory of God, but this is not the idea found in this thought projection of Jesus.

Look first at the story Jesus tells here. A man is travelling to a far country. Before leaving he sends for three of his stewards and places in the hand of each certain responsibilities to be performed in his own country. These responsibilities (talents) were given in direct ratio to the abilities of each man to perform. The two men given the most responsibilities were successful in doubling their commitment, but the other one did nothing with his; he hid it and returned it to his master. Jesus then pictures the rewarding of the first two men and the punishment of the third.

This story is not built around the "plantation-steward" relationship, but more in line with the king and subject relationship.

The crowd could not avoid noticing that the story places the burden of stewardship upon each man. The king is sharing a part of his kingdom with them. They are his agents working for him. They are charged to make a profit. No limit is placed upon this. Each is given according to his own ability and charged with only that amount. Each is expected to make the same percentage gain, and two receive the same words of praise for doing this, even though the amounts of money gained are not the same. Each makes a 100 percent profit.

The third man makes no profit, does not even attempt to make one. He justifies his failure by finding fault with the Master. He calls him a "hard man" and one who makes a profit where he does not deserve to ("does not sow"). Jesus says that this man is judged by his master in the same way he has judged the master. "You say that I am a hard man, then I will be hard in my judgment. You say that I am a man that you feared, then I will give you something that will make you afraid of me."

Too often, we judge the master in this story as being the kind of man suggested by this servant. We overlook the other two men's reports and the response, and treatment of them by their master. The vote from this crowd is two-thirds in favor of the character of the master against one-third vote negative.

What is the application Jesus makes in this thought projection? He is saying that He has a right to expect from each of His followers faithfulness in the task to which each is called by Him. We will be judged by the way we respond to these responsibilities of His kingdom.

God had committed to the Jewish people His Law and Holy Word. He had sent them great prophets to speak to them for Him. They were given "talents" of the kingdom which were to prepare them for the coming of the Messiah. They were the "keepers" of the Kingdom. No other nation had been chosen by God, nor assigned this privilege to share the divine things of God with men.

Jesus is also saying to those around him and to others who will follow in their footsteps, "You are given things of My Kingdom, I am going away for a season, but I shall return to test your stewardship. You are given that portion of My Kingdom's program that you have abilities to perform well. You shall be judged—not by how successful you are, but by how faithful you are with the abilities you possess in carrying out my orders." Faithfulness is the point of emphasis.

This narrative has a lesson, not only for each Christian, but also the churches of the world. No two Christian churches may be given the same "talent" to be used. Some churches are located in areas that call for one type of program for God; another church, because of its location, surrounding conditions, etc., demands an entirely different program. And yet, the world has a tendency to evaluate all churches and the ministers of these churches by one standard—bigness: how large they are, how much money they are raising, how many new members they have received each year, how large their Sunday school is, and so on.

Christ is teaching us in this story that God expects from each of His children a 100 percent effort with the abilities we have to perform, and that He will not give to anyone a responsibility that requires greater abilities than he possesses. We are to be good stewards of the talent (the part of His Kingdom) assigned to us. Nothing less will please God.

Each of us is a steward of one thing—salvation itself. We ought to give the Master a 100 percent profit on this investment in us. We can and do when we bring through our human effort and God's spiritual effort another into His Kingdom.

Thought Projection No. 146: Separation of the sheep and goats (Matt. 25:31-46).

"When the Son of man shall come in his glory, . . . before him shall be gathered all nations; and he shall separate them one from another, as a shepherd divideth his sheep from the goats." This discussion began in Chapter 24 over questions raised by the disciples of Jesus concerning His return. Jesus gave them six "when" thought projections, likening His return to lightning, vultures gathering over carcasses, the budding of trees, the flood of Noah, and to good and bad stewards. He then spoke of the ten virgins and the talents. Jesus now takes his verbal paint brush, and with broad strokes, paints a picture of all the nations gathered before His throne of glory. The people of these nations are passing in review before Him. He then paints out the people and paints in herds of sheep and goats passing before Him. He speaks to these animals as to people, saying to them, "Come, ye blessed of My Father, inherit the Kingdom prepared for you from the foundation of the world." To the goats the King says, "Depart from me, ye cursed, into everlasting fire, prepared for the devil and his angels."

It should be kept in mind that Jesus is not giving a detailed description of the final judgment here. This is done elsewhere in the

New Testament. He is summing up all that he has been saying in the last nine thought projections by painting a picture that shows that in the end there are but two groups of people. One group is made up of His sheep—the redeemed; and the other group is made up of the unredeemed. This is the way they died. He is but recognizing the choices made by them before death. Their decision is His final decision.

The comparison made by Jesus of sheep and goats to the saved and lost peoples of the world is not one of chance. Jesus is pictured as the "good shepherd." He seems to have loved the title of shepherd. In John 10, we have an example of how this word is applied to Him. "My sheep hear My voice and I know them and they follow Me." "You do not believe for you are not My sheep," "I am the good shepherd; the good shepherd gives his life for his sheep." Sheep were dear to the heart of the shepherd, but goats were another thing.

The basic point of value between sheep and goats is not to be found in their former associations, for they lived together. Not in what they ate, for both ate the same grass from the same fields. The difference is not in their ownership, for perhaps the same man owned both the sheep and the goats. This was not uncommon. Their difference is found only in their birth. One was born a sheep and the other a goat. This made them what they were. Some of the sheep were good sheep but other sheep were not. Some goats were good and others were not. Their position as they walked by the King was determined by their birth. The sheep passed on the right hand of the King and were sent into his glory because they were sheep, and the goats passed on the left hand of the King because they were goats. These were sent into eternal punishment because they were goats by birth.

What application is Jesus making here? Jesus is saying to the people before Him that their own judgment will not be based upon their environment. It is true they could claim Abraham as their father—all Jews did this—but they were not wearing Abraham's nature. It will not be based upon their associations in life. A goat could live with sheep all its life and the day it died it would not be one hair nearer a sheep in nature. He would still smell like a goat, look like a goat, and act like a goat: Judas lived as long with Jesus as the other disciples, heard what they heard, saw His miracles, and shared in His love with the rest of the disciples—but Jesus said, "He was not one of us." It is not a difference of "shades" or degrees. A sheep is all sheep and a goat is all goat at all times.

A goat or a sheep has no choice as to its nature. The comparison ends here, for man not only can but does choose his eternal nature. He can become a son of God through Christ Jesus, or he can remain a child of Satan. It is this choice that determines his eternity—its kind, its location, and its joys.

Someone once said, "No one will ever make heaven his home unless he is sensible enough here to set himself to the task of making himself a son of heaven. People who play around at nothing will end up with nothing and will take nothing to hell with them."

33

Matthew 26

Summary: Matthew 26 contains five THOUGHT PROJECTIONS:

147. This is my body (bread) (Matt. 26:26) ALLEGORY.

148. This is my blood (wine) (Matt. 26:27-29) ALLEGORY.

149. When the shepherd is smitten, sheep scatter (Matt. 26:31) METAPHOR.

150. Let this cup pass (Matt. 26:37-46) ALLEGORY.

151. To live by the sword is to die by the sword (Matt. 26:52) METAPHOR.

This writer is well aware that other writers on the parables of Jesus, never consider anything written in the twenty-sixth chapter of Matthew as a parable. But using the "parable" in its truest sense—as a thought projection of Jesus and not merely a narrative—we find there are five in this chapter. Each is a metaphor in speech form, and each has a spiritual message to convey.

Thought Projection No. 147: This is my body (bread) (Matt. 26:26).

"And as they were eating, Jesus took bread, and blessed it, and brake it, and gave it to the disciples, and said, Take, eat; this is my body." The feast of the Passover is over. Their minds had gone back into history to relive the experiences of the liberation of their forefathers from Egypt. On the table before them are the remains of this memorial meal, dear to the hearts of all the sons of Israel. And in the midst of the quietness and hush of the moment, Jesus takes from the same table pieces of the unleavened bread and speaks. The scene is recorded here by Matthew: "And as they were eating, Jesus took bread and blessed it, and brake it, and gave to the disciples, and said, take, eat; this is my body."

301

Christ had not yet been crucified, not been resurrected. His body is the same in substance as any human body. This body had been born of woman like all other human bodies. His conception into the body of Mary was of the Holy Spirit, but the body had to conform to human physical limitations. So when Jesus said to them, "This is my body," they knew that He spoke not of the body they saw before them, but we can be sure that they did not fully understand what he meant then. Later, perhaps, but then, no.

Just as the purpose and spirit of the Feast of the Passover was to become symbolic, so with this newly formed ordinance. When the wives of the Israelites in Egypt, as they fled from Egypt, baked the unleavened bread which was to last for days as food in the desert, they did not know that this same unleavened bread would become an eternal symbol of that experience. This came later. Nor did the disciples at that table with Jesus understand what the real meaning was to be, nor what the act of eating that bread was to become in association with God's plan of salvation for the human race. Jesus was looking forward to His death on the cross, His broken body, the physical pain He would suffer because of human sin cast upon Him (by His own choice). Only He knew the full meaning of Isaiah 53:5-7. He was seeing His body already paying the price, not only for their sins, but for the entire human race for all times—past, present, and future.

Later, Paul warns the Christians at Corinth about misunderstanding and abusing this ordinance. He says that anyone of them not discerning the body of Christ (the significance of the bread) would eat and drink to his own damnation: that was the reason he gave that some of them became sick and some had died. It is a serious thing to misuse and abuse the memorial supper (1 Cor. 11:29).

Only a Christian can really understand the meaning of the bruised and broken body of Jesus. Only a Christian can understand what the death of Jesus was and is for the human race; for without it, there can be no salvation. Jesus here is identifying His sin offering on the cross of Calvary with the liberation of the sinner from his bondage of sin. He is saying, "Henceforth, just as you associate this feast of the Passover with your liberation from the bondage of Egypt, associate this bread with your liberation from sin by Me when I became sin for you and paid your penalty."

"Do this in remembrance" has come to mean many things to

many people. We will remain on safe ground if we let this—as we should with all thought projections—say only what it is supposed to be saying. To some people it has come to mean the actual body of Jesus; to others it is grace to be received for the purpose of making one more acceptable to God. To those who sat around the table with Jesus that night, it was to replace for them their feast of the Passover. This was to be a memorial supper for them in the future to keep alive the memory of His death for them.

Thought Projection No. 148: This is my blood (wine) (Matt. 26:27-29).

"And he took the cup, and gave thanks, and gave it to them, saying, Drink ye all of it; For this is my blood of the New Testament, which is shed for many for the remission of sins." Why Jesus only took two elements used in the Feast of the Passover—the unleavened bread and the wine—we do not know, except that these two elements were sufficient in symbolism to portray the thoughts and ideas he was suggesting. "Without the shedding of blood there is no remission of sins." These disciples had associated the idea of blood and sin from their childhood up. They had seen animals brought to the temple to be slaughtered for their blood offering for the sins of the people. As they looked into the red wine in the cup, in their minds they were seeing the blood flowing from the altar— blood that God accepted in payment for their sins against Him. But they must have wondered at the meaning Jesus was now giving to the wine before them. They did not have to speculate long over His strange words, for it was a matter of hours before they saw Jesus demonstrate what He had said. When the soldier thrust his sword into the side of Jesus and the blood and water gushed forth from his bruised and pierced body, they got the answer to the question of the upper room.

Henceforth, that cup of wine shared with Christians gathered around a table would mean but one thing to them—the sacrificial death of their beloved Saviour. They could have unbroken fellowship with Him and God, because Both loved them enough to allow the death of Jesus on the cross of sin. Again, only the Christian can see and understand the meaning of the words of Jesus when He said, and says to us today out of His Holy Word, "Do this in remembrance of me."

Thought Projection No. 149: When the shepherd is smitten, sheep scatter (Matt. 26:31).

"Then saith Jesus unto them, All ye shall be offended because of me this night: for it is written, I will smite the shepherd, and the sheep of the flock shall be scattered abroad." The way to scatter and destroy sheep is to kill their shepherd; the sheep will destroy themselves. Jesus here is quoting Zechariah 13:7. This chapter speaks of a fountain opened to the house of David for sin and uncleanliness. It pictures a prophet who has arisen with wounds in his hands, of the people being destroyed, with only one-third of them left. These people are scattered because their shepherd is destroyed. The chapter closes with God saying He will hear the cry and call of His people.

Jesus is applying this chapter to Himself. He is trying to prepare his disciples for what is to come. They would be scattered, but they would also be reminded of these words of Jesus. Would they go into the temple and read from the Holy Scriptures (Scrolls) this entire chapter? Did they do this? We have no way of knowing, but as the years slipped by, this Scripture must have taken on fresh meaning for them.

They were scattered. Some wanted to go back to their fishing nets and boats; Jesus did die alone, and Peter, the strong one, the one who was willing to die and did try to die for his Saviour, denied his Lord before pagan men. But they had not lost their shepherd, for He returned to them for forty days to prepare them for the task that would claim the rest of their lives.

Thought Projection No. 150: Let this cup pass (Matt. 26:37-46).

". . . O my Father, if this cup may not pass away from me, except I drink it, thy will be done." "This cup," this strange figure of speech falling from the lips of Jesus opens a floodgate of questions. Was Jesus afraid? Was He asking God to change His plans? Had not God prepared Jesus for what was to come before He left Heaven to take up His human form? Had the heavenly messengers, Moses and Elijah, failed in preparing Jesus for this occasion when they talked with Him on the mount of transfiguration? What was the meaning of the words, "This cup"? What did Jesus see in this cup? These are but a few of the many questions which have been asked by many through the ages. We shall not attempt to give an answer to them here. No man knows all the answers to them.

There is a relationship to this figure of speech and the one used in the upper room, "This is my body and this is my blood." We believe the cup to which Jesus is referring is the total experience of Jesus from the time the mantle of human sin—the sins of all men from the first to the last—is placed on and over Him, until He dies with a broken heart when God His Father turns His face away from Him. This total cup of human sin causes Christ to cry out from the depth of its blackness and awfulness, "My God, My God, why hast Thou forsaken me?" Jesus twice died; here on His knees in the garden, the emotional death of a pure mind and life becoming unholy before it has this sin put on Him; and again on the cross, showing no fear, doubt, or pain, until he reached out for the hand of the Father, searched for the face of the Father, only to find neither. The supreme pure saw Himself become unpure; the sinless became sinful, and the perfect divine became the outcast of the divine.

"Let this cup pass from me" are not the words of a coward or of one seeking a way out of a bargain which has turned undesirable. It is more than this. Jesus facing the hour when He was to become our sin so He could be our Saviour, saw, as no one has ever seen, the awfulness of sin—this even staggered the Son of man with its magnitude of awfulness: He drank it to the last drop—this is the important thing for us: He was the only one who could, and live; and the only one who could have drunk it for us so as to make it possible for us to live.

Thought Projection No. 151: To live by the sword is to die by the sword (Matt. 26:52).

"Then said Jesus unto him, Put up again thy sword into his place: for all they that take the sword shall perish with the sword." This is the last of one hundred and fifty-one thought projections to be found in the book of Matthew. This proverb has proven itself through history. We still refuse to accept its message. The sword is its own enemy.

Only the spirit of Christ in the lives of men and in the lives of nations can give us a warless world. We shall always have wars, and wars will only end when Christ reigns on earth, and this will not be a reality until He returns for His own. The world has been a slaughterhouse for the human race. We have fed the hungry swords of history with the finest young men in every generation—and yet, we have not found peace. When we replace the sword with the Prince of Peace, we will know peace.

34

Matthew 27 and 28

Summary: Matthew 27 and Matthew 28 contain no parables or thought projections of Jesus. They deal with the betrayal of Jesus, His trials, death, resurrection, and return to heaven. God's promise to Abraham found its fulfillment in the person of Jesus Christ.

Chapter 27 is a black spot on the human race that nothing can erase. We have the trials of Jesus recorded here, the attempt of Judas to undo what he has done by returning his "blood money" to the religious leaders. They refuse to accept it and Judas commits suicide.

We have Pilate offering the people a choice between Jesus and a criminal named Barabbas—Barabbas is their choice. Pilate washes his hands of the whole affair and turns Jesus over to the mob to be crucified. Simon of Cyrene is pressed into service to help Jesus carry His cross. When the mob comes to a place called Golgotha, they crucify Him on a Roman cross. They mock Him until the sixth hour, then darkness descends upon them and remains until the ninth hour. Jesus cries out at that hour and dies.

A rich man, Joseph of Arimathea, claims the body of Jesus. He tenderly prepares it for burial and places the body of Jesus in his own tomb. It rests in the tomb until the third day.

Religious leaders go to Pilate and request that a Roman guard be placed before the tomb of Jesus. They say that they are afraid that the disciples of Jesus will steal His body and then claim that Jesus has been resurrected. This request is granted. The tomb is sealed and guards placed before it.

Chapter 28 contains the story of the resurrection of Jesus. In spite of the sealed stone over its opening and the armed Roman guards standing before it day and night, Jesus has left the tomb. He appears to His disciples, talks to them and eats with them. He is caught up into the clouds before the eyes of His disciples and returns to be with the Heavenly Father. He leaves his disciples with a commission and challenge. They are to go teaching and preaching until He returns for them and His church. He promises to be with them beyond the end of all ages.

These two chapters are chapters filled with action. They contain no parables or thought projections. The teaching days of Jesus have ended. The Holy Spirit will take the things He has said and done and become the teacher for man henceforth. Jesus' work for man is over; it is now up to man to accept or reject what He has provided for him, and God will abide by man's own choice.

Bibliography

Allen, Charles. *God's Psychiatry*. Old Tappan, New Jersey: Fleming H. Revell.

Autrey, C. E. *The Theory of Evangelism*. Nashville, Tennessee: Broadman Press.

Barclay, William. *Jesus as They Saw Him*. New York: Harper and Row, 1962.

Boinkammy, Gunther. *Jesus of Nazareth*. New York: Harper and Brothers, 1952.

Bullinger, E. W. *Figures of Speech Used in the Bible*. Grand Rapids, Michigan: Baker Book House.

Buttrick, George A. *The Parables of Jesus*. New York: Abingdon Press.

————. *Prayer*. Nashville, Tennessee: Abingdon Press, 1941.

Chappell, Clovis G. *In Parables*. New York: Abingdon Press.

Crane, George W. *Psychology Applied*. Chicago: Northwestern University Press, 1937.

Davis, John D. *Dictionary of the Bible*. Grand Rapids, Michigan: Baker Book House, 1955.

Davis, Keith, and Blomstrom, Robert L. *Business and Its Environment*. New York: McGraw Hill Publishing Company, 1966.

Erskine, John. *The Human Life of Jesus*. New York: William Morrow & Co., 1945.

Garrett, Constance. *Growth In Prayer*. New York: The MacMillan Co., 1950.

Gifford, William Alva. *The Story of the Faith*. New York: The Macmillan Co., 1946.

Harkness, Georgia. *Prayer and the Common Life*. Nashville, Tennessee: Abingdon-Cokesbury Press, 1958.

Hunter, Archibald M. *Interpreting the Parables*. Philadelphia, Pennsylvania: The Westminster Press, 1960.

Jackson, Edgar N. *A Psychology for Preaching*. Great Neck, New York: Channell Press, Inc., 1961.

Katz, Daniel, and Schanch, Richard L. Social Psychology. New York: John Wiley and Sons, Inc., 1938.

Lockyer, Herbert. All the Parables of the Bible. Grand Rapids, Michigan: Zondervan Publishing House, 1963.

Maltz, Maxwell. Psycho-Cybernetics. Englewood Cliffs, New Jersey: Prentice-Hall, Inc., 1965.

Morgan, G. Campbell. The Parables and Metaphors of Our Lord. New York: Fleming H. Revell Company.

Paul, Leslie. The Son of Man. New York: E. P. Dutton & Co., 1961.

Ramm, Bernard. A Handbook of Contemporary Theology. Grand Rapids, Michigan: Wm. B. Eerdmans Publishing Co., 1966.

Robertson, Archibald Thomas. Word Pictures in the New Testament, Vol. 1. New York: Harper and Brothers, 1930.

Smith, Chas. Edward, and Moorhead, Paul Grady. A History of the Ancient World. New York: Appleton-Century-Crofts, Inc., 1939.

Spence, H. D. M. The Pulpit Commentary, Vol. 15. New York: Funk & Wagnalls Co., 1950.

Stolz, Karl R. The Psychology of Religious Living. Nashville, Tennessee: Cokesbury Press, 1937.

Strong, Augusta Hopkins. Systematic Theology. New York: A. E. Armstrong and Son, 1889.

Tillich, Paul. The Future of Religion. New York: Harper and Row, 1966.

————. On the Boundary. New York: Charles Scribner's Sons, 1966.

Trench, Richard C. Notes on the Parables of Our Lord. Westwood, New Jersey: Fleming H. Revell Co.

Walker, Welliston. A History of the Christian Faith. New York: Charles Scribner's Sons, 1943.

Weatherhead, Leslie D. Psychology, Religion, and Healing. New York: Abingdon-Cokesbury Press.

————. The Christian Agnostic. New York: Abingdon Press, 1965.

Wright, Guy J. The Bible. St. Louis, Missouri: The Bethany Press, 1964.

Wuest, Kenneth S. The Gospels. Grand Rapids, Michigan: Wm. B. Eerdmans Publishing Co., 1956.

————. Wuest's Word Studies. Grand Rapids, Michigan: Wm. B. Eerdmans Publishing Co., 1953.